HOW TO

W I N

IN RENTAL REAL ESTATE

A F T E R

THE DEAL

15 Keys to Mastery & Ultimate Success
in Your Rental Real Estate Business

CASEY DENBY

Cover art by Nhi Cam Nguyen

DEDICATION

This book is dedicated to the love of my life, Chelsey, and to our
greatest blessings, our four children.
May you always have courage, believe in yourselves
and pursue your dreams to the fullest.
I love you all to the moon and back.

CONTENTS

ACKNOWLEDGMENTS

I'd like to thank my forever girl for her unwavering support and for believing I could be an author. You are my number one supporter. There are not enough words to share my appreciation for you, blondie. I love you forever and always, Chetz.

I'd like to thank my business partner and best friend, Austin, for taking this journey with me. Thank you for having faith in me. You are the absolute best business partner I could have asked for, bro!

A big thank you to my real estate mentor, Doug, who encouraged and mentored me before purchasing my first deal. Your advice and knowledge truly inspired me along my journey.

A major shout out to Nhi Cam Nguyen for the amazing cover design!

Follow our REI journey on Instagram

@the_rental_property_dudes

INTRODUCTION

WELCOME TO THE GREATEST GAME IN BUILDING LASTING WEALTH

P ersonal ownership of property is a core tenet of a free, capitalist society. The United States of America was founded on the fundamental human rights of life, liberty and the pursuit of happiness. The founders of arguably the greatest nation of all time understood that private ownership of property and commerce are critical to the ultimate success of a society. True ownership creates a sense of pride and care that is irreplaceable. It promotes the very best in the human spirit. Property or land ownership was and still is a major differentiator between capitalist America and many other nations. The ownership of land and property is a primary driver of any economy. Even most selfish and corrupt government officials understand this. This is why the United States tax code favors owners of real land and property. Real estate is one of the few tangible assets left in the financial world besides cash, which we all know remains on the decline worldwide with the rise of digital currency. Owning a physical piece of property or land is galvanizing to one's soul and remains one of the very best investments you can participate in. Welcome, my fellow real estate investor friends, to the greatest game in building lasting wealth!

YOU BOUGHT YOUR FIRST DEAL—CONGRATULATIONS!

You are *in* the rental real estate game; nice work! This means you have purchased your very first real estate investment and possibly more than that. If you haven't purchased a property yet, and are like the other millions of potential investors who just can't figure out how to pull the trigger, hopefully this book inspires you to get off the sidelines and into the game. There are a vast number of expert real estate books that talk about finding your first deal and getting started. The focus of this book is on the actual investor—not the wannabe—who is in the game vs on the sideline watching others play the game.

Real estate is not just where someone lives. Real estate can be land, a residential home, a residential multi-family, a residential apartment building, an office building, a storage unit, a strip mall, a skyscraper, a tropical island, a sports stadium, etc. Likely, if you are purchasing a sports arena or stadium, you are looking for a different book. The focus here is primarily on residential real estate and helping investors, aka landlords, master their craft. The principles, however, apply beyond just that sphere. Continue forward with me into an adventure of learning and insight that I hope drives you to take action and make some favorable changes in your rental real estate business.

Nolan Bushnell, American businessman and founder of the Atari video game console, shared insight that applies to where you are at this very moment, "A lot of people have ideas, but there are few who decide to do something about them now. Not tomorrow. Not next week. But today. The true entrepreneur is a *doer*, not a dreamer." Are you a doer or a dreamer? I believe that since you purchased your first property, or more, you are in the doer category. Good on you! Now, whether you thought of it this way or not, you are an entrepreneur! The success of an entrepreneur depends solely on the entrepreneur themselves, their effort and what they do or don't do consistently. The same applies to you! If you aren't already, learn how to become a doer. Follow the proven principles of success, the pathway that many others have gone down, and get to work. You will be happy you did.

I am a strong believer in the 70-20-10 Learning Model, where Ten percent of what you learn is in a book or a classroom. Twenty percent of what you learn is from a coach or a mentor. Seventy percent of what you learn is by taking action on the job. In short, what we learn and retain most is what we *actually do* and *practice*. Therefore, the process of taking action is critical to your ultimate success. Mark Twain understood this principle when he said, "The secret of getting ahead is getting started." I congratulate you for getting started, because you are getting ahead!

WHY RENTAL REAL ESTATE IS A GREAT AND SAFE INVESTMENT

We've established that you have already purchased your first deal and are officially 'in' the rental real estate game. Let me affirm your excellent decision and cement your confidence! President Franklin D. Roosevelt shared this about why real estate is a worthwhile venture, "Real estate cannot be lost or stolen, nor can it be carried away. Purchased with common sense, paid for in full, and managed with reasonable care, it is about the safest investment in the world." I don't recommend paying for rental real estate in full, at least early on, though the former president is spot on. The remainder of this book covers the specifics of this quote in great detail. I'll be clear that no investment comes without risk, though relative to other investments, real estate has created many millionaires over and again. Andrew Carnegie, the billionaire industrialist shared, "Ninety percent of all millionaires become so through owning real estate. More money has been made in real estate than in all industrial investments combined. The wise young man or wage earned of today invests his money in real estate." You have made a really great business decision. Let me help you on your pathway to winning in this great game of rental real estate!

Here is my take, that I constantly repeat for why I chose rental real estate for long-term wealth, people will *always* need a place to rest their head at night and store their personal belongings. These two reasons are why real estate is an incredibly safe, dependable and smart investment. Let's be realistic though, it is still an investment. Investments carry risk. Investments go up and down in value. Often times without the investor having any control over the fluctuation. This is primarily due to external market conditions. However, with real estate, you have the unique opportunity to impact that value and the overall results of your investment more so than most other investments. You don't get this flexibility with stocks, bonds or even REITs. Russell Sage, American financier and railroad executive, went a step further when he said, "Real estate is an imperishable asset, ever increasing in value. It is the most solid security that human ingenuity has devised. It is the basis of all security and about the only indestructible security." Another powerful testimony from a another very successful American businessman.

Be sure to buy right, manage your investment well, improve the value of your investment and follow the best practices shared in this book. Over time, the real estate market increases in value. Keep in mind there are ebbs and flows, with potential shock periods such as the great crash of 2008-2009. However, the trend of real estate values does increase over time. In my lifetime, the same home my parents purchased 30 years ago for $145,000 in the northern Seattle suburbs is worth $650,000 today! A 448% increase in value. The first home my wife and I purchased in 2011 for $207,500 sold for $334,000 just four and a half years later in 2015! A solid 61% increase in value. Our second home, which we purchased for $375,000 in 2015 sold for $579,000 in 2019! Another 54% increase in value. With both of these homes, we increased the value and overall appeal by improving the property through kitchen, bathroom, flooring and other upgrades. In our second home, we finished the basement, which added nearly 1,300 square feet of living space along with an additional bedroom and bathroom. The real estate market in Colorado was booming during this period. We were fortunate enough to purchase our first home close to the bottom of the market as it was just beginning to recover from the 2008-2009 crash.

Armstrong Williams, a political commentator, entrepreneur, author and talk show host sees the incredible value of real estate as he shared this, "Now one thing I tell everyone is learn about real estate. Repeat after me: real estate provides the highest returns, the greatest yields and the least risk." The amount of wealthy and successful people that share these feelings about real estate are numerous. Perhaps this is an indicator of something. Could they all be wrong? *Doubtful*. I recommend learning about real estate as Armstrong said. This book is a *great place to start* with rental real estate.

Where do you focus when starting a rental real estate business? Your rental real estate business should be focused on two specific areas of value: *cash flow* and *equity*. Maximizing your cash flow and equity is your path to ultimate success and long-term wealth. Equity in real estate is a fancy term for the value of your ownership. If you have 40% equity on a $100,000 property, you own $40,000 of that property outright. Repeat after me, "Cash flow and equity should be the focus of my rental real estate business!" These aren't the only financials that matter in your business. However, they are both influencers to each metric that does matter. We will go into more detail throughout the book. In the end, remember that people need a place to rest their head at night and store their personal belongings. This is why you invested in rental real estate. I'd love to help you reach the next levels of success in your rental real estate business!

YOUR BUSINESS WILL GO AS FAR AS YOU WILL TAKE IT

Do you want a successful rental real estate business? Of course you do! Otherwise, you would not have purchased this book. Ask yourself, do you want a large or small rental real estate business? Do you want to grow and expand every year or stay small and simple? What are the dreams and aspirations you have for your business? Whatever they are, they will only go as far as you are willing to take them! Your business depends 100% on you for it to succeed. If you take the right steps, stay on top of your business, and do what is necessary, you will likely find some level of success. If you want to build a real estate

4

empire or a thriving rental real estate business, it will require much more intentional effort and focus. That falls on your shoulders. Don't hope for someone else to grow or improve your business.

Renowned real estate expert and best-selling author Brian Buffini stated that, "Real estate is the purest form of entrepreneurship." I firmly believe he is spot on. Entrepreneurs don't depend on others; they know they can only depend on one person, themselves. If you understand this early on, you are better off. This book shares the keys to becoming successful in *rental real estate*. It covers most everything you need to know to win in this most wonderful game. Will all that read this book win? No, I don't believe so. Why? Because they won't do what it takes to be successful. Unfortunately, most book readers do just that, read. Without incorporating the lessons learned from the reading, one cannot grow or succeed as a result. The power and growth come from the intentional and proactive action taken from the learning. Be a *reader*. Be a *learner*. Be a *doer*. Your chances of ultimate success will skyrocket.

EACH RENTAL REAL ESTATE JOURNEY IS UNIQUE

Not everyone inherits millions of dollars or a number of investment properties. For me, rental real estate was a distant dream. One day, I decided to shorten the distance between reality and my dream of being a real-estate-investor. I realized what was possible if I would just focus, commit and put forth the effort. Yes, it is challenging. Yes, it is time consuming. Yes, it has been stressful at times. Yes, I had to sacrifice good things that I wanted to get the best things for my future and the future of my family. Yet, I still did it. I subscribe to the mantra that the best things in life come from *intentional effort* and *sacrifice*. One must put in the effort to reap the reward. Do I sound like a broken record yet? *That's good!* Because the record is true and repetition is how people best retain information.

My wife Chelsey and I began our post-graduate lives in the state of Colorado without much in savings. I started my first 'professional job' in the corporate world at a $46,000 salary, with no bonus or other cash benefits. That was it. We purchased our first home in early 2011 when the market was still recovering from the 2008-2009 crash. After a few years, I went back to school to obtain an M.B.A. in Strategic Management. I took out student loans to cover the expenses. In 2016, while in our second home, we decided to venture into rental real estate. This was a pipe dream of mine since I was a young 19-year-old volunteer missionary in the third-world country of Ecuador. My dream involved investing in real estate and more specifically owning my own hotel chain. I know; it's a lofty goal! However lofty my goals, I never lost sight of investing in real estate. That was always a business venture I wanted to get into. It took me a while to gain clarity into where and how I would begin.

I jumped into the rental real estate investment world with a mere $15,000 saved up. It wasn't much, but *I was determined*. I sought out an experienced and successful mentor who guided me and shared some critical advice that I will share throughout this book. I was ready to get into the game and my outlook was positive. I executed proper due diligence during the search process and established my buying criteria. I narrowed an initial list of 30 properties down to 11, which we visited one by one. I narrowed that list down to three, made an offer below asking price, and it was accepted! I officially became a real estate investor in February 2016 when we closed on that property. That's where my pipe dream turned into reality. I was driven to make it a successful one. The rest of this book includes specific, real stories from my personal investment experience in rental real estate, where I also share with you best practices to follow and pitfalls to avoid along your own personal rental real estate journey. Now let's dive in!

ONE

MINDSET, MENTORSHIP AND MOTIVATION

R ental real estate is similar to any other activity or business venture in the sense that we must be in the right mindset, seek mentorship and find our motivation in order to truly succeed. The world-renowned motivational speaker and author Zig Ziglar put it simply by saying, "Your attitude, not your aptitude, will determine your altitude." How you approach your rental real estate business is the most important factor in determining how successful you will ultimately become. This chapter focuses on the three *M's* that I believe separate the contenders from the pretenders: mindset, mentorship and motivation. Which are you: a contender or a pretender? Your daily mindset with respect to real estate investment will determine how far you will go in this venture. It isn't just a casual investment where one puts very little thought or effort into it and then magically it grows into rivers of unlimited cashflow. It is quite the opposite. You must have business acumen and be savvy or you may end up going the way of so many real estate investors who gave up. Either they didn't know what was required or weren't willing to put in the work. This chapter focuses on how to avoid that result by starting with the right mindset and then provides specific actions to take in order to create your success story.

MINDSET MATTERS IN THIS BUSINESS—THIS IS WHY

Mindset matters in all aspects of life. It is usually the differentiator between success and failure, happiness and sadness, or hope and misery. The way your mind approaches an activity determines the action or inaction that produces the end result. Mindset has been the separation between prisoners of war returning home or succumbing to their circumstances in captivity. Mindset also separates in those that pursue their dreams and those who only dream. It is a powerful reality that shouldn't be taken lightly or brushed aside. Academy Award-winning actor Gregory Peck said, "Tough times don't last. Tough people do." This isn't referring to your physical strength; he is referring to your mental toughness. Mindset is a primary reason why many that attempt building a rental real estate business fail and exit stage left before the show is concluded. A positive, strong mindset is also a major reason why many others succeed in the exact same venture. Let's dive a bit further into why a positive, growth-based mindset is essential to your approach in rental real estate.

Mindset is a tone setter for how you approach business. Your thoughts precede your actions. Thinking alone doesn't produce results. The way your mind processes thoughts determines the actions that follow. Mindset isn't just a thought, it is an established pattern of thinking that has evolved over time, which heavily influences the actions you take. If your mindset is one of criticism and judgment, for example, you will be constantly looking for things to criticize and judge. This will turn into vocalizing those criticisms or judgements, likely resulting in your consistently unhappy, unsatisfied or negative state. If your mindset is one of optimism, you will tend to look for the positive in every scenario, while filtering out the bad or learning to overcome it. You will be more resilient, happy and full of kindness. Author and mindset expert Steve Maroboli illustrates this point when he shares, "Once your mindset changes, everything on the outside will change along with it." In essence, one must change inside in order to change the outside, such as: words spoken, behaviors exhibited and actions taken. Change can be for good or worse. One must be prescriptive and intentional in how they fine-tune their mindset.

Don't take this the wrong way, the road will *not* be easy. You will have to do difficult things. My personal friend and longtime mentor Peter Lynch, renowned speaker, author and podcaster, shared the following about this in his podcast "The UGLY Advantage", "Your brain is a liar, it's going to lie to you. Our brain has evolved to protect us from danger. Guess what...if you want to grow, build a business or sell a product you have to do things that are dangerous and scary. Your brain will try to find ways around it. There are no ways around it. You have to go *through* it! Instead of letting that fear direct what you do, use it as a compass...and move towards that." *Growth is uncomfortable*. Being uncomfortable is a sign you are growing, move towards that as well. Don't let your brain keep you comfortable.

How does one change their mindset? Zig Ziglar argues, "Your mind is a powerful thing. When you fill it with positive thoughts, your life will start to change". In this quote, you can substitute 'life' with 'business' to apply it to your rental real estate business. Science proves that what we fill our minds with impacts the actions we take and the results we see. Actions and results aren't inherently positive or successful. People take action that is detrimental and damaging, which turns into very poor results. Make sure to fill your mind with knowledge, positivity, successful experiences, uplifting ideology and more that will lead to your ultimate success.

I can't finish this section on mindset without sharing a quote from Carol Dweck, best-selling author of several books on mindset, who is also an award-winner for her research on the human mind and how it impacts behavior. She states, "Important achievements require a clear focus, all-out effort, and a bottomless trunk full of strategies. Plus, allies in learning." If you believe the results of your rental real estate business are important, which you should, then it's time to get focused and put in the effort required. Nothing happened in my business until I took action. Basic, fundamental learning was the very first step. Taking action was what propelled my business forward! Had I learned everything necessary in rental real estate before I took action? Of course not! Did I know enough to avoid the major mistakes and guide me along the path of likely success? You bet I did! I have been learning every day since how to get better and build a better business. The difference maker was a clear focus and all-out effort, as described by Carol Dweck. *Learn, then do, then learn some more*. Everyone can do it if they are focused and put forth the effort. *Why not you?*

YOU ARE RUNNING A BUSINESS—NOT A PASSIVE INVESTMENT

There are countless people out there that claim to be experts in the financial or investment world that categorize real estate investing as a 'passive investment'. This could not be further from the truth. Real estate is not a stock. You don't just buy real estate then sit around and check the internet to see if the value of your investment has increased or decreased on any given day. If you bought real estate with the idea that your investment was 'passive' and that it would just make you magically wealthy with little to no effort, you need to change your mindset or get out of the real estate business today. In fact, reach out to me and I will consider buying you out. If you conduct your business passively, you may as well just be giving money away. Eventually you will fail. *A passive approach produces passive results*.

By purchasing rental real estate, you are buying into a business and into an idea that you are ready to take action to ensure your investment succeeds. Focused action is what separates successful real estate investors from those that achieve mediocrity or fail. Before you can even get into the real estate business you had to have taken a course of action. Unless you are a silent or purely capital partner who has an active or operating partner that manages the operations of the business. But that isn't you. Do you know how I know that? You wouldn't have spent your hard-earned money to buy this book! A passive partner isn't involved in the day-to-day operations. They invest capital and trust the operating partner(s) to earn them a return on their investment. You, on the other hand, are here because you performed the necessary due diligence, raised the capital, did your homework, then pulled the trigger and bought your first deal.

Get ready to put in the effort. If not, prepare to become another statistic or bumbling idiot who claims that rental real estate is for losers, is a bad investment or makes up another lame and misguided excuse for not staying in rental real estate. Can you sense my passion? *Good!* I have low tolerance for quitters, for excuse makers and for losers who blame their failures on others or external factors to justify their failure. Effort and grit are rewarded in rental real estate. Those willing to put forth the effort, get their hands dirty and commit are the ones that take their business and their life to the next level. What do you want to become? What would you like to achieve? Are you willing to do what it takes? If so, keep reading to learn how and to continue in your journey of growth and ultimate success.

This Happened to Me – Not falling for the 'passive myth'

Throughout my life I have heard the terms 'real estate' and 'passive' being used as a pair or in relation to one another. Hearing this for so many years burned the correlation of the two terms into my mind as a truth of sorts. I thought, "Real estate is a passive investment and that's the catchy thing right now. Maybe I should invest in some passive real estate?" As I began to educate myself about the real estate business, more specifically rental real estate, I realized one critical truth: rental real estate isn't a passive investment.

I read books, listened to countless podcasts and absorbed any and all learning I could from other real estate investors. It became clear as day that rental real estate was not a passive investment. It required hard work, focus and commitment. I wasn't deterred. I was more educated and mentally prepared. After further education and coaching, I made the commitment that I would do what was essential to succeed in my rental real estate business. The positives were too numerous to outweigh the fact that the investment wasn't 'passive'. In fact, the truth that I was becoming a business owner with my real estate investments pumped me up!

It added some motivation fuel to my tank. I wanted to create, form and improve my business. I was committed to growth. I'm glad I educated myself first to truly understand what was required.

YOU CAN LEARN THIS BUSINESS VIA FOCUSED AND INTENTIONAL EFFORT

How do you learn how to be successful in rental real estate? It requires focused effort and three things that aren't specific to real estate itself: education, mentorship and action. Let's start with the education side of the house.

Education. It feels almost silly to state that before you do something, you should learn about it. This is even more true if that something is important. Important can mean a variety of things to each individual. In this instance, you are spending significant amounts of time, money and effort to build a successful rental real estate business. Is this important? Check! I always wondered why medical professionals have to go through so much education before they can begin their practice or career. In terms of their customer, human beings, and the very nature of their work, physical health, it makes sense. A good friend of ours chose to become an oral maxillofacial surgeon—obtaining both his DDS and MD. He went through 16 years of post-high school education before he could open a business and begin to practice. In real estate, studying anything for 16 years before getting started would be business suicide. The realities of real estate are constantly changing and therefore consistent learning and re-learning is required. The basic principles do remain the same, though the unique tenets of real estate change over time. What was once a strong market can become weak. What was once a good investment is no longer such. What was once a good investment strategy, is now obsolete. The market itself changes, highlighting the importance of continuous education.

Education is not synonymous with formal classroom or lecture. Education is simply the process of learning something new. You can learn anywhere, at any time, always. In fact, the best learning is done outside of a formal setting or classroom. Going back to the 70-20-10 Model from the Introduction, the best way to learn is by DOING. You may be woefully bad at first, however, with continued effort and practice you will get better. The first time I played a full round of golf at the age of 13, I wasn't any good. I was determined to become competitive. I practiced for years, spending most summers as a youth at the 'chip and putt' at the Super Range facility, fine-tuning my short-game skills. Today, many years later, I am a single handicapper with an excellent short game. Practice, commitment and perseverance over time helped me become a respectable golfer. It is also the same formula I have implemented for mastering rental real estate. I consider my consistent education and implementing new business practices the 'short-game focus' that I applied to my golf game.

Education is the process of collecting information. This can be done via various mediums, the most popular being: books, classroom, certification, licensing, seminars, conferences, podcasts and more. Before I invested in my first real estate deal, I read two books, "Rich Dad Poor Dad" by Robert Kiyosaki and "The Millionaire Real Estate Investor" by Gary Keller. I have since purchased and read over 30 real estate books. I became a dedicated student to the real estate business world with a strong pursuit of becoming an expert in my craft.

Part of your success plan should be ongoing education. *Never stop learning*. We will dig deeper into this in the next chapter. The key is that your education is ongoing and fluid. Don't be the person that educates themselves out of a good deal or a good market. Take the time and effort to learn, then *take action* on what you've learned. There is never a perfect time to pull the trigger. There are certainly better times than others, but waiting for the perfect time is like trying to predict the bottom of the stock market.

I find it very challenging to complete any sort of action successfully without first having obtained and retained some information about the subject. I would not recommend purchasing real estate of any kind without first becoming educated enough to have guidelines and best practices to follow. Similarly, I would not suggest performing surgery of any kind without the proper education, mentorship and training. I would not suggest playing a sport without first understanding the rules of the game. This is no different; you should not go into this game with blinders on. You need to be awake and alert with a square head on your shoulders. Success will more likely follow suit as a result of following this counsel.

Mentorship. Whether you are brand new to the real estate industry or are a multi-year veteran, you should have a mentor! I recommend every single person have a mentor or better yet, *multiple*, regardless of what you do for your career. Mentors guide us and counsel us. They teach us and hold us accountable. Every successful person I know has a mentor. If you don't have one, get one. You will not regret it.

Why do you need a mentor in real estate? For the same reason you need a mentor in any industry. Mentors help show you the way. They have been where you are and most likely sit where you want to go! Their advice is invaluable and they can also help shape your confidence in the decisions you are making or the path you are heading down. Before I purchased a single property, I sought out a mentor who was very successful in real estate. He happened to be a friend of my father-in-law. My real estate mentor's name is Doug. Let me share with you some of how we got started.

This Happened to Me – My story of mentorship

I contacted Doug toward the end of 2015 when I had some cash saved up after receiving my annual bonus from work. Doug is a very kind and generous man. He owns and operates his own multi-million-dollar real estate company in the Greater Denver Area. Doug owns a rental portfolio of more than 200 properties in the area that are his cash cow, generating the majority of his business capital that drives his other fix and flip projects. He flips on average 1-2 properties per month and employs around 40-50 people in the process. He has accumulated a significant amount of personal wealth as a result. All of these reasons and more made Doug more than qualified to be my real estate mentor.

When I approached him, he was very willing to assist. I didn't go empty-handed though. I prepared about 15 questions for him after wildling them down from over 40. His time was precious and I knew that. I wanted to get the most out of our time, yet also be respectful of his. During our first meeting, I went to his office where we sat at his main conference table. He asked me, "WHY do you want to get into real estate?" I believe I answered something along the lines of, "Well, I have seen others in the industry succeed and I believe it is a great way to build long-term wealth for my family." I guess that was an acceptable answer, however, he could sense I wasn't quite ready to jump into the game.

One thing he told me that day forever changed how I view investing in real estate, he told me, "Most people that invest in real estate fail. The most common reason is that *they aren't ready*. They just jump in because they know other people are making a ton of money and they perceive it to be a get-rich-quick scheme. When reality kicks in, when their tenants destroy their property, when they aren't cash flowing, when a major expense comes out of the blue and they aren't prepared, they quit. DON'T BE THAT PERSON!" My entire perspective changed. I didn't want to do this because it was a get-rich-quick scheme, however, I was rushing to buy my first property. I hadn't done the research. I wasn't ready. He gave me some homework on the way out that first day. I was to purchase and read the book, "The Millionaire Real Estate Investor" by Gary Keller. I completed the homework and went back the next week having absorbed the entire book I purchased off Amazon with same-day shipping!

This time, loaded with a new set of questions, I returned to his office. He saw I was more prepared, more knowledgeable and ready to dive in. I had done other research before meeting with him. This wasn't the first book I read. In fact, "Rich Dad Poor Dad" was the book that inspired me to get into the real estate game. I didn't want to just work for the rest of my life, be average and have a decent pile of money for retirement. Life is much more to me than just being average. I feel like I settled with being average my entire childhood and it doesn't sit right. When I became a father, it changed so much for me. Now I was living FOR my wife and four kids. Our kids bring us joy and give us reasons to achieve more and become something greater. I want them to see that success is achievable through hard work and dedication.

When serving as a volunteer missionary in Ecuador as a 19-year-old kid, I had many self-discoveries. One of them was learning how to dream big! I didn't have others around me that pursued their dreams and took the risks necessary to do so. I was rarely encouraged to chase my dreams and become great. I was counseled to be safe and do what everyone else does like go to college and get a good corporate job. The vast majority of people are average. I didn't want to be average. There was always something stirring inside of me to be more. While out on my own, in a country with people I didn't know, speaking a new language, adjusting to the heat, humidity and cultural differences from my hometown, I could spread my wings and learn how to fly.

This stirring inside of me drove me to action. This was my WHY. I told Doug during this second meeting that I was ready and explained much of this to him. After demonstrating knowledge obtained from my studies, he concurred I was ready. He knew how much cash I had on hand to buy a property and knew that if I purchased in the metro Denver area, I could barely afford a major fixer and would have no money for renovations. He told me that six months prior he began investing in another town and said I had enough, due to the lower property values, to purchase a rent-ready home there. He was right! Within a week I had researched over 100 properties, selected 11 to go tour, and hit the road with my realtor. I did end up purchasing one of those homes for 17% below market value! That one property is now worth more than twice what I paid for it and has been a cash cow. I owe this stellar start to my real estate investing career to Doug, my mentor.

You may be wondering where to start in finding a mentor. Ideally, your mentor should be someone who does what you aspire to do well. Someone who has the experience and related success in their own journey. Someone that can show you the way, teach you the pitfalls to avoid and provide the encouragement necessary having gone through the process themselves. Look within your network first. I found Doug from my wife's network, which over time has become an extension of my own. A mentor doesn't have to be someone you know personally. In fact, I've had folks reach out to me for mentorship because they've seen the path I'm taking and believe I can help them in their journey. One tip I will give you is to make the time with a mentor worthwhile for them as well. Invite them to coffee or lunch and pay for their tab. *They are helping you*; be sure to return what you can. Thank them and provide progress reports. One ironic event that happened with my mentor Doug is that we actually purchased one of his rental properties from him two years later! It was a win-win for both parties.

Action. You have educated yourself. You have sought out and found a mentor. Now, it's time to take action! You act based on what you've learned and been counseled to do by someone, a mentor, who has done it successfully. Robert Kiyosaki, best-selling author of "Rich Dad, Poor Dad", stated, "Real Estate investing, even on a very small scale, remains a tried-and-true means of building an individual's cash flow and wealth." This is why action is the most important step of them all. The cash flow and wealth don't come by sitting on the sidelines as a forever student. You already decided to suit up and get into the game. Taking more action is the answer to most of your business problems. Don't sit and wait for good things to happen to your business. You must make them happen!

The Founding Father and principal author of the Declaration of Independence Thomas Jefferson, an elite action-taker, stated, "I'm a great believer in luck, and I find the harder I work, the more I have of it." Just like working on your physical fitness produces results with hard work over time, doing the same applies to your rental real estate business. Be a worker. Thrust yourself into action. Take one step at a time, though take many of them. The time to start taking action is *right now*. If you are taking action, *take more*. There is no limit to what you can build or the amount of success you can have.

Grant Cardone, billionaire real estate investor and author of "The 10x Rule", preaches taking action in his books, his public appearances and each week on his podcast. Grant states, "Success is not something that happens to you; it's something that happens *because* of you and because of the actions you take." In other words, success isn't a magic card that descends from Heaven to pour success upon you. Your success is in direct correlation with your actions.

Take a moment to reflect on what success means to you. One of my favorite podcasters is Tony Grebmeier, a self-made millionaire and author. In his podcast, "The Be Fulfilled Podcast", he begins every episode by asking his guest, "What is your definition of success?" As you reflect, answer this question for yourself. The answer is personal to you and should carry significance. Is it money? A big house? Fancy cars? A happy family? Financial freedom? What about traveling the world without the worry of money? The answer is unique to each individual. Whatever the answer is for you, post it somewhere so that you are constantly reminded of what is truly important to you.

I mentioned that my real estate mentor Doug told me to read the book, "The Millionaire Real Estate Investor" by Gary Keller before he would continue to provide additional advice. Gary Keller is a very successful real estate entrepreneur and best-selling author. He is the founder of Keller Williams, which is the largest real estate company in the world by agent count, closed sales volume and units sold. He is the current CEO and Chairman of the Board at Keller Williams. In short, he is very experienced, incredibly successful and extremely qualified to give advice to others who join the real estate game. He shared, "Success is actually a short race—a sprint fueled by discipline just long enough for habit to kick in and take over." Anyone that wants to find success in the real estate business needs to be disciplined in taking action. Take action long enough to build healthy and successful habits. Those habits will ultimately lead to one's success in this game. Now go ahead and make it a reality in your business.

I DID IT—WHY NOT YOU?

Seattle Seahawks star quarterback Russell Wilson is noted for recounting the three words his father used to ask him when he was a boy with big dreams of playing professional sports, "Why not you?" Those words stuck with him his entire life, especially after his father passed away at a fairly young age before Russell was drafted into the NFL. He started a foundation called the "Why Not You Foundation", which is focused on young kids achieving their dreams in life. Russell is not the prototypical NFL quarterback. He is barely 5'10" and wasn't expected to be given much of a chance at the pro level. His college coach at North Carolina State replaced him with a taller quarterback who, in hindsight, isn't half the player today that Russell has become. This particular coach told Russell he'd never make it in the NFL. Well, Russell has made it indeed. He is a Super Bowl champion, many-time Pro Bowler, has a top 3 all-time QB rating, and is among the winningest quarterbacks of all-time. He took his father's words to heart and it became a personal mantra for his life.

I am no Russell Wilson. I grew up in a Seattle suburb in a lower-middle-class household as the second of six children. We didn't have a bunch of money. There was no allowance. Chores were rent, not a paying job. I worked as a paperboy from the ripe young age of 11 so I could buy things for myself. I worked throughout high school and all of college. In high school, I worked a part-time job year-round, even while participating in after-school sports for most of the year. I left college without student loan debt due to my commitment to both education and work. I managed a local Papa Murphy's for my entire undergraduate studies, working 50-55 hours most weeks while enrolled as a full-time student year-round.

I didn't get a scholarship for sports or academics. Nobody offered me an amazing opportunity in life or paid my way. I worked hard, put in the effort to gain an education and then took action the best I knew how. My parents worked extremely hard to provide us with the essentials of life and then some. However, they also came from large families. My father is the second of nine children and my mom is the youngest of seven. Neither of their parents were wealthy. They had to craft their own path. My dad didn't complete his degree from the University until he was in his late twenties, putting him behind many of his peers. My parents were busy each day doing their best to provide a living for my siblings and I, which I commend them for. My mom has overcome great adversity in her life, providing me an example of perseverance. My dad is the hardest-working person I've ever known. Though even he would admit he wasn't the best cheerleader or mentor. I didn't hear much, "Casey, you can do anything you put your mind to", or "You can become anything you want with the right focus and work." My motivation and drive were intrinsic. I wanted to become more than my life's circumstances. Although I had a miniscule chance of living out my childhood dreams of being a professional baseball player in the MLB or being a professional golfer on the PGA Tour, I knew I could become great by taking another path in life.

My wife and I had to borrow money to purchase our very first home because we didn't have enough saved up for the full down payment. Now, a father to four incredible children ages 11 and under, my heart's desire is to give them the very best life possible. They deserve the best I can offer. As a kid myself, I never dreamed of owning a respectable real estate portfolio or being an author. In fact, I didn't particularly enjoy writing. I have come a long way through education, hard work and persistence. I have new life dreams that I am fulfilling and my happiness is at a new peak. Most people that come from my background with a good-sized family can make a decent living, though most never become wealthy. I don't consider myself to be wealthy at this point in my life, however, I am surpassing most expectations for someone my age. I have constantly told myself that I can do more, become more and fulfill more dreams than most ever expected me to. So, if I can build a successful real estate portfolio and multiply my net worth 14 times in just 5 years' time, *why not you?* It all starts with your mindset. Believe in yourself and then put in the work. Success is a more likely result with this formula.

LET'S WRAP A BOW ON THIS CHAPTER

Congratulations, you've finished Chapter One and learned something new to improve your rental real estate business! The focus of this chapter is to baseline that success isn't solely dependent on your skillset or abilities. Success is heavily influenced by your mindset and motivations.

Mindset Matters in this Business—This is Why. Mindset matters in all aspects of life. How you approach your rental real estate business greatly influences whether you succeed or fail. Many people leave the game in the first half because they weren't mentally strong.

You are running a business—not a passive investment. Rental real estate is absolutely a bona fide business venture. It is also by no means 'passive' in nature. A stock is a passive investment. A rental property is quite the opposite. It requires attention or it will fail. Understanding this is critical.

You can learn this business via focused and intentional effort. I would argue that being successful in owning a rental real estate business has little to do with your industry knowledge. It hinges on a focused effort through education, mentorship and action.

I did it—why not you? If I can be successful owning a rental real estate business, why not you? I'm not trying to demean myself when I say this. My intent is to encourage you and help you believe in yourself like star quarterback Russell Wilson's dad believed in him.

TWO

BE THE VERY BEST AT WHAT YOU DO

L ife is full of opportunities to be our best and give our best. From grade school to athletics to employment and to parenting, we want to be our best and give our best. Your future depends heavily upon the efforts given in your youth. Your athletic performance depends heavily on how you approach practice and crafting your skills. Your job performance depends heavily on your level of effort and commitment. Your parenting success depends heavily upon your focus, desire and patience. Why should your performance as a landlord be any different? Disclaimer: *it isn't*. Your success as a landlord depends heavily upon your effort and commitment to being your best and giving your best. I believe each landlord should care as much about their performance in this regard as in any other life pursuit. It is *your business*. It is *your name*. It is *your reputation*. Michael Jordan, the all-time great basketball star paints it clearly by saying, "Some people want it to happen, some wish it would happen, others make it happen." Football legend Steve Young shared additional insight around being your best when he said, "The principle of competing against yourself. It's about self-improvement, about being better than you were the day before." From the mouths of two greats: don't settle, make it happen, improve each and every day. This chapter offers specific actions to be your best and give your best as a landlord.

BE A STUDENT OF THE GAME

If you like sports as much as I do, you have probably heard this phrase before, 'Be a student of the game'. In football, being a true student of the game can be the difference between mediocrity and greatness. Studying situations, players, tendencies, teams, defensive or offensive packages, route concepts, plays and more will give you the edge on an opponent who isn't as studious. *Advantage student*. In baseball, you see the shift on defense implemented often in today's game. This is a direct result of data and studies conducted over time of the batter's tendencies to hit the ball in certain locations on the field. *Advantage defense*. In golf, a good study of the course itself is what will benefit you. There is even a term for this, 'course management'. A golfer's chances of success increase dramatically when they practice good course management. An example of this would be on a par 5 where a river or stream runs between the fairway and the green. The smart play is to lay up on the second shot to then hit a high-probability third shot onto the green that can setup a birdie opportunity. The high-risk play would be pulling out the 3-wood and attempting to reach the green in two shots to setup an improbable eagle putt. The lay-up path has a 60% success rate to score par or better. The green-in-two path has a success rate of just 17%. *Advantage course management golfer*. The data teaches you which path is the most prudent or has the higher likelihood of success. Your level of skill is also a huge factor. The percentages are going to be much different for a PGA professional vs myself. The penalties for going into the water or out of bounds outweigh the smaller potential benefit of having an eagle putt. Remember, the lay-up route still has a good chance of scoring a birdie on that hole. Be a student and take your learning to the course, field, court or whichever venue you play the game. *Advantage, studious athlete*.

In rental real estate, it is similar. Being a student of the game means you are reading books from experts, studying the market you plan to invest in, learning about the current state of the economy, researching the real estate outlook, seeking out a coach or mentor, taking advice from a real estate expert and so on. Remember: your real estate journey is a business. It is not a hobby on the side that you occasionally check in on. Doing so would be a disastrous approach to investing. *Always be a student*. Always be learning. Turn your learning into action as early and often as possible. You will be grateful you did. *Advantage real estate student*.

THE BEST TEACHER IS EXPERIENCE

You will notice that a common theme of this book is around experience. The old adage, "The best way to learn is by doing", is no different with real estate. I'll repeat that 70% of what we learn is by taking action, not by studying alone. My eight-year-old daughter doubts herself often, carrying low confidence before she gives herself a real shot. The truth is, she is rather talented. She has natural athletic tendencies, is a skilled dancer, happens to be very smart and has a knack for being good at things. If you asked her though, you would not get that impression. We are working through anxiety, self-esteem and talent recognition exercises with her. The other day, I asked her if she wanted to play baseball in the backyard with her brothers. She replied, "No, I suck at baseball." To which I inquired, "How would you know if you've never tried? How will you know if you never do try?" This actually made sense to her and after I gave her a very brief demonstration, she stepped up to the plate. To her utter surprise and shock (not mine) she started making solid contact in the first round of balls, including pegging me once or twice. She hit several balls farther and harder than her brothers. "Dad, I guess I *am* awesome at baseball. It's like I'm a natural", she expressed with a smile beaming from ear to ear on her cute little face. It brought joy to my soul. This experience reminds me of how I started my real estate journey. I realized that I would never learn or even know if I could be successful if I didn't take the leap and see for myself. Here I am, five years later with a respectable portfolio that brings in gross annual revenues exceeding $375,000. I made mistakes, lots of them. However, I learned from each and every one. I view mistakes as learning opportunities and so should you. Don't be afraid to make mistakes. Don't be afraid to fail. Don't become paralyzed by your fears. Take action and learn from experience.

Given that you are already an investor, this is not theoretical for you. It's happening right now! Some of you may not be official investors yet and are looking to get a preview into landlord life. You too can learn from this book's contents. Now, for the investors, you should already be learning from experience and I commend you for that. Go ahead; pat yourself on the back! You are miles ahead of the many who never jumped in or when they did, they never got their feet wet and truly learned the game. They burned out and gave up. Good riddance I say to them! They weren't built for this game like you and I.

Your experience may be limited and that is alright. Maybe you decided not to manage your own portfolio and instead hired a property management company to do that for you. Maybe you realized that they will never care for your property like you will. Maybe you realized they didn't actually screen tenants as well as they should have, which resulted in disaster for you. Maybe you realized that you haven't been as diligent in running your business as you should have been. Maybe you realized that you had been burned repeatedly. Maybe you have come to the realization that you are doing alright but want to be doing great. Regardless of your reason for being here and for reading this book, I will tell you this: You are in the RIGHT place! *I applaud you.* I can also assure you that if you are studious and implement the best practices shared in these pages, you will be more successful in the future than you are today. Your family will thank you. Your kids will notice your success and admire you for it. Your spouse or partner will be grateful and commend your hard work. Others will notice and admire from afar. Most importantly, you will be proud of what you've accomplished and more fulfilled in the future you are building.

THE S.T.A.I.R. MODEL

I have been taught throughout life to choose between good, better and best. They are all positive results, though choosing best over good or better requires intentional effort and focus. In rental real estate, the same principle applies. We can be good landlords with a good business. We can be better than good landlords. Or we can choose to be our very best, and in the process, achieve results that others only aspire to. Each of you can reach that level and I fully intend on providing you a formula for getting there with more efficiency. Let me introduce you to the S.T.A.I.R. Model as a great methodology for becoming a mastery-level landlord. I created this model in thinking of how the most successful real estate investors reached that point. Let me break down each of the different steps of the model for you and why they are worth your attention.

Study

Try

Assess

Iterate

Repeat

Grant Cardone understands the principles of the S.T.A.I.R. Model. He said, "In order to get to the next level of whatever you're doing, you must think and act in a wildly different way than you previously have been. You cannot get to the next phase of a project without a grander mindset, more acceleration and extra horsepower." In other words, you must forge onward and not settle for where you are today. Continuing in the same patterns of behavior will not produce different results. Constant learning, taking action and iteration will lead to greater success. Let's review the S.T.A.I.R. Model in detail together.

Study. In Chapter One we covered the importance of continuing education throughout your real estate investing journey. I believe that trying something is generally good. Though trying something of consequence such as investing in real estate, without having taken any thought or time to learn beforehand, is unwise. I would never dare to drive a motorcycle before having studied what was necessary and passed the written and driver's examinations. I also wouldn't allow my children to prepare and cook food without proper education or training. Nor would I want to be a passenger in an aircraft where the pilot was a beginner! I consider investing in real estate without having performed the proper study and research to be foolish. This isn't a lemonade stand on the street corner that you can setup and open in a matter of hours. The investment of capital and time into real estate is significant. On the other hand, I will be the first to admit that I don't believe the lifelong student who never takes any action is prudent or wise either. Taking action is the best way to learn. However, nobody should jump into the deep end before knowing how to swim first. Study and prepare your very best to ensure the highest probability of success. *Learn first*. Everything else stems from there.

This Happened to Me – The seventh grade 'golf cart crash'

I was a seventh grader and it was 'take your kid to work day'. My dad was busy that year so I tagged along with a friend whose dad owned a used-car lot. There was a golf cart the staff used to drive around the lot. My buddy Johnny and I decided to take it for a spin. His dad warned us to be careful, but we were in seventh grade. Careful didn't resonate very well. After driving with caution for a bit, I felt the need for speed. There was a dirt parking lot at the end of the property with a bunch of cars near the on-site repair shop. I was going down this hill and somehow managed to spin around at a high-speed going backwards! Desperately trying to stop and knowing what was about to happen, we were headed straight toward an old van. I couldn't stop. Johnny was cursing and yelling at me to slow down. BAM! We collided with the slider door of the van and I was petrified. I downright terrified of what Johnny's dad would do to me. After mustering enough courage to confess my sin, surprisingly he wasn't upset. Apparently that car was waiting to have some body damage repaired on it anyways and that it wouldn't be much more to fix the new dent on the door. I was LUCKY. I also learned a major lesson that day. I learned that even though I wanted to do something, and I was convinced I could do it; I wasn't prepared and I paid for it. Be prepared, study!

Try. There is no substitute for trying something. Once you have studied and become educated to the point where you know enough to be dangerous, it is time to go for it. Trying in the real estate game doesn't mean you purchase a $500,000 single-family home as your first rental or worse a $10,000,000 apartment complex. Start small and work your way up through experience and continuous growth. The study you have conducted should have prepared you for taking this next step. You wouldn't be reading this book if you weren't already in the 'Try' phase of the model. Maybe you did try and things aren't looking so great. On the other hand, maybe you tried and succeeded, though want to learn how to get even better so that you can expand your business. Either way, there is no substitute for trying something. You can study your entire life, though will never become wise if you don't implement what you have learned. Wisdom is indeed the action of taking learned information and implementing it well. Learn, then do. Don't learn and *do nothing*. I know several people who have decided to get a Bachelor's degree, then a Master's degree, then a PhD, all without ever holding a job, gaining invaluable work experience, or earning a single penny in the real world outside of books. Don't be that person when it comes to rental real estate. Learn what you need to. Study what is available. Learn from other's mistakes and successes. Then execute. *Do something*. Try and try again, my friends.

Assess. This step is one that many forgo because they believe it is either too hard or not important. Neither are true. In order to truly become successful, one must assess how they are currently doing. Without true and thorough assessment, there is no lasting and continuous improvement. Conducting an assessment of how well you are managing your rental property business is essential if you'd like to become great at this game. How are things going? Are you successful? Is what you are doing the most effective route possible? Where can improvements be made? How can you be more profitable? Where can you cut expenses? How can you increase rents and margin? You will only know the answers to these questions through analysis and assessment. Otherwise, you are flying by the seat of your pants, taking your 'best guess' operational method and approach to this high-stakes game of rental property investment. Don't be that investor. Be better. Do better. Assess the realities of your performance, then take action to improve in the next step. You will be far better off.

Iterate. Once you have made it through the assessment phase, you will need to know that the next step is not perfection. The next step is iteration. That simply means that you tweak the way you are currently doing things based on your assessment and study. You make a small change here or a major change there if it's merited and the data supports it. Iterate until you get better and start seeing improvement. Another common academic phrase for this step is *'trial and error'*. You must try something to know if it will work or not. This is no different. Lower the rent. Raise the rent. Upgrade the bathroom. Paint the interior. Change your screening system. Update your rental management software. Change your marketing approach. Expand your rent collection options. During the assessment phase you should be identifying areas of opportunity. Within those areas of opportunity, you have decisions to make. Not all decisions will be ideal and that is alright. Based on your study and assessment, make the best decision possible. Then put it into action. From there, check to see if it worked. Was it more or less effective than the previous method? Did the cost change? Was it more work? Did it bring additional revenue or improve margins? The answers to these questions should all be telling you it worked and was more effective. If not, continue iterating until they do.

Repeat. Zig Ziglar put it eloquently when he said, "Repetition is the mother of learning, the father of action, which makes it the architect of accomplishment." Repetition allows for continued improvement and skill refining. The cycle repeats once you get through the steps. Tiger Woods doesn't stop practicing on the green or the range after just one bucket or one session. He repeats the practice to fine tune his skillset. Nobody can hit a stinger like he does without many hours of practice over the course of many days, weeks, months and years. This applies to everything in life. You can't improve your reading unless you read again and again. You can't improve your speaking skills unless you get in front of an audience again and again. You can't improve your golf game unless you practice again and again. Likewise, in the real estate business, you can't improve unless you fine tune your skills as described in this book again and again and again. The more you repeat an intentional action, the higher likelihood of success you have.

This Happened to Me – S.T.A.I.R. to better tenants

The first major mistake I made in rental real estate is also one of the worst to screw up: the screening and selection of tenants. The first tenants I chose were a young, unmarried couple that ended their relationship in a bad way, which resulted in a messy split from each other and the property as well. The very first tenant my business partner and I selected is now in federal prison serving a lengthy sentence. Needless to say, I swung and missed a few times. However, over time, through learning from my own mistakes, further educating myself and also iterating time and again, my tenant selection quality has improved dramatically. I even created my own screening system that I leverage in my business, which I share with you later in the book. This doesn't mean that every tenant is a home run for my business. Though it does mean my batting average has gone way up. No landlord is perfect with tenant selection because we can't predict human behavior with 100% certainty. Nor can we predict the economy or other market factors that have an impact on our tenant's ability to pay rent or fulfill their end of the rental lease agreement. The principles taught in the model work. I have put them to the test time and time again. The single most important factor in whether I succeed or fail in rental real estate, being tenant selection, is no longer a liability in my business.

The concepts in the S.T.A.I.R. Model are not new. I didn't create them for the purposes of this book. I simply thought long and hard about what makes the most successful real estate investors so successful. I reflected on how I personally attained the point I am at. Once I went through the process and identified several of those key attributes, I worked to develop the model itself. I created the acronym S.T.A.I.R. because I view it similar to the process of climbing stairs. You climb one stair to reach the next then the next until ultimately you reach the top of the staircase, which in this case is your target. I view success as not a moment in time, though a journey to the top. Each stair you take is a point of success reached. Climbing all the steps will result in ultimate success. This leads us to another concept that many consider to be the pinnacle of expertise around a particular skill or area of focus, that is *mastery*. Mastery is the pinnacle of success in a particular area of focus. Let's review how leveraging the S.T.A.I.R. Model can help us reach *mastery* within rental real estate.

MASTERY IS THE ULTIMATE GOAL

Collins English Dictionary describes *mastery* as, "Outstanding skill, expertise, full command or understanding of a subject, expert skill or knowledge." It also states that, "If you show mastery of a particular skill or language, you show that you have learned or understood it completely and have no difficulty using it." This all sounds pretty awesome to me! If you attain mastery in real estate investing, you are essentially an expert who has full command and understanding of the business. You have also amassed a great deal of financial success. This is an ultimate and very worthy goal of any real estate investor. I am certainly seeking mastery and am well on my way there. Though I realize I must persevere in continuous learning and growth, following the principles in the S.T.A.I.R. Model. I have also heard it said that spending 10,000 hours on something will result in mastery. I believe this is *almost* true. it should state:"10,000 hours of intentional learning and action will result in mastery of a subject." The keyword is intentional. Our actions must be intentional for them to count toward growth. True desire, focus and commitment are essential to reach mastery in any subject. Rental real estate is no different.

In my position as Vice President at RE/MAX World Headquarters, we preach mastery of concepts to our network of franchise owners and agents around the globe. Our core curriculum and success framework focus on business fundamentals that are foundational and critical to success in their business. We teach, train and consult our network around certain leading principles. Mastery can be attained by a franchise owner or agent who commits to what is required. A consistent message that we share is that of *doing*. Think of the 'Study-Try-Assess-Iterate-Repeat' or S.T.A.I.R. Model I just introduced. The core tenets of this model are built around how to attain mastery. You can't get there by skipping steps or being mediocre. Mastery requires the entire cycle and being intentional about attaining it.

There are stories of Michael Jordan taking thousands of shots in pursuit of mastery. Kobe Bryant practiced again both after a team practice session and a game. How many people do you know that will practice immediately AFTER a game? For me, I'm not sure I know any. How many people do you know will study again AFTER they take a test? Tiger Woods built a practice facility on his personal property so he can practice both common and uncommon shots and putts for hours at a time, day after day. He does this when he isn't competing on the golf course somewhere. Russell Wilson of the Seattle Seahawks is known to invite his receivers to Southern California during the offseason, where he owns a home, to train and condition together. He even pays for their travel! He runs route concepts with them until they feel comfortable passing and catching together. It is proven that chemistry between a quarterback and receiver is what makes all the difference between the good and the very best. There is a reason these people are considered the absolute best in their sport. They are INTENTIONAL in what they do: in constantly working to improve their game, in their focus on being the very best.

LET'S WRAP A BOW ON THIS CHAPTER

Congratulations, you've finished Chapter Two and learned something new to improve your rental real estate business! The focus of this chapter is to become a student of rental real estate who learns through study, experience and eventual progression toward mastery.

Be a student of the game. Always be a student. Always be learning. Turn your learning into action as early and often as possible.

The best teacher is experience. The 70-20-10 model is proof that the best learning is by doing. Seventy percent of what we truly learn comes through experience. Education is important, though until coupled with action it is simply theory.

The S.T.A.I.R. Model. Study, Try, Assess, Iterate, Repeat. The S.T.A.I.R. Model is a reminder that success requires multiple steps, including education, action, analysis and making changes for better.

Mastery is the ultimate goal. Intentional learning and effort are required to attain mastery. This should be your ultimate goal. Mastery can only be attained through repeated and disciplined action over time. Start now!

THREE

YOU CAN'T WIN ALONE—THIS IS A TEAM GAME!

I n life, I've noticed that there isn't much that can be truly accomplished alone, without the help of others. Children learn to talk and walk through the help of their parents, siblings and others. Students learn reading, writing and arithmetic through teachers and tutors. Athletes learn to improve their skills from a coach or trainer. Employees learn to enhance their performance through mentors and bosses. In each instance, other people are the ones whom we learn and grow from. Yes, we can learn through self-study. However, what are you studying? The behavior, experiences and research of other people! Technically, even self-study requires the help of others. Even professional golfers, who compete in an individual sport, have swing coaches, caddies and conditioning coaches that help them compete at the highest level. Just like most other endeavors in life, teams are essential in the game of rental real estate, or being a landlord. This chapter will cover everything from why you need a team to how you go about building and maintaining that team through lasting success.

WHY YOU NEED A TEAM

You are the investor. Typically, though not always, it is your money being leveraged to invest in your real estate business. You may also have a business partner or two. However, this is not the team I am referencing here. Real estate investors will only go so far alone. In fact, I feel very confident in saying if you take this road alone, you will likely become one of the failure stories that starts scaring other people out of investing in real estate. "Oh, it is so hard." "There isn't money in rental real estate." "It's not what it's made out to be." These are the excuses that come from people who either (a) don't know what they are doing or (b) knew what to do and didn't execute well enough. You may be asking, are these people part of the investing team? Do we split our profits with this team? Who is this team you are referring to and how do we find them or build one? Let's walk through how to build a *great team*.

For starters, the group of people that will form your team are as follows:

- Business Partner
- Real Estate Agent
- Lender
- Handyman
- Insurance Agent
- Property Manager
- Attorney
- Electrician
- Plumber
- Inspector

HOW TO FIND YOUR TEAM

Finding your team is the most challenging step in the building process. It's worth giving the team an acronym because I think it makes certain concepts easier to remember. Let's go with R-E-S-T (Real Estate Success Team). I will promise you this: you *will rest* better and easier if you build your R.E.S.T. the right way. Be sure to continuously add value on your end. I recommend three specific methods of building value as you begin building your ideal team, in order of effectiveness.

Look through your network for people you may already know. This is a great place to start. I started this way with my real estate agent, my original lender and my insurance agent. This helped with my confidence getting into the game because I knew these people would have my best interest in mind and would not take advantage of me. Luckily, this proved to be the case in my personal experience. People don't want to let you down. Especially if their reputation and livelihood are on the line. Not everyone that started on my R.E.S.T. is still there today. As your business changes, so will the people in it.

Ask for referrals. There are plenty of simple and painless ways to ask for recommendations these days. The most obvious may be leveraging your social media network. Perhaps you know people who are in the real estate business and you seek them out for a referral. The Bigger Pockets network is another example of a social network full of people you don't necessarily know first-hand, though can aid in connecting you with others you may be looking for. Ask your family if they know someone. Ask your friends. Ask your agent, your lender, your insurance agent, or anyone else that may know.

The cold-call approach. If you need a real estate agent because you just moved to a new area and don't know anyone, crack open the digital phone book and start dialing! More agents than not will be interested in your business because you are potential income for them. On multiple occasions, I have cold called lenders, shopping interest rates, lending terms and other critical factors when looking for a solid lender. In fact, it was because of this approach I was able to close most of my deals. As my rental real estate business grew, I could no longer rely on a typical lender. I needed to branch out into the commercial world. I made the dials and found two lenders over time that have proven to be a major reason why I was able to grow my business at the pace I did. Don't be afraid to make the call. Keep in mind that in this case you are the type of cold call they will be excited to answer! There won't be an insurance agent that wouldn't return your phone call, for example. What you are doing here is not just looking for a good fit, but also the best deal!

HOW TO GET YOUR TEAM ONBOARD AND ON YOUR SIDE

You may be thinking, why do I need people to be onboard? What do you mean on my side? I'll go back to the introduction of the chapter; you can't do it alone. Nobody scales a successful business all alone. Ask any millionaire or even billionaire if they reached the pinnacle of success all on their own. There won't be a single one that says they didn't do it without the help of many other incredibly talented and intelligent people working alongside them. Neither will you. Are we in agreement? Great! Let's continue.

Imagine this: your real estate agent finds an amazing deal that would be ideal for your portfolio. Do they bring it to you? The answer is, it depends on how you have invested in that relationship. How you treat people and invest in relationships matters. It doesn't require an over-the-top amount of attention or money. However, make a call to check in. Send a text. Send them a message on their birthday. Take them to lunch. Bottom line, add value and you will stand out among the crowd. Whether they bring the best deals to you first depends on what you've done with that relationship. Zig Ziglar reinforces this when he said, "If people like you, they'll listen to you, but if they trust you, they'll do business with you." In the real estate industry, know, like and trust are still King. If people know, like and trust you they are exponentially more likely to do business with you. It starts there. Personally, I wouldn't want to go into business with or even conduct business with an egotistical dirtbag. Whom I do business with matters as much as the business I'm doing. I'm not the only one who feels strongly about this, so pay attention and do your part.

This thinking applies across the board. In short, the golden rule of life applies here: treat others the way you'd like to be treated and they are much more likely to return the favor. My business partner and I have made a concerted effort to build strong relationships with our real estate agent, lender and our handyman. All of the relationships are important, though I believe these three are the most important. Let me share with you some of the things we've done to build a strong rapport. First and foremost, we are kind and fair. We never talk down to anyone, have ridiculous demands or get angry when things don't go as expected. We treat everyone with dignity and respect. That is the baseline for a positive relationship. Next, we make time to break bread with them. We make it a point to go to a restaurant, have a nice meal, enjoy each other's company, get to know each other better and sprinkle in some business ideas or future plans. We stay in contact and not just for every business deal. It is important for them to know you are around and are interested in maintaining a relationship with them. I make a point to be connected with them on social media and show interest in their lives by sending birthday wishes and engaging in their posts. Our handyman speaks fluent Spanish as do I. I make a concerted effort to speak with him only in Spanish and he loves it! I was also invited to his home for a nice ceviche dish, which I accepted, even though we were headed home after a long day's work. Taking the time to build relationships is worth the effort in gold.

BUILDING A STRONG TEAM

Building a strong team starts with building around your core group of players. In professional sports, the very best teams are built around a core group of elite talent. Each player on the team has a role, though each role is different. For your R.E.S.T. I recommend building with a strong core. Let me introduce to you the Core Four. This is the core group of people you literally cannot be successful without. They are likely to be around for more than a single transaction. They make the largest impact within your business. They are your most valuable players. I'll share briefly about why each of them is so important to your rental real estate business.

Business Partner. This is the single most important relationship in your business. Most people don't get into real estate by themselves. If you do, you can skip this section. Your business partner can be a spouse, a relative, a friend or a network connection. Business partnerships exist because they work. No single person on the planet has every skill essential to run a successful business or enterprise alone. You may have one or multiple business partners. Each business partner should bring something unique and of value to the relationship. One partner may be in charge of operations while another brings the capital and finds the deals. Treat your business partner well. It's important this relationship is positive and a win-win. Strong partnerships can produce amazing results. Many times, the partnership itself is the reason for success. My business partner and I rely on each other's strengths to elevate our business. I am grateful for Austin. He happened to be a friend of mine first, which I share about later in the book. I can attribute the business success we've shared to our strong partnership. The legal entity name of our business is 'Los Panas', which is a slang term in Ecuador that means 'best buds'. I can truly say our business wouldn't be where it is today if he wasn't core to it.

Real Estate Agent. Most people probably think of the real estate agent first when we talk about building a Real Estate Team and with good reason. Agents are essentially your starting point. The words 'real estate' are also in their title. You need a quality agent to help you find deals, get you into properties, access detailed information only they can obtain, inquire of the selling agent, negotiate your purchase price and sales agreement, manage the contract deadlines, coordinate everything from insurance to title, then tell you where to be and when to sign! The real estate agent basically does everything that you don't want to do and shouldn't be doing yourself. They are also very well connected with important people that can help build out or fill out your R.E.S.T.

I hear the question a lot: "Should I get my own real estate license so I can save the 5-6% commission expense on each deal?" I highly recommend *not* doing this. First off, the 5-6% is really only 2-3% because the other half goes to the other party's agent, whether you have one or not. The only way out of this is doing everything yourself and hiring a broker who may charge 1-3% vs 5-6% total. I don't recommend this idea either unless you and the seller are both not represented and can negotiate everything without intervention or seriously offending each other. The agent acts as a great buffer between you and the other party, which is a great benefit. Real estate agents must study and pass a state licensing exam. They must complete annual compliance training and continuing education credits. They must also pay annual dues even if they do zero business, all for the privilege of having an active license. On top of that, in order to practice real estate, you have to hang your license with a brokerage, who will also charge you fees! Let me make this very clear, it is not worth the hassle, unless this is how you plan to make money and provide for your family. Hire a good real estate agent and you will be very happy you did. The best agents know more people and have more relationships. Our agent has brought us about one third of the doors in our entire portfolio and we are thrilled he is part of our core.

This Happened to Me – 'Substitute' agent called up

When I first began investing in a town outside of where I live, I wanted to use someone I knew as my real estate agent because I needed that sense of comfort and assurance to boost my confidence. I used this agent successfully for my first seven deals. He was great! However, I felt like I was doing the lion's share of the work. I would find the properties I was interested in. I would drive into town and complete due diligence. I would most times tour the properties alone or with the selling agent. It wasn't that my agent didn't care, it's that he didn't live or operate in that part of the state. He didn't know the town, the deals or have the right network to be successful. As a result, I changed agents to find someone who did.

On my seventh deal, I was touring the property we would eventually purchase with the seller's agent. We clicked right away and exchanged contact information. He was young and motivated to succeed. Being early in his real estate career, he was going to work harder and go farther than most other agents to win our business and benefit his own. My business partner and I decided to give him a shot at doing just that. Less than a month later, he came to us with a couple of off-market properties that would end up being our first multi-family purchases. The deals he found were not listed on the MLS. They were found as a result of his networking within the community.

The duplex and triplex we purchased in this deal were under contract for such a great price, not even the appraiser could come in at value. The properties appraised for $50,000 *above* purchase price. Not only did we find a great off-market deal, we walked into a significant amount of equity. These properties today are now worth a solid $150,000 above what we purchased them for. Needless to say, this particular agent won our business. We have used him for all of our deals since then. We just purchased our first qualified apartment building, with eight total units. It pays to call on your bench because you never know the true starting potential that lies underneath unless they get a chance to play.

Lender. Money, money, money. Enough said right? Real estate deals don't happen without money (aka capital). For most investors, you cannot start without borrowing money from a financial institution. This is why lenders are so critical to your success. As mentioned previously, we would not have been able to purchase many of our deals without a great lender. A lender can be an individual, a public or private group, or a financial institution at its core. When I refer to our 'lender' I am referring to the individual connection that I have within the financial institution (or bank) that we conduct business with. We have made it a point to find good lenders, then build strong relationships with them. Our current lender happens to own an amazing taco shop in town, which is another great benefit. Our lenders have pulled off the impossible for us and we are very appreciative. As such, we make it a point to build strong relationships with them. We stay in contact with them and ensure they have a sense of where we are financially speaking and what's in the cards next. I wouldn't have a business without good lenders and neither will you because money doesn't grow on trees, it comes from your source of financial capital!

This Happened to Me – The 'environmental zone' loan

It was just the second deal with my business partner, third deal in all. We stumbled across a unique situation that pushed us into ambiguity and discomfort. We had leveraged the very beneficial lending terms of the government via Fannie Mae/Freddie Mac loans to this point. However, this latest property was on the market for a killer price and we needed to act quickly. There weren't many qualified buyers in the market because the property was located inside a geographical area labeled as the 'Colorado Smelter Superfund Area'. As a result, investors couldn't qualify for the government-backed loan. Instead, we had to find a local lender that would do the deal. We knew hard money was not our best option because we didn't have a lot of cash on hand and there was no way we could pay the note back within a year. My network of lenders was only offering government-backed loans, so I had to get creative.

I had read a great tip in a book that establishing a relationship with a local lender could prove very beneficial to my business. I started dialing all of the local lenders in town that would offer financing for the superfund zone.

The first 6 calls I made were unfruitful. Maybe I was asking the wrong questions. I wasn't sure. I was looking for a commercial loan. Many in the banking world also call these portfolio loans. Essentially, the loan is fully backed by that financial institution, not the government. On my seventh call, I came across a very kind and patient lender who answered yes to basically every question I was asking. I became very excited! He did mention the caveat that they only recently started to offer these types of loans as part of their strategic business expansion efforts. "Well, lucky for me!" I thought to myself. In the end, we were successful in our quest to find a local lender willing to take a chance on us. They were able to see the investment potential beyond the imaginary boundary line because they were local. We financed five properties using this lender and built a very strong, mutually beneficial relationship.

Handyman. Rounding out your Core Four, the handyman typically isn't the first member of your team, though they very well may be the most important of them all. Real estate comes with one guarantee: something will break and require fixing. Unless you have all the skills necessary, which most don't, or the necessary time, which most don't, you'd better invest in finding a reliable and trustworthy handyman. We have had some good and bad fortune with this team member. We've had to fire some while giving others more responsibility. The handyman is your go-to person that addresses most every problem your business encounters. If a sink is leaking, a window is broken, the water heater isn't working, a tenant is moving out, a room needs painted, an appliance doesn't turn on...who do you call? Your handyman!

It is best to have a single person for most everything. However, it is hard to find. Our handyman addresses upwards to 80% of all issues our business encounters. The rest is handled by specialists. Our handyman happens to be a plumber, roofer, painter, flooring specialist, gutter professional and much more! Also, if he can't personally handle a situation, he knows the people who can. He is an invaluable member of the team! This is also the one position on your team where having a backup or two riding your bench is expedient. Emergencies and repairs wait for nobody! Finally, your handyman is in front of your customer more than any member of the team. What they do and say is a representation of you as the landlord. Be sure they are professional and trustworthy.

This Happened to Me – The 'I can do anything' guy

Our first handyman was inexpensive and friendly with our tenants, making them feel somewhat comfortable around him. However, he was not an expert tradesman in a particular trade or an exceptional talent in much of anything. He did usually get the job done and was decent in his responsiveness. I will call him Tom as I relate this story to you. After my business partner and I purchased our first rental property, we were on site doing some cleanup and yard work. Tom walked over from across the street and introduced himself. We had a cordial and engaging conversation for the next 30 minutes. Tom appeared to be kind, reputable and honest. He lived across the street with his father and had lived in town his entire life. He knew people in town and considered himself a master handyman, offering his services should we need them.

My business partner and I did not live in this town, did not have a network there and certainly didn't know any great handymen. So logically when the first need of repair came along, we called Tom! He was great and affordable. Our first repair was a success. We subsequently used Tom for a number of jobs, probably 20-30 times in total. We would hear decent feedback from tenants. We did have to send him back a few times to correct some work, though no major red flags. That was, until we got into more serious plumbing repairs. Tom had repaired a toilet, unclogged a sink and cleared a sewer line for us already. However, he didn't always communicate well, do the job right the first time or even have the proper tools to do the work. This resulted in multiple callbacks, having to rent or purchase tools for him to complete the work and some frustration that built between us and Tom. We justified continuing to use Tom because he could do a bit of everything and was saving us money, or so we thought.

We had paid to rent a plumbing snake three or four times and got to the point where we decided it would be more economical to buy one for him to use on our jobs. We'll come back to this later. The call we dreaded came in from one of our tenants. We soon found out why Tom's pricing was so great! Our tenant reported sewage seeping back up the toilet line not long after flushing. The next day they reported the sewage making its way into the bathtub as well! Imagine the lovely scene and smell. There was just one bathroom and one toilet in this property, as is the case with most of the single-family homes in town built before 1970. We called Tom and had him assess the situation. He went over there rather promptly and being the chatty bird he was, he needlessly ranted for 20 minutes about all the possibilities. Of course, he went for the simple route first: the plumbing snake. He started to use the snake that we bought and broke the head attempting to snake out the main sewer line. He took it back and had it replaced where we purchased it from. He made a second attempt, same result. He took it back the third time and the retailer called me in a fuss because Tom wasn't using the equipment properly and forced them to replace the device because it was under warranty. They wouldn't replace the head for him this time. He then explained to us in excruciating detail why he needed to dig a massive hole in the backyard to further assess the situation. A week had now gone by with zero progress. Our tenants were rightfully upset and unable to live in the property. They were staying at a relative's house in town and were being somewhat patient with us. It got worse. Much worse.

Reports came back from the tenant that Tom had dug five or six holes around the backyard that were several feet deep. I called to inquire what was happening and Tom assured me he was on track and almost to the 'root' cause. Well, that *was* the root cause...*tree roots*! Lots of them, in fact. The main sewer line was old copper material and the tree roots had fully penetrated multiple areas of the line. It was so badly backed up because the sewage had nowhere to go. It would get stuck in the roots and then seep slowly into the soil in the backyard. From there, Tom hired a few helpers to dig the holes...with hand shovels! I told him to rent some excavation equipment to which he declined and assured me that everything would be fine.

Ten days had now gone by, still no working toilet, shower or water in general. Our tenants were growing very upset and began to explain the situation on the ground and the level of effort that Tom was putting into the job. It was nowhere near finished. Tom had already demanded labor money to cover his work to that point, which of course we paid. He then told us he needed to remove two trees that were causing most of the root problem before they would replace the damaged parts of the line. I insisted he replace the entire line and he assured me he could and 'knew how'. I also assumed that Tom was using power equipment to remove the tree and its roots. Well, I also found this assumption to be incorrect as they were using shovels and hand saws to attack this monumental beast of a job. It was as if we were living in ancient times...with plumbing and unintelligent laborers.

By this point, we felt so terrible about the situation the tenant was in we offered to put them up in a hotel until this was resolved. This calmed them down for a few days, yet also cost us a pretty penny. We were also not requiring any rent during the downtime for the inconvenience. We were still fairly new at the landlord game. We were getting some serious on-the-job training with this ordeal! Now over two weeks had passed, the tenant was enraged and so were my business partner and I as we learned that Tom had still yet to remove one of the two trees and had made zero progress on the line. His excuses and reasoning were mounting up. He loved to talk about why things were not going as planned and how he could handle the situation. I finally gave up on Tom and posted a desperate ad on Craigslist for help. I received several calls and went with the first three people that had inquired. I asked them all to go to the property, assess the situation and provide me with a bid. In the end, this resulted in finding our current handyman, who *is* experienced in all the right areas. He replaced the entire sewer line in three days. Everything was back up and running. Lost money, upset tenants, frustration, wasted time, lost goodwill and more were the result of our lack of due diligence. In this case, don't be like us: learn from our mistakes!

The Core Four are where you should begin building your R.E.S.T. Build up that group as soon as possible and you'll be grateful you did. As reviewed earlier in the chapter, the people you need on almost any real estate team are as follows:

- Business Partner
- Real Estate Agent
- Lender
- Handyman
- Insurance Agent
- Property Manager
- Attorney
- Electrician
- Plumber

- Inspector

You may need others, such as an accountant or an administrative assistant. Though for the essentials, we will stick with this group. Each is important in their own right. Your business is best served by building a network that includes each in some capacity. Let's review the remaining team members and why they are essential.

The Insurance Agent. Insurance is something you must have. Use it or not, it's essential. Each home or building requires its own insurance policy. You cannot get a loan without first having insurance locked down. Also, you don't want to invest without having an insurance policy. Choosing an insurance agent is important because they can help you find suitable and affordable insurance with speed and convenience. My agent is an independent broker, meaning they can shop different insurance providers for the best coverage and premium cost. The right agent is as important as the right coverage.

The Property Manager. A good property manager or property management company can make all the difference between the success of your rental real estate business or its failure. The property manager is the direct contact with your tenants and repairmen. If the property manager is bad at what they do, it could have a negative cascading effect impact your business. This could be devastating and therefore, this particular team member needs to be strong and reliable. As I've mentioned, I don't currently use a property manager to manage my rental portfolio. For now, I prefer to do it myself because I trust myself more than anyone else. Plus, I want to keep as much of the profits as possible to continue reinvesting in our business. This may change in the near future as our portfolio continues to grow and the demands on our time become more cumbersome. A good property manager can also be a major benefit to your business: helping with tenants wanting to stay longer and finding higher quality tenants that consistently pay and keep the property in good shape. They are an extension of you and your business. *Choose wisely*.

The Attorney. I know, attorneys. I get it. They are not always money-sucking and vile. Attorneys can be a savior to a landlord if they are knowledgeable about the real estate laws in the state in which you conduct business and are client-focused. Our business relies on a good attorney's office to help us through the eviction process. Again, the eviction process is my very least favorite component of being a landlord. However, as shared in Chapter Ten, a good attorney can make this process effective and less painful for you. Having an attorney to counsel you through a rental lease agreement or a case where you are uncertain how to proceed with a tenant or a contract, is helpful. Finally, if you are sued by a tenant or contractor, having an established relationship with an attorney's office will be a huge plus.

The Electrician. Having a relationship with a licensed electrician is always recommended. Sometimes, your handyman can be a licensed electrician, most often they are not. Electrical work, similar to plumbing, is not the area where you look to cut corners and costs. Be smart because lives depend on it. Electrical fires are some of the most common causes for house fires. In the town where my rental portfolio is, most of the properties are older. This means the original wiring would not be up to code for today's standards. Most of the properties have been renovated and the electrical upgraded. However, I've seen more times than I'd like to count that patch jobs or partial upgrades were done to reduce costs. A certified electrician can be the difference between life or death and your property not burning down! I will share with you a story about this almost happening at one of my properties.

This Happened to Me – The 'nob & tube' disaster

At one of our single-family rental properties, there was a repair request reported that was completely unrelated to electrical. There was a roof leak that damaged the interior ceiling. Our handyman had to get into the attic to assess the full extent of the damage. During this assessment, our handyman notified us that even though the rest of the residence had upgraded electrical, there was 'nob & tube' electrical wiring in the attic that was still live. He said there was severe evidence of charring in the attic with several wires completely exposed. It was a dangerous situation that required immediate remedy.

I'll never forget the horrible feeling in my gut when I saw the pictures of the charred wood in the attic. Most house inspectors are not inspecting 100% of the electrical work because it is hidden behind walls, ceilings, and other surfaces. It isn't always caught. If it weren't for this ceiling repair, we wouldn't have discovered this risky reality. Fortunately, our handyman was able to disconnect the power as we had our electrician come by to rectify the situation. The electrical repair ended up being $3,000 and completely unexpected. However, the electrician said we made the absolute right call and he was surprised there hadn't been more severe fire damage. Disaster averted and property saved! This could have had a very different outcome. As I write this, I feel so blessed again to have discovered this when we did!

The Plumber. Having a licensed plumber on your team is extremely beneficial. Plumbing is not something you take chances on. Get it right or pay the price. Someone who simply 'does' plumbing doesn't make them an expert. Be sure they are licensed and have a solid reputation before going into business with them. One rule of thumb I use is to give someone an audition. Hire them to complete one job, preferably a smaller one, before deciding to use them on larger jobs or exclusively. Another rule of thumb I use is to always have two plumbers and electricians in your contacts. These are high-demand professions and having a backup can prove valuable when your primary is booked two weeks out. I also highly recommend your plumber be independent. If they are an employee of a major plumbing company in town, expect to pay a lot more. Our plumber will snake a line for $80 vs the local plumbing company $239 for the same job. It's worth searching for.

The Inspector. Having a reliable and reputable home inspector is a wonderful addition to your team. The home inspector is responsible for thoroughly inspecting the property you plan to purchase and providing you with a detailed report and analysis on their findings. Average inspectors simply accept your payment, complete the inspection and report, then send you a copy. A thorough inspector will invite you to join them on-site during the inspection. They will walk you through the property to review both areas of confidence and concern. They will tell you what is essential to repair vs what can wait. Finally, they will make themselves available for any additional follow-up you have before closing on the deal. A great inspector is a partner of yours who will be honest in their property assessment. You need a thorough inspector on your team. Ask for recommendations. You will be glad you did.

HOW TO WIN THROUGH A PARTNERSHIP

Many people hesitate to jump into real estate because they don't want to deal with everything alone. Being a landlord can be a lonely game at times. You are the sole person responsible for everything in this book! That can be daunting to many. As a result, many people never get started. Even worse, many more get started and then leave the business because of this overwhelming responsibility that comes with being a landlord. Not everyone is cut out for it and that's alright, because it helps others, like you and me, take advantage of these opportunities to grow our businesses. One alternative to this is a business partnership. In most cases, a partnership is an agreement which includes a 50/50 split in debt service, capital expenses, property management responsibilities and profit. Other arrangements do exist, though this form is most common and what I will elaborate on. A real estate partnership can be beneficial for many reasons. I will focus on three that have been crucial for my business: reduction of risk, ability to grow faster, and sharing the burden of responsibility.

Reduction of risk. When you purchase a property on your own, you assume 100% of the risk. The major risk categories of owning rental real estate are taking on debt, bad tenants, lawsuits, repairs and market factors. Alone, you assume 100% of the risk for it all. Together, the risk is 50/50, which is a huge relief for most people!

Ability to grow faster. Alone, you are limited to the capital in your bank account. This may restrict your ability to grow. Most investors don't come with large amounts of capital or rich families willing to front the money. Most people need capital and a bank to loan the rest. Once again, the burden of risk is lower with two people for financial institutions. Their willingness to lend you money alone, vs with a partner, is viewed differently. Together, you can ask for more money and put up more capital. This allows you to grow faster.

Burden of responsibility. I view this as the primary benefit of a partnership. The load can be heavy, especially with over ten rental doors. Property marketing, applications, tenant screening, accounting, rent collection, taxes, insurance, tenant calls, repairs, analysis and more all has to get done. Sharing the burden of responsibility allows for more to get done and your capacity doubles. Plus, you have a built-in consultant or decision-making partner to brainstorm challenges, opportunities and the best path forward.

This Happened to Me – My 'dream' business partner

My business partner Austin and I were beyond excited after purchasing our very first rental property together in March 2016. We met in 2004, as missionaries in the wonderful country of Ecuador. We were assigned as 'companions' during my final stint in the country, serving the incredible people of Guayaquil. We were young, broke and full of dreams! We shared a love for punk-rock music. We shared childhood stories and sang punk-rock songs audibly while sweating profusely as we walked the streets of our 'barrio' called 'Union Civica'. We walked everywhere. It was hot, humid and brutal on our feet. Yet, we carried on in pursuit of something better, in pursuit of blessing the lives of as many people as possible. It was during these long, hot and arduous days that we found solace in sharing our life dreams. We bonded and became great friends in a short period of time. We discovered a mutual interest of owning real estate and decided right there, on the front lines, that someday we would invest together.

We both returned home in the year 2005. I returned to Seattle, Washington and Austin to Orange County, California. We each pursued our advanced education and girls! We wanted to start a family above all. We both met our future wives while attending the university. I was married at 23, Austin at age 25. The Denby's and Kennedy's now each have four children of similar ages and are basically family. My kids refer to Austin as 'Uncle Austy'. Through it all, our dream of owning real estate together never faded. In fact, over the years of gaining education, pursuing girls and starting our respective careers, we would continue this discussion of building a rental property empire. Other life events and priorities like our careers and families took precedence.

In late 2015, I decided that it was time to invest in real estate. I was fully committed to making it happen as I shared earlier. 2016 was the target year. I went under contract on that first property in December 2015 and closed early February 2016. I did it! I was officially a real estate investor. While under contract, I was so thrilled with how everything came together that I couldn't wait to share my excitement with Austin. By this point, our families had grown and we were better established in our careers. I was making decent money and had saved some stock purchase + end of year bonus money as capital. I called Austin to share with him the news one day as I was driving home from the office. When I shared with him all of my preparation, the fact that I was under contract and the numbers behind the investment, he asked, "When can we get started together?!" I told him, "Bro, that's why I called you!! Let's do this together, finally, like we always dreamed of". I mentioned that I had already seen 15 properties before I made an offer on this first one and had narrowed the list down to a top 5 that I would be willing to purchase. I shared with him the top 5 and within a month, we were under contract on one of them. This is where 'Los Panas Ltd.' was born.

The property was in Colorado. Austin still lived in California. We decided he would fly out for closing and then we'd spend 2-3 days preparing the property for rent, doing open houses, meeting people in town and getting the property rented. We were a team again, just like in Ecuador! We had around 10 prospective tenants stop by in those two days. Just one submitted an application. Their names, for confidentiality purposes, will be Joe & Mary.

Joe was tattooed up and always wore a bandana. Mary, his girlfriend, let her age and life decisions show by her appearance. We were not deterred though, because they WANTED TO RENT OUR PROPERTY! We had spent money and time advertising the property, sprucing it up and showing it. We didn't want our wives to think less of us by not renting out the property that weekend. Naturally, we listened to Joe say he would care for the lawn and be *on top of it*. Mary was the tidiest person alive and would be *so great* with the place. They had money in the bank. Joe was paid by a government and military pension every month that more than covered 3x rent. Financially they were set and they wanted to move in ASAP! What more could we ask for at this point? After some due diligence in calling references, confirming income and verifying background we offered Joe & Mary our first business partnership rental property! They accepted and we were off to the races. We signed the lease agreement, did the walkthrough, collected the move-in funds and handed over the keys.

Today, we collectively own and manage 27 doors. I have 10 properties on my own for a personal portfolio of 37. Austin and I built this together while both working full-time jobs, raising four young kids and navigating life's demands. The shared burden of risk, the ability to grow faster and the shared burden of responsibility were all manageable because of our partnership. Above all, we have fun doing it! We commiserate over horrible tenants and painful repairs. It has been a blast as everything was shared, both successes and failures. Our reliance on each other has been a major boon to our friendship and growing business.

Based on the information shared in this chapter, I am confident that you now understand the importance of having a Real Estate Success Team to support you and your business. In the end this is your business and you are the head coach of your R.E.S.T. As head coach, you decide who plays for your team and who to suit up during game time. If a team member is underperforming, you'll need to determine whether to keep them or find a replacement. I recommend having a bench for instances like this. That doesn't mean that you are constantly using two or three of a certain position. It does mean you have built up your network sufficiently to be able to call on the replacements as necessary. You can substitute players on your team or cut them completely if need be. Trust me, there will be a 'need be' at some point. I shared some of those scenarios with you in this chapter that I hope you can learn from. A wise person learns from their own mistakes and of others. The unwise choose to commit the mistake themselves, even though there are plenty of examples for why it's a terrible idea. Be the wise person. Follow the guidance in this chapter to ensure you are winning after the deal.

LET'S WRAP A BOW ON THIS CHAPTER

Congratulations, you've finished Chapter Three and learned something new to improve your rental real estate business! The focus of this chapter is to help you realize that winning in the rental real estate game is not a solo act. Building a successful team around you will allow for more efficiency, less stress, and a higher growth potential.

Why you need a team. You will only go so far alone. Real estate investing requires a team effort with respect to finding property, securing insurance, obtaining funding, managing property and more.

How to find your team. Finding your Real Estate Success Team, or R.E.S.T. should be done right away. Look through your network for people you may already know, ask for referrals and make the dials.

How to get your team onboard and on your side. Invest time and effort into keeping a solid team or you may soon be without those you once depended upon to run your business. Your team brings you business, helps secure funding and then keeps your business flowing!

Building a strong team. Build your team and don't wait! Some positions needed on your team are: real estate agent, lender, insurance agent, property manager, handyman, attorney, electrician, plumber and inspector.

How to win through a partnership. Partnerships can be a great approach for your business. It can speed up growth, limit liability and take some stress out of the process. Being a landlord can be a lonely game at times, consider whether this could be a good option for you.

FOUR

CREATE AND LEVERAGE A WINNING RENTAL LEASE AGREEMENT

R ental real estate is just like all other businesses in that the law of the land is really important to both understand and follow. Understanding the laws and learning how to use them to your advantage will prove beneficial. The rental lease agreement is where the law comes in most handy for landlords. Laws may be lengthy and complicated in your state, though there are methods of learning what you can and cannot do without reading the exact verbiage of each legislation. Many widely available sources do an incredible job in summarizing the law simply for landlords like yourself. States such as California and New York have high amounts of regulation and additional laws that make being a landlord more challenging. Most other states have simpler landlord laws and are relatively straight forward. It's important to research the rental real estate laws in your state to understand your rights, as well as those of tenants. This chapter will cover the essentials of the rental lease agreement, including what it does and how to construct yours to best protect yourself and your business.

A RENTAL LEASE AGREEMENT DEFINED

A rental lease agreement (aka lease) can be defined as "a contract by which one party conveys land, property, services, etc. to another for a specified time, usually in return for a periodic payment." In this instance, you are the landlord who is renting property to your tenant for a specified period of time in return for rental payments every month. Simple enough? Great; let's move on.

A lease for a rental property should be a win/win proposition. Landlords have obligations toward a tenant who occupies one of your rental properties. The tenant also has obligations toward you and your property. As covered in Chapter Ten about deadbeat tenants and getting rid of them, the most effective way is to create a lease with many different, specific clauses that make it easy to prove when such are violated. Clear, simple and direct language is preferred. Being sure to include all common and some less-common scenarios is ideal. The intention of a lease is to clearly articulate each party's set of duties so there is no debate as to what those are, when they should be enforced and other relevant information. A lease takes the 'he said, she said' and 'maybe ifs' out of play legally. If you ever need to go to court and defend your position, your lease is your best defense.

One might think that the longer the rental lease period the better. This is not generally the case. Yes, all landlords would love to have their best tenants stay with them forever, however, having a five-year lease period could be more disastrous than beneficial. The hard truth is that you don't know how the person moving in is going to be as a tenant until they are living in your property. People have a knack for putting on a show or a positive façade, only to later show their true colors, which are much less admirable. The general consensus in the industry is a 12-month lease duration. You could obviously put other timeframes in there—longer or shorter—or even go month-to-month. The 12-month timeframe allows an exit opportunity without too much time passing and also enough cushion to know where your rental income will be sourced for the next year. Once you sign a lease, you are also unable to increase rents until that lease period is over.

ALL RENTAL LEASE AGREEMENTS ARE NOT MADE EQUAL

All rental lease agreements are not made equal. There are many different leases in existence for the very same thing, rental real estate. Most people understand the basic tenets of a lease and what it means for both parties. However, snagging a generic lease from the internet could be a recipe for disaster in your business and something I highly recommend against! We will cover the most common provisions for a lease next, though there are some provisions that are more or less important in certain states than others. For example, in Washington State or Oregon, mold is a very common nuisance for landlords and a potential danger for tenants. I grew up in the Pacific Northwest and mold was a common threat in homes. Moss from trees also damaged rooves if it wasn't properly addressed. Where I live now, Colorado, mold is almost never a problem because of the dry air. However, radon levels from the dirt in and underneath basements is a problem. In Florida, there should be a provision against giant, scary bugs and alligators! I'm only kidding, but I think this proves my point. Each landlord should build a lease for where they operate their rental real estate business. Don't trust Google for everything, especially without doing proper research. Any old Joe can put up just about anything without it being properly verified. Plus, this is a legal document.

When learning about how to construct your lease, I recommend doing thorough research. Look up the most common lease provisions in your state. Look up what should and shouldn't be included in a lease in your state. Yes, you can *start* with Google! Look for reputable sources that are in the real estate business who know your state laws. You can also find certified lease agreements online for each state. These typically come with a cost, though it's minimal, i.e., less than $50. You can also go to a site like Bigger Pockets, where they sell a pre-built lease agreement that has a foundational core, then separate lease agreements that are specifically tailored for each state. This is how I got started with my rental lease agreement. I then customized it further over time through the help of a local real estate attorney. I highly recommend consulting a local real estate attorney. If you bring them a pre-constructed lease, they can review it and provide feedback at a minimal cost. If you ask them to build you a lease from scratch, you will definitely pay more for this service.

This Happened to Me – The 'inherited lease' agreement

Upon acquiring a fully occupied triplex with three tenants, we were excited to begin immediately receiving rent payments and cash flow. It can be exciting when you purchase a rental property that has inherited tenants because you don't have to immediately commit the time to filling any of the units. On the flip side you also inherit whoever those tenants are and the existing lease until it expires! Upon reviewing the previous landlord's lease, we were a bit shocked. It was one page, front and back, had some chicken scratch written in and certain parts were illegible! I mean lease agreement 101 is to be sure everything on the paper is written clearly and neatly if it can't be printed. Apparently, this landlord didn't get the memo!

One of the three tenants was bad news from day one. She didn't pay rent, caused a disturbance with the neighbors and never answered her phone. She was a classic avoider and non-payer. We finally got a hold of her and she lied through her teeth about everything we asked. She was only two months into a twelve-month lease! We inherited a nightmare tenant accompanied by an unenforceable lease because they didn't agree to much at all! If she had signed *our* lease agreement, she would have violated at least 15 provisions, which would each be cause for eviction. The inherited lease allowed for us to evict due to non-rental payment, which was essentially the full extent of the legal reach.

Fortunately, we were able to work out a deal with her so she would just go away and not continue to be a problem for us. In this situation we learned some key lessons about inherited tenants and lease agreements. Once she left, we made some minor upgrades to the unit, cleaned it really well and rented it for $75 more than before! Except before we didn't actually get paid from this inherited tenant, so major upgrade!

This story highlights the fact that not all lease agreements are created equal. The value of each tenant is high. In order to be certain that your rights as a landlord are protected, your lease must be compliant and complete. With inherited tenants, once the lease expires, be sure to immediately replace it with your own. If you decide to renew with the existing tenant, have them agree to and sign/date *your* lease. If the inherited tenant(s) are not worth keeping, be sure to provide them with a 30-day written notice that they must vacate the property. This date must be after the inherited lease expires.

HOW TO CONSTRUCT YOUR RENTAL LEASE AGREEMENT

The construction or creation of your lease itself is not as important as ensuring the most pertinent and beneficial information is included to protect yourself and your asset from physical and/or financial damage. I recommend not building your own lease. This is a binding, legal agreement between you and your tenants that needs to be written with an accurate understanding of the law in your state. I repeat, have an attorney review your lease agreement to ensure it abides by your state's landlord laws. Be sure to review the lease agreement yourself, multiple times, to ensure that you understand what's in there and whether anything should be amended or added.

Having the essential areas covered explicitly will ensure that you are properly protected and *when* the time comes, able to act legally to enforce your lease. I've seen lease agreements from other landlords that were clearly not reviewed by an attorney and missed a significant portion of what I consider to be essential elements. This means that when I inherited these tenants, I had to abide by the previous landlord's lease until the expiration of the term. Sometimes it was a problem that I couldn't avoid. Don't be that type of landlord. Create your lease the right way because it protects everyone involved.

Now onto the actual construction of your lease. First, let me note that this is not every provision you can carry in your lease. Again, states vary in what they allow a landlord to enforce. Be sure to consult an attorney before assuming your lease is a winner. Below is a list of the most commonly included lease provisions and a brief explanation of what they include/why they are important to include:

Definitions, Names, Address, Phone Numbers, Email, Term. These sections are brief, though important. Defining the terms of the lease agreement allows for consistency and a better understanding of the terms used throughout, i.e., landlord, manager, owner, tenant, etc. Names are simply those that are agreeing to the lease. Take the time to get the legal names entered correctly. I recommend collecting copies of government-issued photo identification during the application process to ensure this is correct. If you have a legal dispute or are trying to evict someone and you don't have their full legal name or a copy of their identification, good luck enforcing your lease in court. I include middle names for this purpose. The address is common sense, though be sure to include the correct property address. Phone numbers are important because this is the number by which the tenant agrees to be available. This section includes a clause that a tenant must notify the landlord of a change in primary phone number. I also collect email addresses to connect with them on my rental management software. Collecting more contact information is never a bad thing. Term is simply the beginning and end dates of the lease. My lease includes a quick note that if the lease is not terminated after expiration by either party that the lease and all of its clauses continue on a month-to-month basis to ensure continued enforceability.

Rent. This section has several sub-sections worth noting for someone like you who is looking to build a winning lease.

- **Amount.** The amount you are agreeing for monthly rent.
- **Other rent due.** Any monthly fees, i.e., pet fees or if you collect final month's rent on lease signing.
- **Receipt of money paid.** How much rent and deposits, i.e., security/pet, you have collected from the tenant at lease signing.
- **Next payment.** The due date and amount of the next payment.
- **Due date.** When rent is due each month, including a grace period.
- **Late fee.** When late fees will be assessed and in what amount.
- **Eviction notice.** The landlord will serve an eviction notice, paid for by the tenant, if the tenant fails to pay rent by the due date.
- **Payment methods.** The methods by which a tenant may pay rent, i.e., cash, check, ACH transfer, online, etc.

- **Partial payment.** If the landlord accepts partial payment, they can still call for immediate payment of the unpaid balance of rent.

Security Deposit. This section covers the full spectrum of the security deposit, from what it covers to how it is dispositioned. It covers the time for repayment of the security deposit and what is deductible if the tenant doesn't perform their outlined obligations.

Furnishings & Appliances. This section includes a description of which appliances are provided by the landlord for the tenant's use. It covers the tenant's duty to keep the appliances clean and in good order, plus the landlord's obligation to fix or replace should they malfunction. The tenant covers the cost of any appliance they damage.

Negligence. This section describes the duty of the tenant with respect to any damages caused to the property as a result of personal negligence or willful acts, including any negligence or willful acts of the tenant's guests, invitees, friends, family or vandalism. It also holds the tenant responsible for the hazard insurance deductible should an insurance claim be filed to repair related damage to the property.

Premises Use. This section describes the proper use of the rental property as a residence. It outlines who is permitted to live at the residence, the policy on guests, the legal use of the property and other key behaviors around this subject.

Subletting. This section covers whether the tenant can sublet the property or assign the lease to another party.

Pest Control. This section provides a description of the period of pest control the landlord will cover vs what the tenant will cover and when.

Mold. This section applies universally, however, is much more critical in areas where moisture and weather conditions create a mold-friendly environment. It outlines what is covered and the duties of the landlord and tenant as it pertains to mold.

Default. This covers what happens if the tenant defaults any of the terms and conditions of the lease. It describes the landlord's rights under tenant default, pursuant to applicable laws. Interest charges and other financial penalties are outlined here.

Abandonment. This section describes what occurs if the premises appears abandoned and the tenant defaults in rent payments. It covers how the landlord will handle any of the tenant's personal property and that the tenant can't hold the landlord liable pursuant to the outlined conditions.

Death/Disability. This section covers what happens if a tenant dies before the lease term ends or becomes disabled to the extent it impacts their ability to pay rent.

Utilities. This section describes what utilities are covered by the landlord or tenant. It covers the tenant's duty for transferring utilities they are responsible for and by when. It also describes what happens if the tenant fails to fulfill their responsibilities with respect to utilities.

Sewer/Plumbing. This section describes the tenant's duty when a plumbing issue is caused by them, whether accidental or purposeful. The tenant also has the duty to notify the landlord of any plumbing issues within a certain period of time.

Liability and Renter's Insurance. This section describes that the landlord has no obligation to obtain insurance on behalf of the tenant and they are not responsible for their personal belongings in the event of an accident. The landlord may require the tenant obtain insurance or recommend it—should the tenant want to protect their belongings.

Access and Signs. This section permits the landlord access to inspect the premises at reasonable times by appointment. It also allows them to use the key to enter or enter by force, if necessary. It describes for what purposes the landlord may enter the premises and when. It also covers the landlord's right to display signage.

Maintenance. This section covers the landlord's obligation to maintain the structure, roof and foundation of the premises, along with other essentials (i.e., water, electrical). It covers the tenant's financial duties for any maintenance or damage caused by them directly or an omission of expected maintenance.

Care of the Premises. This section describes the tenant's obligations of caring for the premises, including trash & junk removal, general cleanliness, etc. It also describes the tenant's duty to notify the landlord of any damage or maintenance issues immediately. Any maintenance issues caused by the tenant will be covered by them as additional rent. It also covers what can and cannot be added or changed without landlord permission. My favorite part of this section is that vehicles may never be parked *in* the yard!

Windows. This section covers the tenant's duty for repairing broken glass and damage caused to screens, windows, frames or doors.

Window Coverings. This section instructs the tenant not to use bed sheets or any other coverings over the windows other than actual window coverings, such as blinds and curtains. The tenant is financially responsible for any damage caused to window coverings.

Garbage. This section outlines that the tenant's garbage must fit into receptacles and they are not allowed to dump large items, i.e., mattresses or TVs, in or next to receptacles. Tenants are responsible for extra dumping or the dumping of large items.

Access for Repairs. This section describes the tenant's obligation to allow hired contractors or repair personnel into the premises to conduct their work or the tenant will be assessed a fee.

Pets. This section outlines what is allowed or not allowed with respect to pets. Tenants must have prior written approval from the Landlord and pay additional fees to have pets on the premises.

Smoking. This section outlines that smoking on or inside the premises is strictly prohibited. I outline a fine of $500 for each offense to solidify the point. Be specific with verbiage to avoid ambiguity.

Marijuana and other Drugs. This section describes that tenants are not permitted to have or consume any drugs on the premises. This includes their invitees or guests. It also restricts the growing of marijuana or the commerce of any recreational or illegal substance.

Quiet Enjoyment. This section outlines that tenants are entitled to the quiet enjoyment of the premises and as such must not infringe on the same right of other tenants or neighbors. In other words, they are not allowed to throw major parties, fight incessantly, scream loudly or cause any other major disturbances.

Lawn/Pool Care. This section describes the tenant's obligation as it pertains to lawn or pool care. If there is no pool, this doesn't apply. It also outlines restrictions for trampolines, spas and other items without prior written consent from the landlord. I also outline in detail what the tenant is responsible for with respect to lawn care, such as weeds, because this is a problem where my business operates.

Yard Care. This section goes into detail about yard care obligations of the tenant from the prior section. I outline the specifics around weeds, trees, shrubs and trash plus the consequences for not complying.

Other Landlord Liability. This section details that the tenant will not hold the landlord liable for any injury or damage to themselves, the residence or their personal property as a result of defective or non-functioning items, i.e., the food inside a defective refrigerator.

Uninhabitability. This section provides liability coverage for the landlord should the residence or property become uninhabitable due to a fire or act of God. I include not being liable for any moving or other expenses the tenant incurs as a result.

Parking. This section describes parking requirements for tenants and their vehicles. For example, they cannot park their vehicle on the lawn or sidewalk. The vehicles must be in working order and registered.

Swimming Pools/Hot Tubs/Trampolines. This section specifies that swimming pools, hot tubs, trampolines and fish tanks are not permitted on the property unless prior written consent from the landlord is given. Violations incur a fee and possible eviction.

Alterations. This section outlines the requirements for making any changes to the property. In essence, tenants may not make any repairs, improvements or alterations without prior written permission. The most common here are interior painting and minor landscaping.

Keys and Lockouts. This section describes the tenant's duty with respect to keys and the consequences for a lockout or lost key. It also specifies the tenant is not allowed to change the locks for any reason unless written permission is granted by the landlord.

Smoke and Carbon Monoxide Detectors. This section outlines how many smoke and carbon monoxide detectors the property is equipped with and that the tenant agrees to keep them in working order.

Move In. This section outlines the agreement of the landlord and tenant(s) upon move-in with respect to property condition, including that of appliances. The tenant agrees to the condition of the premises and their satisfaction with such.

Move Out and Cleaning Instructions. This section details the requirements for a tenant when they move out, including the 30-day written notice. The cleanliness obligations of the property are outlined in detail here, including the penalties for non-compliance.

Premises Relocation. This section outlines the process for if a tenant wishes to relocate to another unit or property owned by the landlord.

Personal or Bodily Injury. This section is an agreement of the tenant to release the landlord from any liability for personal or bodily injury that occurs on the premises regardless of cause or fault. This includes the tenant's guests, invitees, friends, family, etc. it's important to protect yourself as a landlord from major liabilities.

Environmental or Hazardous Condition. This section is an acknowledgement of the tenant that the landlord has no liability with respect to environmental or hazardous conditions and that the landlord will address such issues as they arise and are reported.

Legal Rights Acknowledgement. This section details that by signing the lease the tenant affirms they are giving up certain legal rights.

Notices. This section outlines that any notices required by either the law or this lease may be hand delivered or mailed to the tenant.

Attorney/Collection Fees. This section outlines that the tenant is responsible for any legal fees incurred by the landlord should legal action be required. It also includes a clause on interest collected for outstanding rent or fees.

Early Termination. This section details what financial and other obligations the tenant has if they terminate the lease early, including penalties and other costs. This section is optional, though I added to my lease because circumstances arise and it's best to predefine it.

Indemnification and Liability. This section details that the landlord should not be held liable for any acts, injuries or damages to any persons on or about the premises. Essentially, this is another 'cover your a$$ (CYA)' for the landlord should something terrible occur.

Invalid Clauses. This section outlines what happens should any provision in the lease be found unenforceable or invalid. The rest of the lease remains valid or enforceable.

Subordination. This section outlines the lease is subordinate to all existing/future mortgages, deeds of trust and other security interests.

Waiver. This section describes that even if the landlord chooses to not enforce a clause within the lease that the rest of the agreement is still enforceable and applicable.

Attachments to the Agreement. This section outlines other attachments or addendums to the lease agreement, such as a lead-paint advisory, a marijuana addendum or a pet addendum.

Entire Lease. This section details what constitutes the lease, including addendums, and that only a written instrument signed by both the landlord and tenant can change this.

Governing Law. This section defines that the state in which the unit is located governs the agreement and state laws take precedence.

Headings. This section explains that section headings or titles are simply for convenience and shall not be deemed part of the lease.

Pronouns. This section describes that even when references in the lease are singular, the same shall be deemed plural and vice versa.

Waiver of Jury Trial. This section waives the right of both the landlord and tenant from a right to a jury trial for any legal action taken by either party.

Notice of Landlord Default. This section outlines a tenants' obligation should the landlord default on any clause within the lease and when the landlord can cure such default.

Covenants, Conditions and Restrictions. This section outlines that the lease and the tenant should be subject to the recorded covenants, conditions and restrictions affecting the premises.

In Witness Whereof. This section describes that the tenant acknowledges they have read the lease and understand both the tenant's and landlord's rights and responsibilities and agree to the terms set forth within the rental lease agreement and addendums.

To finalize the rental lease agreement, I have the tenant(s) initial each and every page, acknowledging they have read and agree to each, plus sign/date the final page. As mentioned before, this isn't every single clause that can be included in a lease. Certain clauses are applicable vs not in the state and county with which your rental properties exist. This covers all major and most important sections of the lease agreement for your business.

HOW A LEASE AGREEMENT PROTECTS YOUR RENTAL BUSINESS

A rental lease agreement is a legally binding contract between the landlord and the tenant(s). Its intention is to state clearly the landlord and tenant's duties, along with the term of the agreement. More than this, the lease is a protection of both parties. Without a lease, a 'he said, she said' type of legal situation could arise. It can be very difficult to prove who agreed to what and what is enforceable by law. Having written and legally binding documentation with all of these parameters clearly defined is essential.

I've worked in corporate America for more than a decade and one thing I learned early on in my career was the importance of documentation. If you have an underperforming employee who is causing more harm than good, it can be extremely difficult to terminate them without probable cause backed up by documentation. In today's world, it's too easy to get tangled up in a lawsuit because a defendant can claim a false bias or accuse a company or individual of malpractice. With documentation, no sweat. Without it, it's best not to pursue termination until you can get the documentation.

In real estate, the lease is your best friend as a landlord. It's what you can hold your tenants accountable to. Yes, they can also hold you accountable as well. It goes both ways. However, the document itself serves more to protect the landlord against damage, poor tenant behavior, abuse of property and much more. Use it to your advantage and use it the right way. Don't skimp out on a lease. Don't just find one online and use it without second thought. Be sure you have all potentially applicable clauses or sections included, or you could end up in a situation where you can't enforce a certain behavior because said behavior wasn't identified in the lease. For example, the section that outlines peaceful behavior towards neighbors makes it very clear up front to a new tenant that there will be absolutely no raver parties being thrown or loud behavior late at night without the likelihood of consequences to the tenant, such as fines and possible evictions.

Though the title of this section centers around protecting your business, a lease is just as critical in protecting *you*. I believe you and your business are not separate entities, therefore when one is impacted, so is the other. However, it is important to differentiate the two in the sense that you can be impacted negatively in a major way if your lease doesn't offer the essential protections it should. Be sure to include the provisions that protect yourself and your business, such as: waiving the right to a jury trial and the tenant not holding you personally liable for bodily injury caused by accidents. Were those provisions not to be included, you could potentially be on the wrong end of a very hefty financial settlement or judgment via the judicial system. Not every real estate investor understands the protections they should have by setting up the proper legal entity, for example. Having a properly written and very thorough lease can be a major protection lifeline. Be sure to do it right the first time. This is best done by having a qualified real estate attorney review your lease.

This Happened to Me – The 'crazy witch lady' says she'll sue

There was a report of a toilet backing up from one of my tenants that soon turned into the strangest and most ridiculous repair situation I've experienced. Long story short, the main sewer line from the house to the main out back was broken and sewage had been dumping underneath the house for an unknown time period. This house had an addition built before we'd purchased it and the construction was not to code. There was no access to the sewer line under the house! As a result, our repairman had to rip up floor boards in the master bedroom to gain access and fix the problem.

The repair was a nightmare. I paid for this family to stay in a hotel for NINE nights. I did my best to accommodate them and checked in daily. The repair access was incredibly challenging. There was heavy cleanup involved and lots of manual labor. Now that you understand the situation, I'll get to the good stuff. The husband was an iron worker and fairly normal. The wife on the other hand, was unique. She and my repairman did NOT get along. She was passive aggressive with him and he was just plain rude back. She'd complain about everything nonstop while he was just trying to finish the job. His best trait is not customer service or soft skills. I would get text messages almost daily where my tenants would complain about the repairman, both what he did and how he was working. I took each complaint seriously and addressed them via phone with my repairman each time. There were two sides to each story I heard.

At one point, they were all screaming at and threatening each other! The wife was so mad that she posted a note on the front door, claiming to be a witch who could call upon the powers of witchcraft and strike down my repairman. The note read, "CURSE YOU. You should NEVER MESS with a BRUJA! Te maldigo. Nunca deberias meterte con UNA BRUJA!" She was cursing my repairman, claiming to be a witch and casting evil wishes upon him. You can't make this stuff up! He responded by walking off the job and refusing to go back there. When I confronted my tenants about the note and showed them the picture of it, her response was she could post anything she wanted on her door and it wasn't intended for the repairman. It was WRITTEN IN SPANISH!! My repairman's name is Javier and he is from Mexico. His English is great but Spanish is his first language. This lady thought I was going to buy that. It took miracle working on my part for the work to resume. I had to schedule hours where one party would be allowed and the other wouldn't be present. Each side literally hated the other.

At one point these tenants left the dog unrestrained intentionally to attack the workers! In response, my repairman left the dog inside the home all day where the dog did its business. The husband confronted Javier and then Javier threatened to beat him up and then proceeded to curse them out in Spanish! Personal property was being damaged due to lack of care or concern from Javier and the tenants not moving their belongings for days when asked. By the end of this fiasco, I was surprised nobody went to jail or was murdered. It was that intense. I was hearing one side of the story each time I spoke to them. At first, I sided with my tenants because I want to believe what they say. They are my customers after all. I'd been working with Javier for several years and he is trustworthy, even if not the best mannered. As it turned out, both sides were just acting childish and had crossed lines of irresponsible behavior. I was mediating between immature kids.

Once this nightmare was over, things calmed down for about a month. All seemed fine. I was still recovering mentally from having to manage this chaos for nearly two weeks nonstop. When rent was due for the month I inquired of the tenant when it was a day late. He responded telling me they had moved out. He continued with a threatening text stating that there were toxic fumes inside the property, which were unsafe to their young child and his wife and that if I didn't prorate rent for that month and return their entire security deposit, they were going to sue me. In fact, they told me they already had spoken with a HUD lawyer and intended to take me to court if I didn't meet their demands. They still had several months left on their lease. This was the first report of 'toxic fumes' that were 'unsafe for inhabitance'. I asked for proof and received nothing. They claimed to have evidence, including pictures and more. I doubted everything and pushed for proof. I had Javier go back and check for toxic fumes or odors of any kind really. He reported nothing. This turned out to be the case.

The tenant continued with threats for another couple of days until I replied stating that I'd be happy if he took me to court because the unpaid rent, plus damages left behind, plus unpaid pet fees for pets they lied about having were in excess of $4,500 after the security deposit. I never heard back from them again.

The primary lesson this experience taught me was to communicate well and document everything. I was very glad to have a lease that protected me had they actually followed through with their hollow legal threats. There were no toxic fumes. They were trying to intimidate me into returning them money I didn't even owe them. The truth is they were dishonest and irresponsible adults. The tenants that replaced them are wonderful. I was just glad it was over. This reassured me of the importance of having a solid lease to protect me against liability that otherwise could be extremely destructive.

THE MOST COMMONLY BROKEN LEASE PROVISIONS

Continuing with the theme of protection that comes with a rental lease agreement, let's cover the most commonly broken lease provisions. Your lease agreement, if written properly, can protect you from each of these commonly broken lease provisions. They are as follows:

- Unapproved roommates
- Unauthorized pets
- Junk & trash outside
- Smoking inside the property
- General housekeeping & cleanliness
- Breaking the lease early

What happens when one of these items happens? As a landlord, you have a few choices. The first is to ignore it. Now I obviously don't recommend this option. Though some landlords choose to ignore certain lease-violating behaviors simply because the tenant is paying rent each month. What I've learned is that you give a tenant an inch of leniency, they take a mile of irresponsible freedom! Be sure to enforce your lease. Call out tenants for poor behavior and document it via text, email or letter. This is *your* property they are damaging.

The second option is to send a formal notice that they must comply with the lease within a specified period of time, typically 7 days or less. This is something I recommend regardless of whether you choose to pursue eviction for non-compliance. This sends a strong message to a tenant that they will abide by the lease 100% or you will pursue action against them. Just like a child who isn't properly disciplined, a tenant will stretch the lines of acceptable behavior unless you hold the line. This option may also be accompanied with a fine for non-compliance of the lease. If you choose to impose a fee, be sure your lease states that you have the discretion to do so.

The third and final option is to send the tenant a notice to vacate the premises as a result of a lease violation. This option is the extreme choice, though sometimes it is the best option. For a rent-paying tenant who hasn't given you much trouble, this may be a second or third offense route to take. For trouble tenants, the real headaches, this may be your best option because you can get them out of your life expeditiously! The courts will likely uphold the eviction of a tenant for breaching their lease obligations. Be certain that before you pursue this route, the offense is serious enough to not be laughed at in court. Smoking inside the property, unapproved guests, trash and junk, and unauthorized pets are all valid and solid reasons to pursue eviction against a headache tenant. For likeable tenants though, do your best to make it work first. Make sure they understand the seriousness of the offenses and that obeying the lease is most essential. I've had several of these direct conversations with tenants I preferred not to evict and had zero problems from then on. Assume that your tenant has not read through each clause of the lease, kind of like a privacy statement that is 12 pages from your life insurance company. I don't read those, though I do read all lease agreements and so should your tenants. The communication can clear up expectations rather quickly.

This Happened to Me – The 'I didn't know' smoker

I partnered with a program that placed three tenants in the same apartment building we own over a period of six months. This particular program helps people get back on their feet after they've had a felony on their record. My business partner and I were really busy at the time managing over 20 doors so the easy, quick placement was attractive. This program also covered their security deposit and rent for a period of time, plus conducted inspections and background. The first tenant we placed was a success story. The next two, quite the opposite. This one guy that came through their program came highly recommended. I made an unannounced visit while marketing another property within a week of him moving in. I knocked on the door, and after about 30 seconds of shuffling around he answered, with an intense wave of cigarette smoke coming with him right into my face. I introduced myself as the landlord and the look on his face showed his surprise. After a brief conversation, I told him we had a strict 'no smoking' policy that he was already violating. He claimed he 'didn't know', to which I quickly referred to the lease he signed. He committed to not doing it again.

I was foolish enough to believe him. I went back months later to the property and while there decided to conduct a follow-up. He happened to be two days late for rent and I hadn't heard back from my attempts to reach him. This time, when he answered the door, I was shocked to be welcome with a potent marijuana smell! Naturally, I inquired. His answer was 'I didn't know' I couldn't smoke pot inside the apartment. I thought it was clear that smoking inside the property was strictly prohibited. In his mind, I was only referring to cigarettes. Honest mistake, right? Wrong! He was either playing me for a fool or incredibly unintelligent. He tried to say it was medical in nature and essential for his health. I reminded him that his essential meds must be consumed *outside*.

I could have evicted him, but didn't at the time. I couldn't fine him because a consequence wasn't explicitly mentioned in my lease. I have since added a specific clause to my lease stating that I can fine someone $500-$750 for violations of the 'no smoking' policy. I had no schtick other than pursuing eviction, which is time consuming and expensive. This guy was out less than one month later and it cost $2,000 to remove the odor.

Having had success with the first tenant, the lesson learned was that nobody will conduct due diligence as intensely as I would. Another person wouldn't come to the same conclusion about a prospective tenant as me either. The truth is, we chose the easy route. What we thought was the path of least resistance became the path of ultimate regret. I share my stories of failure with you because I sincerely want you to learn from my mistakes. If my story can help prevent you from making the same or similar mistake, I consider that a victory.

THE MOST VITAL CLAUSES OF A RENTAL LEASE AGREEMENT

One can argue that every provision or clause in a lease agreement is important. In short, this is true. However, specific clauses carry a much larger weight of importance than others. The two determining factors of importance are that these clauses protect you as a landlord from financial liability and give you the legal right to evict a deadbeat tenant. Be sure to include these clauses as they are likely to save you headaches, legal fees and allow you more freedom as a landlord.

Default or Breach. This clause explains your legal right as a landlord shall your tenant breach or default on their obligations within the lease. The intent here is to define for the courts that your tenant has agreed to abide by specific lease provisions. This clause outlines your rights as a landlord when breach or default occurs. This clause should include the right to pursue eviction of the tenant with the courts and termination of the lease.

Premises Use. This clause outlines how a tenant may or may not use your rental property. Defining that the tenant can't run a business out of your property, grow marijuana, or allow friends and other family members to stay beyond 48 hours will allow you to take action if and when these events occur. It may seem self-explanatory that a tenant shouldn't conduct illegal activity within the property, though including it protects your rights as a landlord should they be in violation of such. Outlining the consequences for violation of this clause is essential.

Rent and Fees. This clause again seems obvious, however specificity around the agreed upon monthly rent, plus any fees for pets or storage, eliminates any he said/she said if you end up in court. Be specific with what rent is due, when it is due and the consequences for not complying.

Subletting. This clause is a security blanket if your tenant attempts to sublet the property and you didn't have the clause in your lease agreement. Include it so you can take action if you need to and also to ensure the tenant understands what is allowed vs not.

Care of the Premises. This clause outlines the tenant's obligation for maintaining and caring for the property. The tenant must understand their obligation in caring for the premises, including landscape, and what happens if they do not hold up their end of the agreement. Be sure to include this as cause for eviction for repeated violations.

Landlord Liability. This clause outlines what the landlord is and more importantly is not liable for. This section should specify that the tenant shall not hold the landlord liable for things such as a natural disaster, a broken pipe, a fire, personal or bodily injury and more. Prevention of liability is a major purpose of a rental lease agreement and as a landlord, something you should include while taking seriously. It's best to be thorough vs assume that a tenant won't attempt to hold you liable for something out of your control or ridiculous in nature.

Waiver of Jury Trial. This clause should be in all rental lease agreements because you don't want to face a jury, ever, as a landlord. Landlords can have a bad reputation and juries are known to award unreasonable penalties. The waiver is for both parties, the landlord and the tenant. It's best to include and stay away from a jury at all costs.

Move Out Instructions. This clause outlines the tenant's duty for notification of move out, plus their responsibilities before vacating. Outlining the specific expectations here can save you later when deducting expenses from a security deposit for the lack of cleaning, weeding, left over furniture or garbage, broken or damaged items, etc. Be specific as this clause is additional protection for you.

CRAZY THINGS TENANTS ASK AND WHY YOUR RENTAL LEASE AGREEMENT SAVES THE DAY

Current tenants, ex-tenants and even prospective tenants all get creative with questions they ask and actions they decide to take. Having a solid rental lease agreement, as defined clearly in this chapter, is designed to help you navigate these situations. Let's cover a few of these scenarios and how you might respond.

Tenant: We agreed on a move-in date one week from now, what are the possibilities of moving in a few days early at no additional cost? **Landlord:** For liability reasons, I won't be able to let you move in before the agreed upon date unless I modify the lease and collect the additional rent. I will be delighted to modify your lease if that's what you'd prefer.

Tenant: It's not a pet, it's a frog. **Landlord:** If it isn't human, but still a living and breathing creature, then it's a pet.

Tenant: A five-day grace period means that rent is not really due until the fifth, right?

Landlord: All rent is due on the first of each month. I assign late fees after the fifth of the month. The grace period exists for when a holiday weekend, challenging circumstances or life's realities get in the way. If rent is late past the fifth, I will pursue eviction that same day.

Tenant: Why can't you give my deposit back the day I move out?

Landlord: I need proper time to conduct a thorough investigation and determine what work, if any, is required to make the residence rent-ready. Also, if work is required, I need the work to be fully completed in order to calculate the difference vs what will be returned.

Tenant: Just use my security deposit to cover last month's rent.

Landlord: The rental lease agreement specifically states that the security deposit cannot be used for the payment of rent. You are not allowed to dictate how the deposit is used. The security deposit is for damages and other expenses incurred after you move out.

Tenant: I'll sign the one-year lease if I can get out of it whenever I want.

Landlord: I'm sorry but what you are asking for is a month-to-month lease agreement. I typically don't offer this type of agreement, however am willing to discuss it with you. Just know that rent will be charged at a premium.

Tenant: My guest broke down the door and put a hole in the wall, I shouldn't be held responsible for that.

Landlord: The lease agreement clearly states that all damage to the property while you are a resident is your responsibility. This is true regardless of whether it was your fault or that of a friend, guest, family member or visitor.

THIS IS A WINNING RENTAL LEASE AGREEMENT

This chapter has covered the basics of a rental lease agreement, why you need one and the essential items to include in said agreement. Now, what is a winning rental lease agreement? It's simple. A winning lease is one that protects you, protects your investment and outlines the obligations of both the tenant and the landlord. The lease can be both a weapon and a shield for the landlord tenant(s). I consider the following to be the three most important factors of the lease itself.

First, the lease should protect you, the landlord, from being taken advantage of by a tenant or from financial loss as a result of the tenant's non-compliance. Second, it should protect your investment, specifically from a tenant damaging your property. Third, the lease outlines the obligations of both the tenant and the landlord. This results in being able to resolve disputes that may otherwise go unresolved or land you in court without a proper defense. It is always best to have a fully executed lease that covers each of the essential obligations for all parties. More importantly, the lease is a safety net for landlords who get stuck with irresponsible, destructive and dishonest tenants. The lease must be written in such a clear manner that a landlord can sever the relationship with any tenant at any time for violating the provisions within the lease agreed to by the tenant. That, my friends, is what I consider to be a winning lease. Be sure to have one working for you and your business right away!

LET'S WRAP A BOW ON THIS CHAPTER

Congratulations, you've finished Chapter Four and learned something new to improve your rental real estate business! The focus of this chapter is for each and every landlord to understand the importance of a rental lease agreement, what needs to be included and how to enforce it.

A rental lease agreement defined. A rental lease agreement is a legally binding agreement between the landlord and tenant(s). This document conveys the agreed upon living timeframe, rental cost and overall expectations.

All rental lease agreements are not created equal. Be careful to use a rental lease agreement that applies to the state in which you conduct business. Provisions can vary by state depending on what is applicable, either legally or naturally. Do your research! Consult a real estate attorney to ensure you have a winning lease.

How to construct your rental lease agreement. Ensure the most pertinent and beneficial information is included to protect yourself and your investment. Don't build your own lease agreement. Ensure the lease is in compliance with your state laws and has been reviewed by an attorney.

How a lease agreement protects your rental business. The lease protects your business to ensure you can evict a non-compliant tenant and enforce the agreed upon expectations throughout the duration of your lease term. Your lease is your best friend if you ever have to go to court.

The most commonly broken lease provisions. Your lease, if written properly, can protect you from each of the commonly broken lease provisions. When it happens, you can ignore it or you can enforce compliance of your lease agreement through a formal notice, fines and even eviction.

The most vital clauses of a rental lease agreement. Every provision or clause in a lease is important. Certain clauses carry a much larger weight of importance. Be sure those are included and clearly written.

This is a winning rental lease agreement. A winning lease protects you, protects your investment and outlines the obligations of both the landlord and tenant(s).

FIVE

GET IT RENTED! HOW TO FIND THE BEST TENANTS AND AVOID THE NIGHTMARES

I n rental real estate, tenants are your lifeblood. With them, you have a great opportunity at success. Without them, or with really bad ones, your business will suffer. Tenant is just a fancy word for a person who pays rent to live in your property. Tenants are simply human beings, like you and me. They are living life and doing their best to get by. Most everyone at some point in time is a tenant. I was a tenant for several years while attending the university in Idaho so I could further my education. I was a tenant while I lived in Ecuador for two years, serving the Ecuadorian people. I was a tenant when I first moved to Colorado back in 2008. My wife and I purchased our first home in January of 2011. I have been a homeowner ever since. My years of being a tenant were eight in total, though less than two once I graduated with my bachelor's degree. In a report issued by the real estate data firm Zillow in 2015, the typical first-timer now rents for six years before buying, up from 2.6 years in the early 1970s. This is post-college education. The median first-time buyer is age 33. A generation ago, this number was 30 (1). According to a 2020 survey showcased by iProperty Management, there are more renters today than at any other time over the past 50 years. In the USA, the current homeownership rate is 64.4%, while the current percentage of households renting their homes is 36.6%. Almost 40% of renters are aged 45 or older (2). It's easy to see why owning rental real estate in the United States is a very popular long-term wealth strategy. This chapter covers how to get your rental property rented, including specific details about property marketing, the application process, tenant selection and more.

MAKE YOUR PROPERTY ATTRACTIVE

As a young boy, I had to learn about the concept of attraction as my interest in girls grew over time. I was always gun shy, totally afraid and unable to speak to the best-looking girls I had crushes on without looking and feeling a bit foolish. I complained one day to my dad about girls not paying much attention to me, looking for some sort of sympathy. Instead, I got one of the best lessons I'd ever receive from my dad. He said, "Casey, if you want girls to notice you and like you, you have to make yourself as attractive as possible." I thought this was interesting coming from my dad, who was color blind, and could barely put a coherent outfit together because he loved the colors purple and red, due to the fact he could 'see them best'! Regardless, he was right. My hair at the time was parted down the middle. I wore South Park t-shirts almost daily and did the annoying impressions I thought were funny. My shoes were nerdy. Nothing in my outfits coordinated. I had acne, glasses and was fairly immature. It wasn't until I was a senior in high school that girls started to notice me and consider me a viable option. I finally found a good hair style, addressed the acne, coordinated clothes better, stopped wearing south park t-shirts, started wearing cologne and contact lenses. As I made myself a more viable option, my options of quality and beautiful girls increased exponentially. I credit that advice from my dad as part of the reason I landed the amazingly talented and beautiful wife that I did. She is far above my level of attractiveness and proof that the right presentation can land the best suitor!

The same principles apply to your rental property. If you want to attract the most quality people on the block, make your rental attractive. This doesn't mean spend a ton of money. It means you must make the interior and exterior of your property attractive. Here are some simple things you can do yourself, at little to no expense, that will make your property more attractive:

- Clean, clean and clean! Either hire a cleaning service or do a good job yourself.
- Improve the aroma! Buy a candle, scented plug-ins, scented wax, etc. People want to live somewhere that smells nice.
- Make sure the bathroom water, toilet and shower work! People will test them out, trust me.
- Tidy the patio! Clear it of debris, trash, dirt and furniture!
- Clean up the yard. Pick up leaves, eliminate trash, cut the grass, trim the edges, water the grass, trim dead branches, etc.
- Paint ugly walls and doors. You can hire this out or do it yourself if you are talented enough. Paint color and appearance matters.
- Change the light fixtures so they look modern and clean.
- Add new window treatments. Replace the blinds with nice faux wood coverings to enhance the aesthetics!

- Power wash outside. Power wash the exterior of the home itself, the sidewalks and the driveway if there is one.

This Happened to Me – The Denby's get to work

Let me take you back to the very first rental property I purchased with my wife. I had spent most of my capital acquiring the home. Luckily, I scored the place 15% below market value. However, I was still not Tony Wynn. My funds were limited. When we closed on the property, I took my entire family with me to the newly acquired business asset. We had an open house planned and were so excited to get rolling on our very first rental property adventure together! The home was in fairly good condition. It was essentially rent-ready. I was confident we were going to rent it ASAP. That day passed by and there was quite a bit of foot traffic, though just one application from about 15 viewers. The applicant was unimpressive and wouldn't be my first choice. However, it was my ONLY choice!! "What had gone wrong?" I thought to myself. The property was one of the better on the market and I was sure of it. After some reflection, I realized the place wasn't ever cleaned well. There were piles of wet, dirty leaves that were never raked from Fall. There were weeds and garbage around the exterior. The inside was dusty and didn't smell great. The windows were dirty and there was some food left in the cabinets and fridge. Once I realized my mistake, I about panicked! Luckily, my wife talked me down from a moment of high stress and we decided to come back the next week armed to tackle the problem. I was working full-time and this was a weekend 'hobby' I had just embarked on.

My excitement of finally owning a rental property clouded my judgment a bit. As I climbed back to reality I could see where I needed to realign my focus. The next week came and we were prepared with gardening tools, garbage bags, cleaning supplies, brooms, etc. My crew consisted of myself, my wife, our six-year-old boy, three-year-old girl and one-year-old-baby boy. We spent nearly five hours that early February day raking leaves, picking up trash and debris inside and around the property, sweeping floors, washing windows, cleaning countertops and mirrors, trimming the landscaping and general tidying. The open house was set for after lunch and foot traffic was again high, with about 17 viewers. This time we received *six* applications! I was thrilled! My wife helped improve the aroma by strategically adding some glade plug-ins. We rented it out easily with a line of prospective tenants.

LET'S PUT UP THE 'FOR RENT' SIGN

Once your property is ready to rent, the next steps are to create an advertisement, list your property for rent and then start showing it to potential renters! At this point, I assume you have completed all necessary repairs, cleaned the property, verified everything is working as expected and spruced up some trouble areas as best you could. Great! Now, we open the doors to the public. This is done through advertising, open houses and showings.

Advertising. In order to rent a property, you must let prospective tenants know that it is available for rent! This may seem obvious, but there are effective and ineffective ways of doing this. In today's world, the internet is the very best place to advertise a rental safely and with the largest reach. Even the least educated and savvy renters know how to search Craigslist or Zillow for a place to rent. I started advertising with Craigslist, however there was no tracking software provided and the quality of tenants seemed to be lower. I quickly switched to Zillow as my primary rental source. When I entered a rental listing on Zillow, it would automatically post my ad to Trulia and HotPads simultaneously. These are two other popular and wide-reaching rental websites. Zillow tracks the inquiries you receive, compares your rental ad traffic to other similar properties in the area and provides you with a far reach of prospective tenants. They charge a reasonable weekly fee to post the ad. The first step after selecting where you will advertise, is to create the ad. Include important details about the property. Be as upfront as possible to what you expect of your future tenants and what you do not allow.

Here is an example of a property description that I posted in a rental advertisement:

This newly remodeled 3-bedroom, 1-bathroom home has all newer vinyl windows, new flooring, a detached single car garage for storage, a huge lot open to your visions of design and a fully fenced-in yard for pets. Other features include the formal dining room, eat-in kitchen, stainless steel range and new refrigerator!

The hardwood floors are beautiful and it boasts a large kitchen! The bathroom is very spacious. With over 1,100 square feet, the home has an open-style concept. Don't miss out on the large back patio with great entertaining space.

This rental will go fast so make an appointment to swing by this coming Friday July 12 or Saturday July 13 by texting or calling Casey @ 101-222-3333! Showings by appointment only!

Please only serious renters. We do NOT accept smokers so please don't inquire if you smoke. Great street and neighborhood with a park one block away! We look forward to meeting you!

Please Note: Owner pays water & sewer. Tenant pays electric, gas and trash. We accept up to 2 pets on a pre-approval basis, subject to additional charges. Rent $1,025. Security Deposit $1,250. $30 application fee for the first applicant, $20 for each additional adult (18+) payable in cash only. Ready for move-in right away!

This is a solid example of how to advertise a rental property. Now, this isn't perfect by any means and each market is going to differ. You will not market a penthouse suite in New York City the same as an apartment in Knoxville, TN. This book isn't written for the owners of that penthouse suite in NYC. It's written for those who, like me, are starting small and building a rental real estate business. To successfully market a property there are four components: essential information, property highlights, quality pictures and a call to action. Let's cover each one of these along with other helpful information.

Essential Information. Include the essential information in your rental advertisement. When marketing a property for rent, be sure to share the basic information that a potential renter would need to know to help them determine if the rental is even an option for them. Here is a list of what I consider to be essential information to market:

- Property address
- Monthly rent
- Security deposit
- Number of bedrooms
- Number of bathrooms
- Livable square footage
- Date of availability
- Utilities covered vs not
- Do you accept pets, if so, what type and how many?
- Basic lease information
- Application fee amount and payment options
- Next steps in the application process

- Primary contact name and phone number
- Pet deposit and fees, if applicable

Property highlights. Basic information is great, property highlights are even better! What would a tenant want to know about the property? What are the stand-out features? This is the time to pique their interest. These features are selling points for a prospective tenant. Here are some property features you could include in your ad:

- Covered patio
- Fenced-in yard
- Garage access
- Off-street parking
- Upgraded appliances
- Close proximity to a park
- Walking distance to the elementary school
- Firepit
- Tool shed
- Basement storage
- Vaulted ceilings
- On-site laundry or washer/dryer hookups

Quality pictures. Listing 101 teaches you must have quality pictures for your rental advertisement, period. If you don't, good luck attracting quality tenants. In today's world, people do research before the research. Pictures can replace most words. *Don't post low-quality images*, it will turn off prospective tenants. Post clear and high-quality images that will draw people in. Frame your shots well. Don't include the less attractive features in your pictures. Include enough pictures to show the goods, but don't give it all away. The objective is to get them to want to visit and look further. Show no more than ten pictures. Include at least one exterior photo, though focus on the best features of the property. Put the *best* featured picture as the cover photo of the ad. For example, if the kitchen has the best features, tag that for the cover photo. It will attract more eyes and interest. The newer smart phones have high-quality cameras that can do what you need here. If you are renting a higher-end unit, consider a video tour and professional photos. I'm not personally in the high-end market, so phone pictures work well.

Call to action. Many forget to leave a call to action. Be sure to provide your email and phone number, along with your first name so they know who to contact. Share details of an upcoming open house if you plan one and how to set an appointment. Provide details on how to apply and where to submit the application fee. Tell them how to work with you. Most renters searching through the rental ads are lazy. By this I mean they just click the 'I'm interested' button without doing anything else. I include the call to action in every ad and then reiterate it when people express interest. If they don't respond at that point, they are not a serious candidate.

Some other things to include are the property address so a tenant can conduct a drive-by of the neighborhood and see the property from the exterior to determine their true level of interest. Include all the other information listed above. This way you don't get thirty questions when speaking to them before a showing. If they start down the line of questioning, simply direct them to your well-written ad for all the details. One thing to be aware of when posting a rental ad is the potential fraud. Fraudsters seem to target rental ads as a quick way to con an unsuspecting target, such as renters. It has happened to me on multiple occasions. I share one instance below.

This Happened to Me – The 'New York City' fraudster

We posted one of our properties for rent on Craigslist. I believe it was our third property. We started to have some inquiries come in via phone like normal. After a couple of days on the market, we received a call where the person asked if we were from New York. Naturally, I was confused, so I inquired further as to why the question. This candidate went on to explain that she had called this ad for my property. It was a New York City phone number and a guy with an accent. He fabricated a story that he was unable to show the property right then because he had to leave town to New York and address a family emergency. However, he was willing to guarantee them the property if they sent him $800 cash via money remittance. Sadly, this lady fell for it and sent this guy the $800! She said, "This guy has your property for rent in a separate ad!" He literally copied my ad, but undercut my rent by $200 to make his more attractive. This phony had zero association with the property, though he took the information and pictures from my ad and reposted as his own. He then pretended to be the owner and defrauded whoever was ignorant enough to believe him.

Once I discovered the behavior, I actually located the ad and called the guy pretending to be interested. Sure enough, he tried the same fraudulent scheme on me, not knowing I was the actual property owner. I called him out after he tried to get me to send the money and told him I was coming after him. Now I couldn't do much about it, but it did scare him off. The ad was reported and removed. I was able to rent the property later that week. Unfortunately, this lady wasn't the only one who fell victim to the fraud. There were three others who reported this guy back to me, but they weren't ignorant enough to fall for the scheme.

The moral of this story is that people will pretend they are you to take other people's hard-earned money because they suck at life and have no moral compass. I wish there was more I could do to catch these dirtbags and have them prosecuted. Unfortunately, fraud is pervasive in society. This is why I strongly recommend being 100% transparent with applicants and know that they are likely suspicious of you from the start because of this reality. Be careful and search for duplicate ads of your properties to report them as fraud so you don't come under the gun. Posting an effective ad goes a long way toward finding the best tenant in an acceptable timeframe. Now, let's cover open houses and showings as effective methods for getting your property rented.

Open Houses. Another popular way to get a property rented is to hold an open house. This is similar to an open house when a property is for sale, with the exception these are prospective tenants vs buyers. Most people, in fact about 97% of people that I have rented to, have wanted to physically see the property for themselves before they decide on moving forward with the application process. Since I don't live within a relatively short distance of my rental properties, it is incredibly inconvenient for me to show the property one at a time and on different days of the week. I have been working a full-time corporate gig the entire time I have owned rental properties and as a result I am limited in my options for showing the property to prospective tenants, or so I thought. For now, let's keep rolling with open houses. They are a fantastic way to have people come and tour the property without having to over coordinate. You schedule the day and time window, then market that in your ad. We share this information in the ad and with those that who have inquired. This approach doesn't always work effectively, which is why I prefer showings by appointment.

Showings. Showings are different than open houses as they are pre-scheduled appointments. Showings are very effective because they are personal and very focused by nature. All of your attention, or that of a property manager, is on the individual or party viewing your property. Take the time to point out the positives and showcase key features of the property while answering any questions or concerns that arise. This is also a great opportunity to get to know the prospective tenants and assess your overall impression of them as actual tenants. Don't underestimate the importance of this. You must be observant and aware of what you see and hear during the showing. Take notes! Look for red flags during your interaction. This could be anything from unpleasant odors, their appearance would frighten a normal person, they mention something that makes you question their character, etc. On the other hand, be on the lookout for positives that might make this person a great tenant. This could be a professional appearance, they are clean and groomed, they share their love for your property and all the wonderful things they would do to decorate once they move in, perhaps information about their job and how they work well with previous landlords.

Showings are, in my experience, the number one method of finding a tenant to rent your property. It is likely that every showing scheduled was a result of the prospective tenant finding your property through an online ad. Be prepared to answer these inquiries! They are gold in the landlord's safe! If you don't acknowledge them, they are worthless to you. If you do, your probability of renting your property quicker and for longer is much higher. One important note to make is that unless you are spending a morning or afternoon doing showings at a property, it is inconvenient for you to do showings one-by-one. A few best practices you can implement for the highest chances of success are:

- Schedule all showings for the week during a certain day and time period, say 2-4 hours during a single day and schedule showing appointments every 15 minutes.
- Don't schedule more than two appointments for the same time. The idea is to show there is interest, though not an overwhelm of traffic or they will feel there is no shot and won't apply.
- For multi-family buildings, you can have a neighbor from one of the other building units show the property for you. TIP - you will need to pay for this option via cash or reduced rent. I usually place a set price for this service and then a cash bonus once a lease is signed.

- Hire another trustworthy, reliable person to manage this process for you.
- As you greet people, share the key features, point them in the right direction and let them check the place out alone. Don't be a creeper and follow them around everywhere. Nobody likes that!
- If you have a property manager, they will handle all showings.

This Happened to Me – The open house 'fail'

The second house that my business partner and I purchased was a cute, newly remodeled 3 bed 1 bath with 1,100 square feet of living space. The issue was that even though it was on the side of town with the best renters and surrounding areas, it wasn't on the best of streets. Each street is like its own neighborhood in the town we invest in. This street happened to have some characters living on it and proved to make it more challenging for us to rent out. We decided we would hold an open house on closing day, Friday, and then again on Saturday. We marketed the open house as we had done before in the Craigslist and Zillow ads. There was plenty of pre-open house interest. We were expecting over ten parties to come by. We brought our folding table, our music, some snacks, a stack of applications, some other supplies and a couple of lawn chairs to relax in when we weren't actively showing the place. We were scheduled to be there from 10 AM to 4 PM. The first few hours were a bit slow, as in nobody came. We expected this on a Friday and that it would pick up after lunch. Well, time came and went. It was 4 PM without a single soul having stopped by. We tried to follow up on the Friday confirmations to no luck. The saving grace, there was an 80-year-old bakery across the street where we bought some sandwiches and cookies for lunch and made friends with the store crew. The day was a total bust!

We had another list of folks who were interested that were planning to come by on Saturday. We almost had a repeat of Friday. One family came in, toured the place, and left awkwardly when they weren't interested. The second and final tour of the day came, showed interest, and ended up putting in an application. Just *one* total application over two full days spent showing the property. We felt defeated. One application isn't ideal. As a landlord, you want options. We didn't end up choosing them.

One lesson learned from this experience was that we were never going to operate an open house that way again. Learn from your own mistakes and those of complete strangers like me. I always tell people; I don't have to try cocaine to know it's not a good idea and is terrible for my mind and body. You don't have to hold an empty open house because I already made that mistake and you should learn from it. The next weekend I had to show the property again, this time with some more luck. We had three applications and the tenant we selected lived in the home for two years, paying on time and causing little trouble.

Have you ever seen the show Friends? Naturally you have because you aren't a Neanderthal! The episode where Ross buys a sofa that he can't seem to get up the stairs and into his apartment is a learning lesson for us all. As Ross and the team lifted the sofa up the stairs, Ross would yell multiple times, "PIVOT", in order to turn and adjust the position of the sofa so they could proceed successfully up the stairs. In the episode, they didn't pivot correctly and ended up cutting the sofa in half, then trying to return it badly damaged to the store! Don't be Ross. *Pivot* when you need to! The pivot we made was that we would do the following going forward:

1. Contact everyone with interest in your unit via text, phone call, email or all three.
2. Set a specific viewing time/appointment with that individual to see the property.
3. Confirm the appointment the day before the showing.
4. Send application requirement basics to each interested party via email so they come prepared.
5. Confirm the appointment the day of the showing.
6. Call, text or email if they don't come within five minutes of the scheduled showing time.

This simple method has increased my foot traffic on showing days by over 300%. It promotes accountability for both parties. Here are some of the benefits of following a successful methodology:

1. If you contact everyone on the list and reach out multiple times as necessary, the higher your chances of booking an appointment and securing a quality tenant for your property.
2. If an appointment is set, there is more of an obligation and likelihood that your prospective tenants will actually show up.
3. If you confirm the showing the day before you increase your odds of them showing up.

4. If you send the application requirements via email beforehand you increase the probability of prospective tenants coming prepared.
5. If you confirm the viewing the day of, you'll know who is actually coming and will increase the total number of viewings.

TENANT CRITERION AND PRE-SCREENING

You should have an established criterion for your tenants, just like you do during the dating process, a college search, a job search, a house search and so many other big decisions in life. Have I said that tenants are a big decision yet? Yep, I did! I will keep saying it as well. How do you know you've found what you are looking for if you don't know what you are looking for? Exactly my point. The criterion you set for potential tenants shouldn't be exhaustive, though there are a few areas to consider as you narrow down your selection process. Let's review the criterion that I use and any landlord can easily leverage to better screen potential tenants.

- Do they appear competent and serious?
- Do they communicate well?
- Are they punctual?
- Do they follow-through?
- Can they pay rent?
- Do they meet all requirements as expected?
- Can you confirm their income and identification?
- Do they appear to be a good person?
- Are they consistently impressive?
- Do their references show positive signs?
- Are they courteous and respectful?
- Do they appear well kempt?

As you look to see if they check the boxes, I also recommend a pre-screening before you go further down the line with an application. It's just like with a job applicant who is seeking employment. The original pool of applicants is massive. When an employer screens applicants, there is a pre-screening criterion to determine whether or not an interview is requested. There is another set of criteria, which compares all applicants, that factors into who is invited for the final round of interviews. Once at this stage, pulling and confirming references is essential. Then of course a drug test and sometimes more. In the end, one lucky applicant is offered the position. A similar process exists for renters. As a landlord, you must determine who makes the first, second and final cut. You can't make an accurate assessment and solid decision without clear-cut criterion and expectations. In my process, I conduct an unofficial pre-screening, where I look at the following:

General vibe. How did you feel during each interaction with them? Did they offput you or were they engaging? Look for positive and negative signs. Do they have face tattoos? Can you smell the odor of their cigarettes or marijuana? Are they dressed nice? Do they treat you with respect? General vibe is all about how their actions and appearance made you feel about them.

Application. Was it completely filled out? Was the writing legible? Did they take thought into completing it or was it a rush to the finish? Were additional bonus details included? Did they submit any other documentation along with the application? Did they return it to you promptly? You can determine what type of tenant someone will be by the answers to these questions.

Social media. Check a potential tenant's social media account for clues as to who they truly are via photos, posts, groups and interests. Do they have pictures partying or do they appear to live a calm, normal life? Are they following fringe groups and love Marilyn Manson music or do they follow a charitable group and like classical music? Social media accounts can tell you a lot about people. Don't forget to leverage this screening source when screening tenants.

Move-in timeframe. When a prospective tenant plans to move in is another factor to take into consideration. You may prioritize someone willing to move in within a week or two over someone who is six or more weeks out. Financially speaking, the sooner you can fill a vacancy the better, assuming the prospective tenant is of good quality.

Follow-through. This one is big for me. Do they do what they say they will? Did they come to the scheduled open house on time and without reminder? Did they complete the application timely and follow up with you? Did they provide all the required documentation? Did they reply to text messages or calls promptly and with urgency? How they show up during the screening process is likely their best foot forward. If they don't impress here, it goes downhill from there if you choose them as a tenant.

Let me be the first to tell you that you should not rent to anyone and everyone that is interested in your property. *Don't do it*! Less-experienced landlords are more susceptible to this practice. However, I know of plenty experienced landlords who continue to make this mistake. Just because someone is living and has interest in renting your property, does not qualify them as a good 'tenant investment' for you. A tenant investment is a term I use for tenants that you choose to invest your time, hard-earned money and faith in. Each tenant you allow to live in one of your rental properties is 100% unequivocally an investment. Don't be fooled in thinking they are doing you a favor in living there and paying rent. *Everyone* needs a place to live and *everyone* must pay for that right. I use the term investment because you are handing them something of capital value, the rental unit, expecting them to in turn pay you a return, in the form of rent. This is no different than you investing money in the stock market and expecting a return on that investment. It is no different than the bank lending you money and expecting interest paid as a return on their investment in you. You are investing hard-earned capital (aka your money) on whatever tenant you select to live in your property, with the expectation that they return payment on that investment plus interest each and every month in the form of rent.

This Happened to Me – The 'desperate' landlord

As my business partner and I were holding an open house at our first rental property. We had around ten people stop by in a two-day period. We received just one application. Their names, for confidentiality purposes, will be Joe & Mary. Joe was tattooed up and always wore a bandana. Mary, his girlfriend, let her age and life decisions show by her appearance. We were not deterred though, because they *wanted to rent our property*! We had spent our money and time advertising the property, sprucing it up and showing it to prospective tenants. We didn't want our wives to think less of us and to be failures by not renting out the property that weekend. So naturally we listened to Joe saying he would care for the lawn and be on top of it, while Mary was the tidiest person alive. They had money in the bank. Joe was paid by a government and military pension every month that more than covered 3 times rent. Financially they were set and they wanted to move in ASAP! What more could we ask for at this point? After some due diligence in calling references, confirming income, and verifying background we offered Joe & Mary our first business partnership rental property! They accepted and we were off to the races. That very week I signed the lease with them, did the walkthrough, collected the upfront money owed and handed over the keys. Fast forward 14 months, when Joe left our property in handcuffs, before their lease expired, escorted out suddenly by the FBI.

Be careful renting to the first person or only person that applies if they don't meet your pre-established rental criterion. Know what you are looking for and don't settle for the bottom of the barrel of quality.

THE RENTAL APPLICATION

The rental application process you choose to follow is critical to ensure you attract, select and retain the best tenants. It is a primary step in the tenant selection process. To ensure the very best people reach the application process, you must buy right, prepare the property, create an effective ad and be thorough with your follow-through. The application process is the gateway to keep bad tenants far, far away.

You must have a rental application process, bottom line, no questions asked. If you don't have one and simply hand over the keys to the next stranger who expresses interest in your rental, you will soon be in a regretful situation. Trust is an interesting term in the rental game. My take, after years of experience, is this: *trust nobody*. I mean it. Don't believe a single word that applicants tell you. Not even 'trust but verify'. Not innocent before proven guilty. Bottom line, don't believe what anyone 'tells' you. They are and should be trying to convince you that they are the right tenant to choose for your property. Treat every interaction, whether via phone call, text, email or in-person as part of the rental interview process. You are the boss in this situation and they are the job applicant. They want to live in *your* property. They must prove they are worthy! Strong words, I know. Let's get real though. If you don't want to be fleeced over and over again, follow this counsel. Now that we have covered that, let's get to the application process itself.

Keep your application simple. The longer your rental application, the more headaches you invite. If people are unable to complete the written application within 15-20 minutes on average, it is too long. The application I currently use is one page, front and back. All of the pertinent information is on the front page. The back page is simply two disclosure statements, my tenant qualifications and signature lines.

Every person 18+ should fill one out. Yes, an 18-year-old child of a tenant, cousin or grandpa that plan to live at your rental property should be completing their *own* application. The questions on the application should be specific to an individual, not to a group of people or a family. Each adult (18+) living in your rental property is a responsible party to fulfilling the lease obligations. This includes paying rent. They must complete their own rental application. Don't only trust the person who is the head of household. It is very possible that their cousin, who plans to live in your property, is an ex-gang-member, current-gang-member, drug dealer or convicted felon. That matters to you as a landlord. That matters to your reputation with neighbors and the city you invest in. Choose the right people to occupy your rentals.

Include the most important details in the application. The application should be concise, yet focused on what matters most. Don't ask people what their favorite color is or if they are planning to conduct illegal activities inside the property. In either case, it doesn't matter if the question is there or not. The answer is either completely irrelevant to whether they would make a quality tenant or they will lie to you even if it was true. If someone was planning to conduct illegal activities at your property, they surely wouldn't be telling you in the application. If they do, consider this a super red flag.

Here are some critical things I ask for on the rental application.

- **Personal Information.** Name, social security number (for background & credit checks), date of birth, driver's license number, phone number, email and who plans to live at the property
- **Rental History.** Current address, previous addresses, move-in/out dates, landlord names and contact information, monthly rent and reason for moving
- **Employment Information.** Current employer, position, supervisor and phone number, gross monthly income, hire date, other sources of income
- **Candidate Questionnaire.** I ask the following questions because I want to know the answers! You should too, because it may make all the difference in the world. You'll notice that they are succinct and straight forward. They invoke truthful answers. Here they are:
  - Why do you want to live here?
  - How long will you live here?
  - Why are you moving?

- o   What pets do you have?
- o   How many evictions have been filed upon you?
- o   How many felonies do you have?
- o   Have you ever broken a lease?
- o   Do you smoke?
- o   How many vehicles do you own?
- o   Is the total move-in amount available now?
- o   How do you plan to cover the move-in charges?
- o   When would you like to move in?
- o   For what reasons could you not pay rent on time?
- o   Do you have a bank account? What is the balance in each account?
- o   Emergency contact information
- o   Why should we rent to you?
- o   What else would you like us to know?

As mentioned above, the back side of the application has two disclosure statements, my tenant qualifications and signature lines. Having this disclosure and requiring their signature will cover you from liability and ensure you are being compliant with the Fair Housing Act. You must collect as much information as possible. State on the application that if not filled out completely, in other words, every question is not answered, you will return the application until it is or deny their application. It is the candidate's responsibility to ensure they completely fill out the rental application. If they don't, they are likely omitting facts you would want to know about, or won't make a good tenant in general because they don't pay attention to small and simple details. If they don't pay attention to this, why would they pay attention to things that matter, such as paying you rent each month. Be aware that the best screening system for keeping bad tenants far away is you. Nothing can replace your instincts or your systems.

The application isn't the only thing you should be collecting.
Don't be silly, the application itself is not enough. You must collect supporting documentation to confirm what the candidate is stating on the application is true. This is another test. Are they exaggerating the amount of money they have on-hand, the quality of their previous tenant performance, or even basic information like name and birthdate? Trust me, it happens. I have seen it all. Some of what you ask for them to include on the rental application are automatic

disqualifiers based on your rental criterion for tenants. Perhaps smoking, a pit bull, a violent felony or an eviction. These are all red flags that you should know about before ever offering your property to anyone. The more information you have, the better decision you will make. When you apply for a mortgage or car loan, they don't just hand you the keys to the house or the car. They conduct due diligence. They do this by collecting supporting documentation and running a credit/background check. All of these screening methods give them a clear and true picture of who you 'really' are vs who you represented yourself to be. Confirming the representative version of a tenant vs the real version of the tenant is the objective. Collect this information, or you will likely be bamboozled:

- Copy of their valid driver's license
- Proof of income (paystubs)
- Two month's bank statements (checking & savings)
- Proof of employment
- Proof of government assistance, i.e., HUD, if applicable
- Letters of recommendation (optional)

Charge an application fee. There are certain areas of rental property management that should be emphasized as more important or critical than others. The application fee falls dead square into that category. If you don't charge an application fee, you will be accepting applications from a host of deadbeat candidates who have half-hearted interest in your rental. You will waste your own valuable time processing a stack of applications that will never merit you a penny. The processing of an application requires time, your time, and no small amount of it. From my experience, each rental application requires a minimum of two hours work. Between the background check, reference checks, social media check, credit check, employment confirmation, income verification, and other basic application information you are easily at two hours. Your time is worth something. Also, tenants expect to pay an application fee. This is standard procedure. Make sure you do it. I charge $30 for the first applicant and another $20 for each additional applicant 18+ years of age who will be living in the residence. Some landlords charge $50 per applicant. Many apartment complexes charge between $75-$100. I don't charge that much as I would drive away most applicants from ever applying. You want to be fair, not too high, though certainly not zero. Study what others are charging in your area and be around the average. I collect the application fee upfront, in cash. If they don't have the cash or need to pay later, I hold onto the application until they pay. I won't process it until they do. I make this very clear upfront. If they pay, they are a serious applicant. If they don't, they aren't. For out-of-town applicants, I have allowed payment via PayPal or Venmo. However, I still require upfront payment before application processing. Trust me on this one, charge the application fee. Do it *every single time*. Someday, you will thank me.

PROSPECTIVE TENANT DUE DILIGENCE

Due diligence is not fun; let's start there. It is purely administrative work. However, it is 100% the most important component of the tenant selection process. You can't adequately assess a tenant without conducting proper due diligence. I don't purchase a rental property without first asking the right questions, conducting a full property inspection, viewing the property appraisal or understanding the market. Therefore, why would I offer my rental property to a prospective tenant without first conducting the same level of due diligence, if not more? Like I've said numerous times throughout this book, tenants *make* or *break* your rental real estate business! I will walk you through how to find the best tenants and avoid the nightmares. Let's go!

Thoroughly review each application. We've already covered what to ask for on the rental application. Now, review it thoroughly to ensure all the relevant information is there. I don't process incomplete applications and neither should you. It is the prospective tenant's obligation to fill in the entire application. Each and every field of the application should be relevant and help you make your decision. If information is missing, you can't conduct a complete assessment.

Social media check. Not every landlord conducts social media checks. I think that is a major mistake. Social media checks are 100% free and employers of all types are doing this, so why not you? The most common accounts to check are Instagram, Facebook and Twitter. Facebook is my go-to as it provides the most information, whereas Instagram can be set to private. It is completely within your right to request social media usernames to screen prospective tenants. If they refuse, it may indicate they are hiding something.

Verify employment. Employment is the primary income source of most tenants. Verifying the source and history is a must. Employment can be verified through a phone call to the employer, a W-2, tax returns and background checks. I don't typically ask for tax returns, but if employment can't be verified through the other sources it may be necessary. When I call current or former employers, I leverage the opportunity to ask character questions vs just confirming employment. Not all employers will answer these questions, but it's worth a shot.

Intended duration. How long someone plans to stay in your property can be the deciding factor in your tenant selection process. All things being equal, someone who plans to stay more than two years vs someone who is in transition for six to twelve months, the safe choice is the one who plans to stay longer. Turnover is a major challenge in rental real estate and the less you have, the better your business tends to perform over time.

Verify income. Always verify income. The general standard is that their gross income is 3x rent. Some even require 4x, which obviously reduces risk on your end of a default. The first method is to ask for paystubs from a current employer. Don't stop there. Ask for 2-3 months of bank statements as well. Why? Because you can confirm the money went into their bank account and it also gives a clue into how they manage their finances. It also helps with the very next step of verifying cash on hand. Verifying bank statements can also indicate whether or not they have other sources of income.

Verify cash on hand. Cash on hand is a key indicator because without it how will a prospective tenant pay you? Verify they have all the cash required to move in with those bank statements and then some. That should be the minimum requirement. I don't expect tenants to have $30,000 in the bank. However, if their total cash balances are less than $1,000, tread carefully.

Drugs & alcohol. The objective here is to determine whether or not your potential tenants are heavy drug or alcohol abusers. The first objective is the sniff test, literally sniffing them in person to see if they wreak of drugs or alcohol. That doesn't mean you lean in to their shirt or anything creepy like that. If they are smokers, potheads or alcoholics, it will be very evident from a normal proximity. You can also look into their eyes and assess their behavior. If a prospective tenant comes to meet you showing signs of drug or alcohol use, proceed with caution.

Run background & credit. You might be asking, haven't we already asked for this information on the application? Yes, you have! However,

I will reiterate, don't trust anything. Confirm by *verifying everything*! Background and credit checks are a great way to fact-check and confirm whether or not your prospective tenant has a criminal past or is financially irresponsible.

Rental history. Rental history can tell you a lot about how a prospective tenant will behave and treat your property. Call prior landlords and verify rental history. Ask questions about how the tenant behaved. I will share with you the questions I ask prior landlords. Keep it simple and to the point to be respectful of their time.

- Did prospective tenant ABC live at your residence at [insert address here] from [insert timeframe here]?
- Did they pay rent on time?
- Did they fulfill their lease obligations?
- How would you describe [insert prospective tenant name here]?
- Would you rent to [insert prospective tenant name here] again?
- What else should I know about [insert prospective tenant name here]?

Yes, this is a lot of boring, tedious work! It's important and worth your time. Another key point to note is that you don't have to conduct the entire due diligence process for each and every applicant. As you filter down tenants, you can eliminate some early on in the process if they don't pass an important item within your rental criterion.

TENANT SELECTION AND MOVE-IN

The most important decision you will make about each of your rental properties is who you choose to live there. That's right, your choice of tenants is the most critical decision you make as a rental real estate business owner. It is what determines whether you succeed or fail! No pressure. Actually, that's not true, there is a *lot* of pressure! Don't fret though. I'm here to provide best practices to make this pressure-packed and stressful decision more manageable. My hope is that you have more confidence to make better tenant selection decisions.

With the pre-screening process and prospective due diligence steps now complete, you are ready to move on to tenant selection. I leverage a prospective tenant scorecard in helping me make this most important decision. The reason? Because it takes emotion out of the equation and brings true qualification to the forefront. People can make a good impression, even when deep down they are not who they portray themselves to be, in order to get what they want. Being fooled as a landlord happens more often than you may imagine. The solution? Have a system that leverages hard facts and verified information to aid in decision making. Choose the most qualified candidate, not the one you get along with or that 'impresses' you the most in person. Yes, it is important that they don't give a terrible first impression, however their qualifications should knock your socks off more than their personality! With that being said, let's cover the prospective tenant scorecard that I created and am sharing with you for buying this book.

Prospective Tenant Scorecard. To help simplify the process for me and put a number rating to each prospective tenant, I leverage a scorecard when conducting evaluations. Each of the pre-screening and post-screening categories has a 1-5 score associated with it. Each category is also weighted to the level of importance I assign to it. Not every category is created equal. Each should factor in, though there are a few categories that should be of the highest importance when making this critical decision. I leverage the SUMPRODUCT formula in Microsoft Excel to help calculate the weighted average of my scorecard based on the assigned weighted percentages for each category. You can see the difference below between the normal average, which is just an average of all categories, vs the weighted average that factors in level of category importance.

The 'Income Ratio' in the third to last column is the income to rent calculation, total income/rent = X. The "Normal Rating", in the second to last column, is a simple average calculation of the columns 'General Vibe' to 'Credit'. The 'Weighted Rating' in the final column is the weighted-average given for the same categories using the associated weights provided in the top row. This is the final rating that I use to make my decision. I added conditional formatting to the cells where any score below 4.0 is RED, 4.0-4.4 is YELLOW and scores above 4.5 are GREEN. The below graphic only shows the black & white version. Here is what that translates to:

- 4.5 – 5.0 GREEN—High Quality Score
- 4.0 – 4.4 YELLOW—Average Quality Score
- 0.0 – 4.0 RED—Inferior Quality Score

Prospective tenants ranked RED, or inferior-quality score, will not be offered residence in one of my properties, regardless of whether they are the only candidates. Prospective tenants ranked YELLOW, or average-quality score, are unlikely to be offered residence, though they are not completely eliminated from contention. Prospective tenants ranked GREEN, or high-quality score, are immediately in contention. Obviously the higher the score within that scale the better. I feel comfortable offering prospective tenants ranked GREEN residence in one of my properties. I prefer to have a score of 4.8 or 4.9, making the decision much easier to make. If there is a tie, I first look at intended duration to see who plans to stay longer. This usually is the deciding factor. If the intended duration is similar, I go with my gut! Feel free to use the prospective tenant scorecard tool below in your business to rent out your property with more confidence.

Here is my prospective tenant scorecard. The below is from a property I rented out, with real prospective tenant ratings. I excluded last names for privacy reasons, though this is how I go about my rating process. In this particular scenario, I have 3 prospective tenants that ranked GREEN. Not even 24 hours after I collected applications, I started the process. Eden & John didn't impress me much in person; however, their application qualifications were off the charts. She just started a job as a psychology teacher at the local University. I reached out for more information, but she had just accepted another offer. No surprise, her income and cash on hand were off the charts. I moved on to the second and third options. In this instance, Randi & Laken were coming from out of town and couldn't move in for several weeks. They didn't reply to my inquiries right away and intended to stay for 12 months. Savanna & Michael were also coming from out of town, but they did come to the open house after driving all night to be there first thing in the morning! They wanted to stay for a few years and were timely in their responses. As a result, I offered them the property and they accepted with excitement! They have been a joy from day one.

Prospective Tenant Scorecard												
Weighted Average	8%	8%	10%	10%	10%	18%	13%	10%	13%	100%	Normal Rating	Weighted Rating
# Candidate Name(s)	General Vibe	Social Media	Employer	Landlord	Intended Duration	Income	Cash	Smoke	Credit	Income Ratio		
1 Tamika	5	4	4	3	5	3	3	4	3	3.1	3.8	3.6
2 Hope	3	4	4	5	4	3	1	5	3	3.1	3.6	3.4
3 Randi & Laken	5	5	5	5	3	5	5	5	5	6.5	4.8	4.8
4 Stephanie	4	4	5	3	3	3	1	5	4	2.1	3.6	3.4
5 Myranda & Thomas	4	2	5	5	3	5	5	4	4	4.0	4.1	4.3
6 Eden & John	5	5	5	5	5	5	5	5	5	4.8	5.0	5.0
7 Savanna & Michael	5	5	5	5	5	4	5	5	5	3.3	4.9	4.8
8 Alvaro	4	3	5	4	3	3	4	5	3	3.0	3.8	3.7

What I just shared with you is best practice, not a guarantee of any kind. The truth is that tenants are human beings and their behavior changes over time. Also, many are excellent liars and can deceive even the most diligent landlord. I mean, deceit has risen to the highest levels of power, fame and government. So, if and when it happens to you, take comfort in knowing it happens to us all. It's just another bump in the road. By following the prescription defined above, you are much more likely to succeed and avoid most of those deceitful people along the way. At least with a scorecard, you can proceed with more confidence and less risk.

Deposit to Hold Agreement. Once you have offered a property to a prospective tenant and they accept, the very next step should be completing the 'Deposit to Hold Agreement'. I wish I had learned about this best practice earlier on in my rental real estate career. In essence, the agreement benefits both the landlord and the prospective tenant. The landlord agrees to hold the property for the tenant until the designated move-in date and the prospective tenant agrees to pay a deposit for this hold. The deposit should be significant. I ask for $500 minimum. This should be paid within 24 hours of acceptance. Once they complete the document, sign it and pay the deposit you are locked in as a landlord and cannot offer the unit to someone else. Now, if there is any issue prior to lease signing, you can always return the deposit funds and not move forward. Once the tenant signs the full lease agreement, the pre-deposited funds roll into the security deposit. If the tenant backs out for whatever reason, they are forfeiting those funds to you. I have had this happen and it's the absolute worst. Since implementing this practice into my business, it has only happened one time. And guess what? I kept the $500 and offered the unit to my runner up who moved in a few days later. By implementing this practice, you are avoiding the 'ghoster fail'. The ghoster fail is when you offer the property to a prospective tenant who ghosts you before lease-signing day. Who loses? You do. Only you. By then, your runner up has likely already found a property and likely your third best option if you had one. Once the prospective tenant pays the deposit, they have a lot of skin in the game and are invested in signing a lease with you. Otherwise, they are out $500 or whatever amount you decide to charge. I have had zero people push back on the deposit to hold as they see the benefit for them as well. Many people run scams out there and nobody wants to be victim of fraud. This is a legally binding document and I share a copy of the one I use below.

Deposit to Hold Agreement

Date: _____

Property Address: _____

Congratulations for being offered the property! In order to guarantee possession of this property come the agreed upon move-in date, this agreement must be completed, signed and the 'deposit to hold amount' must be paid in full.

This agreement is made between the **Prospective Tenant**(s) _____

and the **Landlord**(s) _____.

Move-In Requirements are as follows:

- 1st month's rent must be paid in full totaling: $_____
- Security Deposit must be paid in full totaling: $_____
- Pet deposit or other agreed-upon funds pain in full totaling: $_____
- All utilities as predefined must be transferred into the Prospective Tenant's name.
- The rental lease agreement must be fully executed by all parties.

Deposit to Hold Execution:

Landlord acknowledges receipt of the Deposit to Hold totaling $_____ from the Prospective Tenant(s) as a non-refundable holding fee for the property listed herein. Prospective Tenant(s) understands the holding fee secures the property until a rental lease agreement and all move-in requirements described above are completed. The deadline for completion is by ____/____/_____.

Once all move-in requirements have been completed and Prospective Tenant(s) given possession of the property, the Deposit to Hold funds will be rolled into the Security Deposit. Security Deposit rules are defined in full in the rental lease agreement. Prospective Tenant(s) fully understands and by signing this document is in agreement that possession of the property will not be granted until all move-in requirements are completed.

If the Prospective Tenant(s) do not complete all move-in requirements by the defined date and time, Landlord will post the property for rent publicly and the entire Deposit to Hold funds will be forfeited to the Landlord to cover lost expenses including, but not limited to, advertising costs, lost rent, holding costs, marketing costs, etc.

By signing this Deposit to Hold Agreement I am confirming my understanding of all defined above.

Prospective Tenant _____

Prospective Tenant _____

Landlord _____

Landlord _____

This Happened to Me – The 'ghoster' applicant

I showed a property that had a decent amount of interest. By the end of the day, I had received three paid applications. After completing due diligence, I offered the property to one of the applicants. They seemed excited! They accepted immediately and we set a lease signing date for two weeks out when they would be ready to move in. I assumed everything was in order. I created the lease agreement, but didn't reach out for any confirmation until lease signing day. I texted in the morning on my way into town, no response. I figured it's early, I will give them a few minutes to respond. Thirty minutes go by and no response. By this point I have texted multiple times and am starting to sweat a bit. I try calling, no answer. Now I am getting frustrated. I keep driving to the property in hopes they had phone problems or changed their number and were at the property waiting with my move-in funds. Nope, nobody was there. I was screwed. I could do nothing about it. I tried calling the second and third people on my list to see if they were still interested and they had both found a place already. I had already removed the listing and had zero new leads. I was back at ground zero and learned a very valuable lesson that day: Do not trust anybody on their word alone.

I give people the benefit of the doubt unless they give me reason not to. This is who I am. As a landlord, nobody gets the benefit of the doubt. I assume everyone is lying until I can prove otherwise. I know, it seems harsh. But think about it. You are just meeting these people. They likely have low credit scores and income. They are going to show their best selves to impress you. They are going to say the right things and appear the part. I have learned to believe nothing and verify everything. I learned the hard way that day, but that learning has not gone to waste. I collect the deposit to hold funds with every new tenant, unless they are associated with a government program. In those cases, I work directly with the program contact and am guaranteed payment.

Since implementing the deposit to hold system in my business, I have had zero prospective tenants back out. I highly recommend this practice. Now that you have selected your tenant, it's time to move them in! This is an exciting day for both parties. There are six simple steps I recommend for a successful tenant move in.

1. **Tour the property.** When arriving at the property with a new tenant, conduct a walk-through inspection with them and answer any questions. Show the tenant the most common 'things to know' about the property. A more thorough walkthrough should be conducted by the tenant within the first week of living there.

2. **Cover expectations.** It's *very* important to cover expectations with your new tenant before signing the lease agreement to ensure they understand how you operate and how you expect them to behave. This is covered in extensive detail in Chapter Seven. Be sure they know the essentials of paying rent, maintenance, repairs, communication and more.

3. **Collect move-in funds.** Always collect move-in funds prior to signing the lease agreement! Be sure the required funds are paid

100%. Don't accept cash or personal check. I recommend only accepting a cashier's check or a money order. This is guaranteed money where you cannot succumb to fraud. Don't bend here and collect *before* signing legal paperwork!

4. **Review and sign the rental lease agreement.** Review the key points of the lease with the tenant. I recommend sending them a copy of your lease via email prior to move-in day so they have an opportunity to read it and bring any questions they have to the lease signing. Be sure to answer any and all questions. Finally, sign the lease! Be sure to have tenants initial each page so they acknowledge the full contents and sign/date the final page.

5. **Leave behind the move-in/out condition report.** Now it's time to leave your new tenant with the move-in/out condition report. Instruct them to conduct a thorough inspection of the property within the first seven days of move-in. Instruct them to complete the form and return it to you to ensure both parties agree on the property condition upon move in. You can find many versions of this form online and customize for your business.

6. **Hand over the keys.** You've done it! The most challenging component of owning and managing rental real estate is now complete. Hand over the keys, enjoy the moment and celebrate!

Renting your property to a qualified tenant is the objective each time you have a vacancy. Vacancy is a landlord's worst enemy. Vacancy means you are not collecting revenue for that property. Track your vacancy rates. Follow these best practices and greatly improve your ability to fill each and every rental property in short order.

LET'S WRAP A BOW ON THIS CHAPTER

Congratulations, you've finished Chapter Five and learned something new to improve your rental real estate business! The focus of this chapter is simple, yet critically important; your business depends on whether you find the best tenants and avoid the nightmares. Tenants are your lifeblood, without reliable and decent ones, your business will collapse.

Make your property attractive. People want to live in a clean, welcoming environment. You are best served by making your property attractive to prospective tenants in order to attract the very best. Follow the list of inexpensive improvements to spruce up your rental.

Let's put up the 'for rent' sign. Advertise your rental where the best prospective tenants go to find a place to live. Be sure the ad is complete, well-written and includes quality photographs.

Tenant criterion and pre-screening. Know what kind of tenant you are looking for upfront. Pre-screen each and every prospective tenant well. Screen them on your general vibe of them, how they completed the rental application, their social media accounts and whether they follow-through/communicate.

The rental application. Asking for the proper information can aid or impede your ability to make a sound decision. Only process completed applications. Charge an application fee. No exceptions.

Prospective tenant due diligence. Take your time to follow the due diligence procedures, be thorough and you will be glad you did. This is where you find the best tenants and avoid the nightmares.

Tenant selection and move-in. Leverage the best practices in this chapter to select the best tenant. Key factors to include in this decision are employment status, previous landlord references, proof of income, verification of cash on hand, signs of drugs & alcohol usage, expected move-in timeframe and intended duration in the property. Use a scoring system or scorecard to take the emotion out of the process.

SIX

YOU ARE DOING THIS TO MAKE MONEY!

R ental real estate is a business venture, and just like any other business venture the objective is to make a profit that can sustain you. You are an official business owner. Start thinking and operating like one, if you aren't already. This is a common mistake of many landlords. They purchase a rental property or several in hopes of making some extra money or saving for retirement. Unfortunately, many don't understand that just like any operational business, your rental property business needs an active operator. Markets change. Rents change. Tenants change. Environments change. Properties age and change. Are you staying on top of all these changes? If not, you are not an active operator in your business. I have encountered many different rental property owners that are not true operators. They are ineffective and aloof in their own business. Peter Lynch, an American investor, mutual fund manager and philanthropist, wisely stated "Know what you own, and know why you own it." Readers of this book own rental real estate, though do they know why they own it? Ask yourself that question and be sure you understand the answer. If your answer doesn't include making money or building lasting wealth, you may want to reconsider your path.

Each multi-family property that I have purchased was from a seller who poorly managed the building and their business. The rents were almost always undervalued. I took one building's overall rent from $3,600 to $5,200 in the span of just one year, that is a 44% increase in top line revenue and ultimately bottom-line profit in less than one year. I accomplished this through property improvements, rental renewals and turnover. It wasn't complicated, but it did require a focused and intentional effort. This chapter will cover the basic purpose of your rental real estate business, making money!

THIS IS ABOUT LASTING WEALTH

If you got into this business to get rich quick, you walked in through the wrong door. There are signs, advertisements and promises all over the place that claim, "Real estate will make you rich!", "I will teach you to make it big in real estate for the low cost of $20,000!", "Get rich fast with real estate!". False, false and false is what I say to this garbage. Rental real estate is about lasting wealth. This requires hard work, focus, concerted effort and consistency. If you want lasting wealth through rental real estate, then pay attention and take some notes! This book provides the winning strategies to help you get there. Whether you achieve lasting wealth is a direct correlation to your ability to learn and your commitment. Don't get me wrong. There *is* money in rental real estate. There can be *big money* if you play your cards right. If you had extra cash lying around and invested $1 million in real estate back in 2009-2010, you are likely worth over $100 million today. You can get rich doing real estate. Though it is never 'quick' and certainly never 'easy'. This chapter about maximizing your revenue, cash flow and overall net income. Let's start with the basics.

This Happened to Me – Burned by 'get-rich-quick' schemes

I have been tempted to delve into 'get-rich-quick' schemes in the past. Each time, I was burned. Each time, I damaged relationships. Each time, it didn't work. The appeal is tempting. Human nature encourages us to do less for more. However, lasting wealth is built upon the foundation of hard work and consistency. While still a college student, I fell for the 'get-rich-quick' mentality twice. The second time, it cost me my entire savings account along with shame and embarrassment for thinking I knew better. All the while my new bride warned me against pursuing the investment. I started investing in real estate because I wanted to finally do it the *right way*. I wanted to build *lasting* wealth through hard work and consistency. When I bought my first rental property, I barely had enough cash to afford the 20% down payment. I used a conventional loan and purchased the property for 12% lower than it was advertised. I followed a simple rule that I wanted to purchase my properties for at least 10% below market value. I was fortunate enough to lock this one up at the price I did to jump-start my rental real estate journey.

That first property has more than doubled in value and provided me with a 125% rate of return on appreciation alone. This was not expected. I didn't buy the property with fingers crossed that it would appreciate like this over time. I invested with two major criteria: buy 10% below market value and it must cash flow a minimum of $400 monthly. I have purchased each single-family property with this criterion. I leverage capitalization rate (CAP rate) as a key purchasing factor for my multi-family rental properties.

When growing a rental portfolio, capital is the name of the game. At first, I didn't have much. After I purchased the first property, I partnered with a good friend, who happens to be someone I trust with my life. We began splitting the capital requirements and were able to grow our portfolio to two doors in the first year, five in the second year, eight in the third year, and 21 in the fourth year. With the first eight doors under our belts, and the market conditions good, we decided to refinance three of our properties into a single loan and cashed out $120,000 that financed the next 13 doors! We invested 100% of our earnings back into our business and lived off the income from our full-time jobs. With that additional cash-out money we were able to branch into multi-family properties. As a result, we more than doubled our total door count in just *one* calendar year, 2019. We also doubled our gross revenues and overall profitable returns!

Today, we find ourselves in a cash-wealthy position each month. This has afforded us the opportunity to make improvements to existing units upon turnover and then increase revenue through higher rents. This has proven to be a very successful strategy. Our collective portfolio is worth over $3 million. This wasn't done overnight. It was accomplished through *hard work* and *consistency* over time.

MONEY-MONEY-MONEY: THE FINANCIAL METRICS WORTH TRACKING IN YOUR RENTAL REAL ESTATE BUSINESS

You are probably thinking about the theme song from Donald Trump's, "The Apprentice" or "The Celebrity Apprentice" when you read this title. The actual song is titled, "For the Love of Money" by The O'Jays. The truth is, you *are* doing this for the money. You need to realize that right now. It's not a hobby or a fun thing to do on the weekends. It is hard work that requires a significant commitment. We are doing this for one primary reason—money. Here is why that money matters to me. Money to provide for my family. Money to pay the bills. Money to take memorable vacations. Money to donate to my church. Money to help lift others. Money to help my kids attain a better life through higher education. Money to build my dreams. Money to take my kids golfing. Money to pay for their sports and activities. Money to pay for the start of *their* dreams. Money to take my amazing wife on dates. Money to travel the world with her someday. Money to achieve my wildest dreams. Money, my friends, is not a bad thing. It is *okay* to want to make money out of your hard-earned ventures. Money has so many positive uses and that's where my money will be going.

As the owner of a rental real estate business, it's important that you understand the basic financial terminology associated with the business. We will cover cash flow, net operating income, net income and capitalization rate. The more knowledgeable you are about the financial efficiency or success of your business, the better off you will be. Now that we have the right perspective about money, let's make some! We will cover the most common methods of making money or earning 'revenue' in your business. It all starts with your cash flow!

Cash Flow. Cash flow (or margin) is a simple business term that defined seems more complex than it really is. Here is one definition from Merriam-Webster, "the difference which exists between net sales and the cost of merchandise sold and from which expenses are usually met or profit derived". The calculation for cash flow is **'total income – total expenses = cash flow'**. I will simplify this. Let's take a vendor outside a sports stadium who is peddling water bottles and peanuts. If they purchased each bottle of water at 27 cents and sold them for $1.00, the margin would be 73 cents. This is a crazy good margin. It is 3.7x what they paid for it. For the peanuts, the whole bag is probably $5.00, which they separated into 10 different bags and sold them for $2.00 each. The margin would be $1.50 per bag or 3x the original value of the product. Not too shabby for the peddling street vendor.

Now onto a rental real estate example. The factors to consider are income vs expenses each month. Let's review how this works.

Income
- Rent: $1,500

*Total Income: **$1,500***

Expenses
- Debt service: $400
- Insurance: $70
- Repairs & maintenance: $100
- Management fees: $160
- Utilities: $90
- Vacancy: $50

*Total Expenses: **$880***

Cash Flow = $1,500 - $880 or $620

Your cash flow for this month would be $620. Vacancy and repairs do not happen each month, though it's encouraged to average them across the span of a calendar year to properly estimate true margin. Without vacancy and repairs, your margin would be $770 for the month. Cash flow is an essential in rental real estate. As in any business, cash is king. The higher the cash flow the better, obviously. Cash allows you to reinvest in the growth of your business. Cash pays for all expenses, planned or unplanned. Without a steady flow of cash, your rental business will struggle.

Annualized Net Income. Net income is more commonly referred to as *profit*. No metric is of more importance than actual profit. Net income is simply the money left over once all expenses are paid. The calculation is **'total gross income – total expenses = net income'**. An example of this is if a business brings in $100 and had expenses of $70, the net income would be $30. Net income differs from cash flow in that it determines the overall profitability of your business vs just cash on hand. It includes all expenses for the business, but not forecasts such as vacancy estimates. I recommend calculating this metric annually, while still tracking monthly NOI and cash flow. Here is an example of how this might look like for your rental business.

Income
- Rent: $250,000
- Fees: $3,000
- Laundry: $5,000
- Storage: $5,000

*Total Income: **$263,000***

Expenses
- Debt service: $75,000
- Taxes: $12,500
- Insurance: $15,000
- Repairs & maintenance: $37,000
- Utilities: $15,000
- Marketing: $1,500
- Legal & accounting: $3,000
- Management fees: $25,000
- Mobile Phone & Internet: $2,100
- Miscellaneous Expenses: $6,250

*Total Expenses: **$192,350***

Net Income = $263,000 - $192,350 or $70,650

Net Operating Income. More commonly referred to as NOI. This is the most important financial metric in your business. The number of income lines is typically one, though I recommend having more. Rent is always the single largest source of income. Savvy investors have learned how to get extra income through utility coverage, storage, parking, a garage, laundry and more. Then, you subtract your total operating expenses from that total income line. The calculation is **'total gross income – total operating expenses = net operating income'**. One expense item not counted in this calculation is your debt service. Debt service is not considered an operating expense. That is calculated with total net income, but not net *operating* income. The net operating income metric shows the efficiency at which you *operate* your rental real estate business.

Examples of non-operating expenses are the debt service, depreciation and capital improvements. Add these to the operating expenses, then subtract the total from the gross income to get to net income. Let's review an example together of net operating income.

Gross Income
- Rent: $1,500
- Laundry: $50
- Parking: $50

*Total Gross Income: **$1,600***

Operating Expenses
- Taxes: $40
- Insurance: $70
- Repairs & maintenance: $100
- Utilities: $90
- Vacancy: $50
- Marketing: $20
- Legal & accounting: $20
- Management fees: $160

*Total Operating Expenses: **$550***

Net Operating Income = $1,600 - $550 or $1,050

This metric is calculated monthly. I recommend calculating annually as well. Compare this to previous months and years to discover trends in your financials that may allow you to identify improvement areas. We don't simply calculate financial metrics to look at them once and move on. We calculate them and subsequently analyze them to identify opportunities for improvement in our businesses.

Capitalization rate. More commonly referred to as *CAP rate*. This metric is a percentage that sends a signal of whether you are making a good deal or a bad deal. The CAP rate calculation is '**(net operating income / purchase price)*100**. This metric is expressed as a percentage. Net operating income is all monthly expenses minus the debt service, referenced above. The CAP rate is often used as an analysis tool to see if you are making a solid investment pre-purchase. However, CAP rate can also be leveraged *after* the fact to determine whether you have improved the profitability of your rental property over time. CAP rate is one of the most commonly referred to terms for shopping investments. CAP rates typically range from 3% – 15%. Some are below 3% and likely indicators of a bad deal. CAP rate is often times given a proforma evaluation when looking to purchase an investment. Here is an easy scenario for you. I recently evaluated a fourplex for sale. The current CAP rate vs the proforma CAP rate was substantial and made submitting an offer worth the time and effort.

Current CAP Rate vs Proforma CAP Rate - Fourplex Comparison							
Category	Value	Unit	Current Rent	Proforma Rent	Expense Type	Current Monthly Expenses	Proforma Monthly Expenses
Purchase Price	375,000	Unit A	625	800	Vacancy	134	160
Current Monthly Cash Flow	1,787	Unit B	625	800	Maintenance	250	250
Current Annualized Cash Flow	21,438	Unit C	675	800	Utilities	275	275
Current CAP Rate	5.7%	Unit D	745	800	Taxes & Insurance	125	125
Proforma Monthly Cash Flow	2,290				CapEx	100	100
Proforma Annualized Cash Flow	27,480	Totals	2,670	3,200	Total Monthly Expenses	884	910
Proforma CAP Rate	7.3%						

Proforma essentially means, at current market rents your CAP rate would be X% higher than what it is currently. This indicates that under better management this investment would be more valuable. It would generate more cash flow, net operating income and a higher overall return. The example above was from a fourplex that I was evaluating. The rents were grossly mismanaged. I knew that we could increase cash flow and net income, which in turn is a major increase in the CAP rate. We purchased the property and did just that. A nearly 2% increase in CAP rate means serious financial improvement. The monthly operating cash flow increased by $504 and the annualized return increased by $6,042! As a rental real estate business owner, CAP rate and the improvement of it on each owned and operated property should always be top of mind.

As an update to this property showcased above, our current rents are $775, $880, $785 and $990 for a total of $3,430 in monthly rents. We outperformed the proforma in less than six months' time! The current CAP rate is 8%. Our investment is already looking very solid.

MAXIMIZE YOUR REVENUE AND CASH FLOW DOOR BY DOOR

The statement this title makes isn't centered around greed, but a focus on good business. This doesn't mean ripping folks off and going 20% above market rent. The single most common mistake landlords make is renting a property *below market value*. I can't remember how many times I have had someone interested in selling me their property tell me the following, "The unit is currently renting for $600, but could easily rent for $800-$900. Oh, and the tenant is on a month-to-month lease." Ok, first, *why* are you not charging market rent right now? Second, *how* do you know you could get $800-$900 when you are only collecting $600? I always find this peculiar because they *know* they are undercharging rent, yet they do nothing about it. The good news for you and I is there are many of these people out there who are looking for buyers. These investors looking to be sellers are a great way to help your business grow.

This Happened to Me - Grandma never raised rent

My wife's grandma, who has long since passed away, used to live in a home that had seven total apartments on the property. She managed the properties herself. She was well-intentioned and far too nice when it came to charging proper rent. For those who stayed with her long-term, she would either never raise rent or raise it ever so slightly. For widows, she *never* raised the rent. Literally, never. She left for a couple of years on a church service mission with her husband and asked her son-in-law, who is my father-in-law, to manage the properties in their absence. When he looked at the rent rolls, he realized that his mother-in-law was charging *only* $50 for several of her units, which included utilities! After doing some simple math, he realized that she was actually upside down on some units as a result of being nice and never raising their rents. For some perspective, some of these people had been living there for 20+ years!! Yikes, I know. Being a businessman and also being asked to manage the properties, my father-in-law did exactly that. He raised the rents for these units to $300, which was *still* under market value at the time and they began to actually realize income on these units. His mother-in-law was floored when she arrived back home, but then soon realized the error of her ways with some enlightenment. Being nice doesn't mean not charging fair market rent. Fair also means for *you*.

Rent is the largest revenue item in your business and number two isn't close. Charging the right amount of rent is critical to ensure you are successful. Charging too much can price you out of the market, limit the number of potential renters and increase the amount of vacancy time. Each of these results will hurt your overall profit. Charging too little will likely attract undesirable tenants, lock you into that low figure for the duration of the lease and reduce your overall profit margins. So, you may be asking, how do I know what to charge? Well, there isn't a matrix for this that makes it overly simple. This is part of your business that you actually have to put effort into. Google and Alexa won't even give you the answer here! This one is up to you and the amount of work you are willing to put in to determine the fair market rent in your area.

This Happened to Me – Increasing revenue door by door

We purchased our very first apartment building with 8 units in October of 2019 from a nice gentleman who owned the building for many years. When we calculated the value of the deal, we realized that most of the units were actually well under market rent. Even with this, the CAP rate was above 10%. We calculated that with some small renovations with the turn of each unit and increasing rents to market value we would be able to clear around a 14% CAP rate. Needless to say, we did the deal. This previous owner had one glaring gap in his property management style—undercharging tenants for rent by 10% or more! Within the first three months of owning the property, which was fully occupied upon acquisition, one of our tenants passed away. Her 1 bed, 1 bath unit was going for $550 at the time. We calculated that we should be getting around $590-$600. With some renovations we could charge as much as $700. We replaced the flooring, added some new light fixtures, painted the unit white, replaced the toilet, upgraded the vanity and gave it a deep clean. With these upgrades, we ended up charging $675 and filling the unit within a week of going on the market. We will now clear another $1,200 per year on this unit alone. Our total spend was less than $3,000 for the renovations. We also added around $10,000 in equity value to the property.

Another unit in this same building was occupied by an older gentleman who one day stopped paying his rent. After two months of no rent, we evicted him. Unfortunately, he was a smoker and dragged the smell along with him into the unit. This unit was renting for $600 monthly. We transformed it, with: new floors, kitchen cabinets, interior paint, bathroom sink, vanity, kitchen sink, kitchen counters, etc. We spent a pretty penny on this one and a tenant from upstairs ended up moving downstairs due to their advanced age and limited mobility. The tenant agreed to pay $700 monthly for the newly renovated downstairs unit and vacated their unit upstairs. We were clearing another $100/month in rent.

A third tenant in this same building gave their 30-day written notice of departure. We negotiated with him and he was willing to vacate early if we found a new tenant in time. It was just a few days and a young couple seemed impressive enough. We offered them the property and they accepted for $150 more than it was previously being rented for. We have since gone on to turn several more units and increase the rents to market value or slightly above with some renovations. The property is performing rather well.

You are running a business and each door is your 'product'. You want to get the best rate of return, or margin, for your product. This is how successful businesses are created and how they endure. If you get stuck accepting below market rent and below average tenants, your business will struggle to grow and so will you. Be sure to maximize your revenue and margin by door! Now, we will cover several different methods for you, as landlords, to maximize your revenue and cash flow per door. These are common practices that every landlord should consider as they manage their business.

Have tenants pay utilities. As a rental property manager, you have the choice to pay for or pass along the cost of utility services to your tenants. I highly recommend passing this cost along to your tenants, unless your property doesn't allow for it. The tenant is the one consuming the electricity, water, heat, etc. Why should you be paying for it? It is just another expense that you can avoid or reduce significantly. If you must pay the utilities because your duplex has a single meter, I recommend charging higher rent to compensate for the increased expense. In hyper-competitive rental markets where you are struggling to find good tenants, it may be necessary to offer paying certain utilities as an incentive to choose your property over another.

Utilities can take a major chunk out of your net income each month, so if you can, pass the expense along.

There is a triplex in my portfolio that has a single water meter, so I pay for water. However, the rent is increased to cover the average cost of water and ensure that I'm not stuck paying for my tenant's water consumption. Our triplex has separately metered electricity, but a single meter for both water and gas. We take the same approach with each of our rental properties. Remember, you are a business person. Maybe you don't think of yourself that way, but it's true. You need to be thinking like one in order to run a successful business.

Raise the rent. Rent is the largest and most important revenue line item in your business. Most tenants expect rent to increase every year or upon lease renewal. If you are charging above market rent and have an incredible tenant you don't want to lose, you may consider leaving rent where it is for a longer period of time. Vacancy is worse than a slight increase in rent. All other reasons aside, the recommendation is to raise rent upon lease renewal. You can incentivize people to sign a 6-or-12-month lease by offering different rent prices. For example, you can communicate that upon their upcoming lease renewal they can pay just $25 extra for signing a 12-month term, $40 extra for signing a 6-month term or $75 extra to remain month-to-month. This takes the burden off you and puts the responsibility on the tenant. It also allows them the opportunity to feel like they have a choice vs just forcing a rent increase onto them. An extra $20-$40 per month is not going to force many people out. Moving is one of the most stressful and disrupting events in people's lives. It is a huge commitment to move. Most people will stay put and pay the extra rent vs going through the hassle of finding a new place, packing, renting a truck, etc. I reiterate, moving stinks and most people don't want to deal with it unless they *have* to. If you hike rent 10% or more per month, this may cause some serious moving consideration by your tenants. Keeping people in place and paying rent each month is usually the best solution.

Charge fees. I know, 'fees' is such a negative word, with good reason. The reality is, fees are not only going to make you more money, they are essential for your ultimate success in rental real estate management. Let me explain. First, you should be collecting fees from the very first step in the rental process, the application. I will run you through some of the more common fees that every rental owner should be charging and the reasons behind it:

Application fee. You should always, I repeat, always collect an application fee before processing an application. I refuse to process them without a paid fee. You collect a fee for three main reasons. Reason one, due diligence requires your time and money. If you process a background or credit check, it isn't free. Also, your time shouldn't be free. It takes more than five minutes to process an application. Likely, it will take a cumulative one to two hours per. Your time is valuable; charge for it. Reason two, this shows that the potential tenant is serious about their application. If you don't charge a fee, you will most certainly receive two to three times the number of applications submitted. More than half of those applicants are not seriously interested. One of the most painful points in managing rental real estate is completing due diligence on an application. Charging an application fee disincentivizes non-serious applicants. Reason three, intent. Submitting an application fee demonstrates that the prospective tenant fully intends to rent the property and accept the property if offered to them. Showing intent is important because you don't want to waste your time. One important item of note, there is a cap to the amount you can charge for an application fee per state; be sure to look it up before you get caught overcharging. The most common fees are between $25 to $40 per application.

Late rent fee. This one is obvious. If a tenant doesn't pay rent on time, you charge them a late fee. Again, be sure to check your state law to ensure your fees are allowed and reasonable. For example, you can't charge a $200 late fee if rent is one day late. You can, however, charge a one-time late fee, plus additional daily fees until rent comes in. It is best if you charge a higher amount right away, then a smaller amount ongoing. For example, $40 for being late, then $10 for each additional day late. This adds up for the tenant and lets them know rent isn't something they can choose to pay when they feel like it or after they pay all the other bills.

Pet fee. I discuss this in detail later because of the importance of accepting pets and managing how you do it to find more success. The pet fee is simply charging an amount above and beyond monthly rent each month for permitting pets on the premises. Most pet fees are between $20-$50 per pet. Trust me, people will pay it and you should absolutely charge it.

Lack of maintenance fee. If the tenant is responsible for yard maintenance as outlined in the lease agreement and doesn't fulfill their duty, you can charge them a fee upon inspection. Be sure to document the issues via picture and written notification. I charge $75 when this happens. The local code enforcement department patrols this type of behavior where we own. This is also a reminder to the tenant that you will enforce your lease agreement.

No-show fee. If you setup an appointment with a professional to repair or service something inside the property that requires someone to be there and the tenant doesn't show after agreeing to be there, you can charge them a 'no show fee'. Usually, the service provider will charge you for a visit even though they did nothing. Charging the fee is a strong reminder to your tenant that they must be responsible. Especially since most of the time they are calling about the repair. Be sure to include this in your lease upon move in.

Bounced check fee. Just like banks, you can and should charge a bounced check fee. Most people aren't using checks anymore, but some still do. I recommend offering other payment methods to avoid this altogether, i.e., bank deposits, ACH transfers or online payments. However, if you do happen to run into this one, charge a fee.

Smoking fee. First of all, you should *not* allow smoking in any of your properties. If you do, you are asking for trouble and to lose serious cash. If during an inspection or some other time you find out the tenant smoked inside the residence, you must have a consequence. I recommend a heavy fee, such as $750 per occurrence. This is high enough to scare people away but not so high that you can get into trouble by the law for charging it. Each smoking violation is worthy of eviction. Your $750 fine becomes a second chance, unless you want this tenant out anyways because they are trouble or will continue to cause you headaches over time.

INCREASE THE VALUE OF YOUR INVESTMENT

Over time, you should steadily increase the value of your investment. By this, I mean you should be *investing* in your investment. Sometimes this is required immediately because you bought a fixer-upper. Mostly though, this happens steadily over time. Here are some great strategies for increasing the value of your rental properties.

Add a fence. Most people want a fenced-in yard. This is true whether they have pets or not. Many tenants have kids, pets or both. Most people want a fence for privacy purposes. It also adds a sense of security. If your property has a fence, though it is broken or not enclosed, you should fix it or finish the enclosure. This may require adding a gate. If there is no fence on the property, you don't necessarily have to add one all the way around the house if it is going to break the bank. Instead, add a fence to the backyard or perhaps the front, depending on the way the property sits. The least expensive fencing option is typically chain link with metal posts. It also requires the least amount of maintenance. Wood fences will always cost more and require ongoing maintenance. Consider these factors when choosing your fencing material.

Replace flooring. Flooring is usually one of the steepest upgrades for any rental, though doing it cheaply will only cost you more in the long run. Carpet does not do well in rentals. Life lived on carpet results in wear and tear, pet odors, stains, etc. I prefer to replace carpet with laminate wood (vinyl) flooring. I recommend ceramic tile in kitchens and bathrooms. These are durable and attractive finishes that remain in style for a long time. The style of colors and patterns will change with time, so stay with something more neutral so it can endure a change in style. Almost every time a property of mine has turned over that had carpet, it has been destroyed. Plus, people want nice floors to walk on and look at. Choose something durable, affordable and attractive.

Fresh paint. This is one of the easiest and least expensive upgrades you can make. Add some fresh paint to spruce up your property. This can be inside or outside, depending on where the need is. Paint is also something that you can do yourself. Many times, this can be as simple as painting baseboards and other trim pieces to freshen up the look. Be sure to paint in neutral, non-distracting colors such as shades of gray, white or beige.

Upgrade plumbing fixtures. This one is quite obvious. Nobody wants to flush a 20-year-old toilet or wash their hands with a rusty faucet, or worse yet, shower under a moldy shower head! Plumbing fixtures are not overly expensive, but they go a long way in attracting and keeping tenants. If a potential tenant walks into the main bathroom, or any bathroom for that matter, and they find a rusty faucet or shower head, the chances of them submitting an application are very slim. Unless of course they are desperate. Let me tell you, you don't want desperate tenants! They are desperate for a reason and that reason doesn't usually result in tidy, clean tenants who pay the full rent on time every month! Offer *quality* or you get what you offer when it comes to tenants. You don't need a tenant who demands the best of everything from Ethan Allen either. Politely decline their application. However, the better tenants usually have a standard that you must be able to match as a landlord. This one will easily result in a 100% or higher return. *Do it.* Trust me on this one.

Upgrade the bathroom. People want a nice bathroom, period. Think about it. Some of your most private moments happen in the bathroom. This is where you get naked to clean your body. The bathroom is where people discharge their bowels and also clean out after having too much to drink or coming down with Montezuma's revenge! Make it a place they feel comfortable in. This doesn't mean that your bathroom is a mirror image of the Ritz Carlton. However, it does mean that the vanity needs to be sufficiently attractive and functional. There should be some storage space. The shower head and faucets must be of good quality. The lighting should be adequate. There should be a fan for ventilation. The flooring and shower should not have chipping, broken or missing tiles. The toilet should not only work, but also be white! Bathroom upgrades may be costly, but it doesn't have to break the bank. You will find a good return on your bathroom upgrade with better tenants and higher equity. This will result in positive things for your business.

Upgrade the kitchen. Kitchen upgrades fall under the most expensive category, though they also translate into the highest return on investment when done correctly. The areas of focus in a kitchen are appliances, countertops, paint, backsplash, cabinets and flooring. Upgrade doesn't always mean replace. Cabinets can be upgraded with fresh paint, a new stain and/or new nobs/pulls. Adding more cabinetry in kitchen spaces where there is room and needs additional storage is also a bonus to tenants. Appliance upgrades or replacements are recommended when the existing appliance can't be cleaned to 'like new' condition, they have broken pieces or fixing them costs close to buying a new one. An upgrade can be a used appliance that happens to be better than the existing appliance. Attractive kitchen appliances attract better tenants. The opposite is also true. Countertop upgrades don't need to be Quartz or Marble. There are several faux materials that have a modern style to them with less than half the price tag. Adding a backsplash can go a long way in enhancing a kitchen and is relatively inexpensive. Tile is an enduring and affordable kitchen flooring material. Consider replacing old or 'out of style' flooring with a newer contemporary look. The easiest, most affordable upgrade is new paint. If the kitchen is painted a mustard yellow or dark green, definitely prioritize new, fresh paint as an upgrade.

Increase storage space. People need somewhere to store their life's collection of stuff. The United States self-storage business is booming because people have so much stuff and not enough room to store it. People also pay through the roof to hang onto items of personal care and attachment. That means, if they are willing to pay someone else to store it, they will be willing to pay *you* if you give them more storage space. The space should be safe and accessible. I have converted sheds and detached garages into storage space. I have also added closets and cleared out basements, otherwise uninhabitable, with space to store belongings. I once converted outside garage space into rentable storage units. This not only increased my margin and CAP rates, it resulted in satisfied tenants because of the convenience! Storage equals money, whether it be higher rents or additional fees for a separate space. Look for the space you do have and convert it to storage where practical and possible. The tenants will love it and so will your pocketbook!

Newer, better windows. Quality windows not only help reduce utility costs by keeping desired air temperatures in or out, they can increase your property value and reduce safety risks! Most of the properties I have purchased were built many years ago, when dual-pane windows weren't commonplace. Single pane windows result in safety risks, i.e., easy break-in. They are easily breakable and they don't maintain a comfortable home temperature. This will result in unhappy tenants and very high utility costs. This is a win-win every time. Just be sure not to overpay when replacing windows. Top of the line is not essential. Be sure to go with double-paned windows that have a 'green' rating.

You might ask, "When do I do these things?" There are three solid times to do this: 1. When you purchase the property, assuming no one lives there; 2. When a tenant leaves, this is considered the vacancy period; or 3. While the tenant is living there. With option number three you are limited to the types of improvements that can be made. For example, don't replace the floor while a tenant is living there. This will be a nuisance and likely cost you a lot more time, hassle and money. Wait until they move out. However, you could upgrade the outside of the property, add a fence or replace outdated plumbing and lighting fixtures. The truth is, properties require updating now and again. Investors who take the time to make the proper upgrades get the most rent and resale value out of their rental investment. Above all, they attract and retain the very best tenants in their area.

LIKE EM' OR NOT—ACCEPTING PETS IS A GREAT WAY TO MORE CASH FLOW

Get on the pet train! You don't have to love pets, or even like them. Believe me when I say this: accepting pets is your best way to a more profitable rental real estate business. The American Pet Products Association (APPA) states that *44%* of all US households own at least one dog and *35%* own at least one cat *(3)*. Americans have a love affair with their pets. It is even more intense with the renter population, where the Humane Society of the United States says that *72%* of renters have pets *(4)*! Many Americans spend outrageous amounts of money on their pets. The reality is that people are willing to shell out cash for their furry friends. Yes, even those with limited means behave this way. If you hold a hard line and refuse to accept pets, two of the worst-case scenarios come into play for you: 1. Your renter pool shrinks by 70%+ and 2. Your 'no-pet' tenants will lie to you about having one. In scenario one, having tenant options is critical to a successful rental business. By eliminating pets, you eliminate some great tenants. Many are the best kind of tenants who happen to have a pet. In scenario two, the statistics don't lie; people love pets! Tenants will lie to you and hide their animals. You may as well make money off the pet love affair vs realizing after-the-fact that they had or purchased a furry friend during their tenancy with you and the pet did some damage to the property. My wife and I were kicked out of our very first apartment together because we adopted a kitten that we named Jones, after Jones Soda. There was a zero-tolerance policy for pets and we had snuck Jones into our apartment where we managed to get away with it for two months. Whoops!

Some real talk for you, pets will more likely than not damage something that requires repair. This is why you collect the non-refundable pet deposit and the monthly pet fees. If this doesn't cover the repair costs, which is unlikely, the security deposit should. There is always risk in rental real estate. Pets are just one of the risks worth taking to improve your financials. I have found tenants with pets to be *stickier* than those without pets, meaning they stay longer. Tenant retention, aka low turnover, is a critical business metric. Let people have pets and collect the necessary funds to protect your investment.

Speaking of protecting your investment. You should do your best to pet-proof your rental. Carpet is a landlord's worst enemy while accepting pets. Actually, it is a landlord's worst enemy regardless! Carpet attracts the worst of everything a tenant leaves behind. You can rest assured that tenants will not be treating your property as if it were their own. Forget about that though. It's like a girlfriend you keep going back to, even though she isn't right for you and keeps breaking it off. Tenants don't care like you care. Accept that fact and prepare for it. Preparing for pets is not always the same. However, here are some tips to protect your investment from pets:

- Use a non-penetrable, hard-surface, easy-cleaning floor. Examples include: linoleum, vinyl wood, hardwood, and concrete.
- Fence in your property to prevent pets from causing issues with neighbors.
- Require that pets be vaccinated for distemper and rabies.
- Request a reasonable and non-refundable pet deposit. I started charging $250 and now charge $400.
- Charge monthly fees on top of rent per pet. I charge $25 - $50 extra per month per pet.
- Avoid aggressive breeds of pets such as Pit bulls.
- Require that a pet be neutered or spayed.
- Limit the allowable species, breed or size.
- Have tenants sign a pet addendum, outlining their obligations.

Time to wrap up the emphasis on being pet friendly yet charging for the convenience. I will repeat that pet-friendly properties are in high demand. Renters with are more likely to stay longer. Charge the non-refundable deposit and the monthly pet fees to increase your chances of success and reduce your overall risk. Let's cover a few scenarios for accepting pets and how it can impact your business.

The Hernandez family wants to rent your single-family rental home. The market rent for a 2-bedroom, 1-bathroom, 975 square foot home is $900. You charge $950 as your property has some upgrades. They have two pets: a German Shepard dog and a Westie dog. This is the impact allowing pets can make on your financials. The first table shows the monthly and annual revenue for this property without pets:

Income Category	Totals
Monthly Rent	$ 950
Monthly Total	$ 950
Annual Total	$ 11,400

The second table shows the monthly and annual revenue for this same property with pets:

Income Category	Totals
Monthly Rent	$ 950
Monthly Pet Fees	$ 75
Monthly Total	$ 1,025
Non-Refundable Pet Deposit	$300
Annual Total	$ 12,600

As you can see, the additional pet fees are $75 per month, which results in an additional $900 in annual revenue! Add on the non-refundable pet deposit and you are looking at a $1,200 revenue bump. In my business, I have had someone pay as much as $150 extra per month to have their pets live in my rental with them. The obsession is real and the money people shell out for their furry babies is no joke.

We've covered several benefits of accepting pets and also some of the downsides. Now, I'm going to take you into the reality of accepting pets. Pets and pet owners are not always one and the same in behavior. The good and the bad of accepting pets usually has a direct correlation with how responsible the pet owners are. Let's walk through some scenarios together.

Scenario A – The 'I don't have a pet' tenant!

One of my tenants swore there was no animal upon lease signing and we believed them. At this point, we gave people the benefit of the doubt. Common rookie rental real estate mistake. This tenant moved into the property and paid rent without hiccup for about three months. From month four onward (they signed an 18-month lease) rent collection was a constant struggle. This particular tenant had *every* excuse in the book: "I'm on my way to the bank", "The bank just closed", "My car broke down", "I'm waiting for my Uber to take me to the bank", "I promise there was money in the bank".

We collected monthly late fees for three consecutive months and decided it was time to pursue eviction. When visiting the property to post the eviction notice on the door, the tenants didn't receive us, though their two scary and vicious dogs did all the greeting necessary at the front door! Now six months into their tenancy, we realized we'd been duped. After speaking with the neighbors, we learned the pets not only had always been there, they were mischief makers in the neighborhood. The tenant was evicted not long after and upon departure, I entered the home for an inspection and turned right back around. The smell from those animals was so horrific I immediately knew a brand-new floor was in store. The reality is, we missed out on $800 in pet fees plus $300 in the pet deposit, for a total of $1,100. The cost of the new floor was $2,100. Had we collected the proper pet deposit and fees; we would have had enough funds to cover the floor replacement. Unfortunately, we didn't and were out about $1,000 with no ability to recoup the cost. A sunk cost and lost opportunity.

Scenario B – The Pet Accumulator!

Another set of tenants moved into our rental with one dog that they had informed us of. After living there for ten months, there was a major repair required. We sent our handyman over. He relayed back to us that the place was filled with animals and smelled horrific. Among the companion pets were another dog, two cats, a turtle and a *bunny*! I immediately called the tenant who admitted to having the pets living with them. I couldn't believe it. I shouldn't have been surprised though; I did it myself one time! We began charging them additional monthly rent and collected a pet deposit, which they agreed to comply with.

Scenario C – The Destructive Devil Pet!

Correct, pets are not humans and they are more likely to cause damage because they are not well trained or their owner is absent. However, I have known my human tenants to be equally as damaging with property and I don't collect extra fees for allowing more tenants into the property per month! The destructive devil pet will happen. It always does. You will have very bad tenants that you expected to be top notch. Pets will be the same. The devil pet does their business inside the house and chews on your stuff. One such pet we had was a dog that literally ate the bottom third of an interior door! Not kidding you. They were locked up in the room and chewed up the bottom third of the wood door. In this instance we had to use some of the pet deposit and pet fees to replace the door and repair some other damage from this particular devil dog.

Scenario D – The Tidy Cash Flow Pet!

It was the purchase of our third property that yielded our first pet-loving tenant. We had just purchased this cute little bungalow, newly remodeled with exposed brick on the interior, a completely redone exterior, fenced in backyard, detached garage and sprawling yard. There was real excitement about this particular property from my business partner, myself and the applicants. It is located in a cute part of town just blocks from downtown and the local Sonic drive-in. After reviewing with diligence our growing list of applicants, we settled on a sweet single mother with her two kids, her mom and their little Westie dog. We didn't understand that we were allowed to and should have been charging a pet deposit. Though we did know about the monthly pet fee. Due to the size and breed of the puppy, we only charged an additional $25/month on top of rent as a pet fee. It has been over two full years since they moved in. We visited the property on multiple occasions for repairs and random inspections. It was spotless! This was not typical with most tenants. More often than not it was a mess when we went to visit tenants. This particular pet and tenant were very tidy and essentially harmless to our property. As a result, we have yielded an additional $600 over the past two years of extra income that will flow straight down to the bottom line.

Presently, 57% of my current renters have at least one pet. I am collecting $1,000 more each month for pet fees and you guessed it, $12,000 annually! I happen to have two German Shepard dogs myself as well as two cats that our family loves very much. You own this business to make money. People want to give you more money to allow them to house their pets in your rental property. Consider it, along with the 72% statistic when making your decision!

Before ending this section on pets, I'd be remiss if I didn't cover service or emotional support animals. Under Title II and Title III of the Americans with Disabilities Act, service dogs are defined as dogs that are trained to assist an individual with a disability by performing specific tasks for that person (6). These animals receive specialized training and as such have protections and privileges that other animals do not. Service dogs accompany their owners everywhere and are not considered 'pets' under the law. Therefore, you cannot discriminate against owners of service dogs and also cannot treat the service dog as a pet. This means you cannot charge additional fees for them.

Emotional support animals are different than service dogs. They are considered pets that provide support for their owners, such as calming anxiety. They do not have to be dogs. They also don't have the same privileges as service dogs.

Unfortunately, many renters try and take advantage of the service dog privileges by misrepresenting their 'pet' as a 'service animal'. Each state has different requirements, which I recommend you research as a landlord. Asking for certification paperwork to verify authenticity is usually OK.

LET'S WRAP A BOW ON THIS CHAPTER

Congratulations, you've finished Chapter Six and learned something new to improve your rental real estate business! The focus of this chapter is to instill in your mind that this is a business and you are doing it to make money. In other words, you aren't running a rental real estate business for the fun of it.

Not a get-rich-quick scheme—this is about lasting wealth. Rental Real Estate is a wealth building, cash flowing and tax advantageous long-term strategy. You can certainly get rich in the rental real estate game, though it is never quick and certainly never easy.

Money-money-money: the financial metrics that matter in your rental real estate business. You own a rental real estate business to make money. Money provides for your family and allows you to build your dreams. It's important that you understand the basic financial terminology associated with the business: cash flow, net income, net operating income and capitalization rate.

Maximize your revenue and cash flow door by door. This is a business and businesses must make money or they close the doors. Know your market rent and be sure to collect what your property is worth. Look for other ways to increase your revenue door by door. Improve and enhance your property. Make it safe and livable. People will come.

Increase the value of your investment. You should be steadily increasing the value of your investment by investing in your investment! Increasing the value of your investment will allow you to earn more now, pay off debt faster, strengthen your properties, better prepare for an exit of your property portfolio and be ready for retirement.

Like em' or not—accepting pets is a great way to more cash flow. Get on the pet train! Accepting pets is your best way to a more profitable business. Most tenants have pets and would pay additional deposits and fees to be able to live with them. Do your best to pet-proof your rental with durable flooring. Accept pets or risk a significant reduction in your prospective tenant pool. Be sure to understand the rules around service animals and emotional support animals.

SEVEN

MANAGE YOUR TENANT OR THEY WILL MANAGE YOU OUT OF REAL ESTATE

I n real estate, as in any business, there are unpleasant realities that one must deal with in order to be successful. Though there are several of these in rental real estate, the topper of them all is managing tenants. The hard truth is tenant management can be frustrating, stressful and emotionally draining. The good news is it doesn't have to be! Each landlord manages this phase of the business differently. Some are just better at it than others. Better doesn't mean they are more capable. It means they are more prepared, more intentional and follow the systems that others have set forth. For the people committed to running a successful rental real estate business, we welcome those that can't handle it and give up. Those are the people we buy properties from at a discount as they exit the business in a hurry. When I first got into real estate, and even before, I heard over and over the same lines, "It's not worth the hassle of dealing with tenants. Being a landlord is the worst. It's not worth it." The lines may vary, though the theme is the same. People who are not committed and willing to be successful find excuses for why they aren't successful and then do their best to deflect personal responsibility by saying that being a landlord sucks. I am a fan of theirs because they make it easier to build my business when they give up on theirs. This chapter focuses on helping you find success in the ever-important realm of tenant management.

SETTING EXPECTATIONS

The landlord-tenant relationship is not like having a significant other. It is a business relationship that requires setting expectations and creating very clear boundaries. However, just like with a significant other, the most important aspects of that relationship are the same: clear communication and mutually understood expectations. Communication is where the success of the landlord-tenant relationship begins from the first interaction to the last. Being clear in what is expected around how you will communicate, how to report maintenance requests, where and how to pay rent and more must be discussed with the tenant upon move-in.

You might ask, "When and how do I go about setting expectations with a tenant?" The short answer is, the first moment you interact with them. This means that you must be consistent in the way you interact and communicate with prospective tenants from the very beginning. Once you list your property for rent, you begin the process of setting expectations, regardless of whether or not an interested candidate becomes your tenant. You can't show up as one kind of landlord during the marketing and application process and become another after someone signs a lease with you. That is called fraud, whether it is criminal fraud or not. *Don't be a fraud.* Be yourself the entire time. However, yourself must be a good business person. A good business person that respects people, their time and your own time. People notice your behavior just like you notice theirs. From the moment I first interact with a prospective tenant about a property I have for rent, I am assessing them. Do they sound responsible? Do they seem put together? Are they sincere? Do they seem to be taking this seriously? Do they come through with the application fee and supporting documentation without requiring follow-ups? All of these are *tells* for me as a landlord. Just like in poker, your tells allow others to see your hand. I am looking for their tells so I know what hand they will be playing and I won't be fooled. Believe me, people are doing the same assessment of you. They are asking, does this person seem responsible? Are they kind? Do they have compassion? Are they going to follow through with their promises? The landlord-tenant relationship is two-way, just like any other healthy relationship. Each party must follow through and be responsible for the relationship to work.

What you do and say from the very beginning will begin the process of setting expectations, however, this is not sufficient to create and maintain a successful relationship. You must be explicit with people as to what is expected of them. In corporate America, one of the most common reasons people are disengaged in the workplace is due to a lack of clear, focused expectations. If someone doesn't know what is expected of them and there is a surprise down the road that catches them off guard, high levels of discontent will arise and likely persist until that relationship is completely severed. Setting expectations with people isn't just a 'nice thing to do' it is *what you should do*. I start setting expectations during the first interaction with a prospective tenant. When notifying people about the application process I set the first formal expectations:

- A 100% complete application
- Full honesty and transparency
- Copies of current Driver's License
- Application fee paid in cash
- Supporting documentation, i.e., paystubs or bank statements
- When I expect the application to be delivered for consideration

I also share with them what they should expect from me. This includes:

- Once the application fee is paid in full, I will process the application
- They will hear from me in 2-3 days with a status update
- How I will go about completing the due diligence in the application process
- The available move-in date for the property

People want to know what the next steps are. It is best to share this with them as soon as possible. People have lives and other obligations. They can't afford to and likely won't wait for you in good faith without first knowing what the next steps in the process are.

The next opportunity to set expectations is when you offer someone tenancy. It's at this point when I share the deposit to hold requirements and ensure they deposit the money within 24 hours. I also share the following:

- A firm move-in date
- A scheduled time for lease agreement signing
- When and where we should meet at the unit for the move-in
- The exact funds that are required at move-in
- How the move-in funds are allowed to be paid (i.e., no personal checks)
- Define which utilities are the tenant's responsibility and the requirement for them to transfer utilities into their name before lease signing

The final and most important time for setting expectations is during the lease signing appointment. You should do this face to face wherever possible. This last and most critical opportunity to set expectations is one that should be taken advantage of. As I walk through the lease with a new tenant, I carefully address all of my most critical expectations. Let me provide you with some examples that are considered best practices:

- Communicate when rent is due and how it should be paid.
- Share the late rent fees and how those will be enforced.
- Discuss eviction up front! Be sure to tell people that you will move to evict if rent goes unpaid.
- Let them know *how* to communicate with you. Preference of text, email, phone, etc.
- Tell them *when* to communicate with you. If you don't tell them, you are asking for around the clock communication. I highly recommend setting business hours, such as 9 AM to 5 PM. If on the weekend, I tell people to wait until Monday except for emergencies.
- Describe what is considered an emergency. For example, weeds are not an emergency. Neither is a broken fence or dishwasher. A leaky pipe that is gushing water? Yes, let me know immediately! The house is on fire? Call the fire department first! Then call me. The list goes on.
- Inform tenants what they are responsible for and that I don't want to hear from them about these things, ever: replacing light bulbs, cleaning the carpet, yard maintenance including weeds, etc.
- Make it clear to tenants about getting written permission before altering the unit in anyway, specifically painting or adding something permanent to the structure.
- Be clear on the fact that they cannot make copies of the key or change the locks, ever.

In short, you are sharing the lease requirements with them and being very specific on how you expect them to behave and more importantly *not* behave. I am very clear with every tenant that they will follow these expectations as discussed and shared in the lease agreement or I will evict them. The word evict is something that scares people. Eviction is a permanent scar on someone's record and credit. Even the worst of tenants don't want to be evicted. The only ones that don't care are people you should have never rented to in the first place! If you ever find yourself in this situation, you likely didn't complete an effective due diligence process. In my early days of landlording, I wasn't as effective in communication and setting expectations. I thought tenants were doing me a favor and I needed to cater to them as much as possible. I am a kind and positive person by nature, therefore I leaned toward this type of relationship and communication. I learned the hard way that tenants, most of them, don't see things the same way. They also don't care about your stuff like you do, (kind of like naughty children, to be honest.) My kids treat things the way my tenants do, with carelessness and a lack of respect. Be very clear what is expected. If not, you will be sorely disappointed.

YOU DRIVE THE RELATIONSHIP

One very important item to remember is that you are in charge of the relationship. You are the *alpha*. That doesn't mean you are an insensitive jerk. It does mean, however, that you are very clear about how the relationship will operate. The previous section went into greater detail around expectations and how to communicate upfront. This is a great start. Though that is exactly what it is, *a start*, to hopefully a long and cordial relationship. Similar to a bad boss, people will leave a bad landlord. So be kind and considerate. Though be the driver of the relationship. Communicate and repeat what is important. If someone didn't remember or care to follow directions of something that has already been communicated, remind them what the expectations are. Make sure tenants know what is required of them. If you don't, they will assume you don't care.

The principle I want to convey is *consistency*. Be consistent with your communication, your engagement and your expectations. If tenants don't follow procedure, simply remind them. If they repeat offend, be a little firmer. I have had tenants call or text me at weird hours before. I simply didn't respond until business hours on the next business day. The requests were not of immediate importance. I have also received inquiries on Easter, Sunday evenings, Tuesdays at 10 PM, and so on. I typically don't respond until the next business day during business hours. I then take the opportunity to remind them in my reply what my office hours are. Most are good at adjusting, even apologizing for the mistake. Those who don't and act as if they should be priority number one in your life for their every demand are people you likely don't want renewing a lease. It isn't worth your time, mental capacity or energy. Most times, people adjust. If they don't adjust after multiple reminders, they likely never will. Let them be someone else's problem. You might say, "But renters are hard to find in my area." If renters are hard to come by, then first do your best to manage them. Reiterate the expectations. Don't, however, cater to them unnecessarily.

This Happened to Me - The 'untenable' tenant

My wife and I purchased our second rental property together and rented it out to what appeared to be a great younger couple. The husband was a 25-year-old veteran who left the service due to a disability. He was very professional at first and promising as a tenant that could live at my property for several years. Then, they moved in. Once he was inside the property, the complaints began. Everything from, "It's dusty." To, "The fridge smells." To, "I need you to change this and change that." I wanted to have a positive relationship, so I appeased a few of his requests. One of them was doing a deep clean of the duct work at the property. I didn't notice anything the multiple times I visited the property, but apparently, I am a normal person. This guy was not. He was sensitive to everything. I had the ducts deep-cleaned and it cost me $500!

After this and a few other things, I realized these weren't 'normal' requests. This guy was unreasonable and I was going to lose money as a result. Things only got worse from there. As I started to push back against his ridiculous requests, he grew more into a captious critic. I knew this wasn't going to end well for me. He had signed a two-year lease agreement and we were barely 6 months in when things became untenable. He started threatening to take me to court for some of his complaints, which were not normal. As a result, I shared, with a bit of tense retort mind you, the specific lease obligations he had agreed to. He came back with specifically researched replies about rental laws, insisting that I was violating many of them. *I was not.*

I once read this quote that says, "Don't let negative and toxic people rent space in your head. Raise the rent and kick them out!" I'm not even certain the quote is credited to anyone. I would alter this quote slightly, to say "Don't let negative and toxic people remain your tenants. Raise the rent or sever their lease agreement and kick them out." It was at this moment I realized signing a two-year lease agreement was actually *not* a good thing for me. This guy needed to go! He became the reason I stopped signing any lease agreement beyond 12 months.

Back to the resolution of this nightmare. After being threatened with multiple lawsuits, for which cause I'm still uncertain, I knew I had to get rid of this guy. I came back to him with kindness and said in short, "Listen dude, I don't want to escalate things any further and I am wanting a happy resolution for both sides. As a result, I'm willing to allow you to terminate the lease early without penalty and return your full security deposit, on the condition that you won't pursue any legal action against me." He agreed. Then I had him sign a document I wrote up with these exact terms of agreement. For me this was a win-win. He was a nightmare and not worth my mental energy. I can always find a new tenant. Unfortunately, the rental laws in most states heavily favor tenants over landlords. As a result, even though I did no wrong, it wasn't worth risking an actual lawsuit where the courts could still choose to reward the tenant.

REMEMBER—IT IS YOUR PROPERTY

At the end of the day, your property is exactly that, *yours*. The fact that you aren't living in the property and may only see it but a few times a year does not mean that you forfeit control of what goes on *at* your property or *to* your property. As detailed in this chapter, you are the owner and you dictate the relationship with your tenants. You also decide what happens with your property. If a tenant wants to change something with your property, they must ask for approval. They want to change the paint color? They must ask for and receive approval in writing. They want to build a shed out back? They must ask for and receive approval in writing. They want to drywall a room in the basement? They must ask for and receive approval in writing. You get the gist of it.

Let's say your tenant wants you to upgrade the property. Remember this, it is *your* property and *your* decision, not theirs. I have had tenants who demanded that I make an upgrade to the property. Others have tried to manipulate me into the same thing using flattery and other tactics. Before you do anything to upgrade your property when a tenant already lives there, answer affirmatively to at least two of the following three questions:

1. Can I afford to make this upgrade?
2. Is there a big enough return on investment?
3. Will this provide a long-term benefit?

The kicker is that the answer to question one always has to be *yes*. Then, at least one more yes from questions two or three are needed to move forward.

1 - Can I afford to make this upgrade? The answer here must always be *yes* before proceeding. What does afford mean? It means that you have enough money in the bank to cover your expenses for two months if no rent were to come in. This is a safe guideline, not a strict requirement. In other words, if you don't have the money, don't pull the trigger on the upgrade. Each of these questions are business decisions. As the owner of your own rental real estate business, you must have the money in the bank to make the upgrade without putting yourself in a weak financial position. If something unexpected were to happen, for example, an urgent and expensive repair, would you have enough money to cover that expense as well? What if you lose a few tenants at the same time resulting in a big cash flow decrease? Can you still cover the upgrade in this situation? If you can comfortably say yes to both of these scenarios, you likely have plenty of money in the bank. At this point, you can proceed to questions two and three.

2 – Is there a big enough return on investment? I strongly recommend having a yes to this question before making any sort of upgrade. A return on investment can come in the form of any of the following to be considered an acceptable qualifier: increased rent, cash flow, equity or occupancy.

Increased rent means that by making this upgrade, you can increase the rent of your property. This is preferable in the short-term, but also considerable for the long-term.

Increased cash flow means that after expenses, your profit margin each month increases. Usually, this means increased rent. However, it can also mean additional fees like storage, pet or parking.

Increased equity means that by making the upgrade your property will be worth more immediately. If the increase in equity is not more than the amount spent for the upgrade, you may want to reconsider the upgrade. Increased equity can help your business with the sale of a property or a cash-out refinance, allowing you access to more investable capital.

Increased occupancy simply means that by making this upgrade, your tenant agrees to stay in the property longer. This will naturally increase your occupancy rate as a result of the tenant staying put. You can ask in exchange for an upgrade that the tenant sign a new extended lease. If they refuse to sign an extended lease, yet the upgrade would still benefit you in one or more of the other ways above, consider making it now or simply wait until the tenant leaves before upgrading. By doing so, you are setting yourself up for success.

3 – Will this provide a long-term benefit? This area is 'grayer' in nature. It isn't quite as cut and dry as the question around return on investment. The reason being, not every upgrade or decision results in an immediate or short-term return on investment. Some upgrades result in benefits further down the road. Some of these benefits can include:

- Your property is still standing.
- You avoid a potential lawsuit.
- You can sell the property and upgrade.

Your property is still standing. This involves repairs or upgrades that don't result in a rent increase or immediate return of any kind. A great example of this is repairing or replacing a roof. Sure, it will look nicer. However, it won't garner more rent. It is *expected* you have a functional roof. It's also important because it keeps your property in good condition for the long-term.

You avoid a potential lawsuit. This sounds obvious, but as a rental property owner you want to avoid the courtroom. To this date, I have never had to step foot in a courtroom for any legal dispute. In fact, we have never been sued or had a complaint filed against us of any kind. Knock on wood! Now that doesn't mean we are perfect landlords and haven't made any mistakes. However, we have been smart and done right by people. Some have very much disliked us, but that had everything to do with them not wanting to pay rent or play by the rules. Another example is fixing the sidewalk in front of your property. We recently had to repair the stairs leading to the front door as the concrete was crumbling, which resulted in a dangerous entry. When we became aware, we made arrangements for a repair as quickly as possible. Another example may be a broken window or unsafe door frame or lock. These types of repairs are not going to win you any equity bonuses or rent increases. However, they will help you avoid the courtroom and the possibility of extensive damages. The largest repair we had to address that fell into this category was a foundation, which I will share more about next.

This Happened to Me – Creating a 'firm foundation'

This property was a 105-year-old restored beauty. It was a two-story home that sat on two lots. It was full of character and enough charm to even catch my wife's eye. During the initial inspection there wasn't any severe warning about the condition of the foundation. In these older homes, most foundations had been upgraded or fortified over time as the building requirements weren't quite the same in the early 1900's. It is common for some soil deterioration around the foundation that requires addressing, though most structural issues require a closer look from a structural engineer. About a year and a half into owning this particular home, we sent our repairman over for an unrelated repair (a leaky pipe in the basement). During his inspection, he noticed the deteriorating condition of the foundation. He told us it was dire and would require fixing within a few months to avoid a potential disaster and subsequent lawsuit. At this time, we were still buying properties and low on capital. The repair would be between $10,000 - $20,000. The labor required was extensive due to the fact that the home was already standing and the labor had to be performed without disturbing the security of the home. It required engineering equipment, foundation jacks and a *lot* of cement along with temporary support beams. The temporary beams were replaced with permanent beams one by one after the area around the foundation was secured. This repair did not make us *any* return on the investment. Though it *did* protect our asset and ourselves. A falling house and potential injury or death to a tenant is *not good* for business. We went ahead and made the repair the following week, spending almost all of the cash we had on hand. We were nervous awaiting the repair and throughout until it was finished and all was secured with the foundation. Fortunately, the repair went smoothly and no unforeseen dangers presented themselves. Unfortunately, we spent $17,000 on the repair! It definitely hurt our pocket book, but the alternatives could have proven much more costly to our business in the long run.

You can sell the property and upgrade. Upgrading requires purchasing a larger, more expensive rental property. The US Government created the 1031 Exchange for rental property owners to avoid taxation. If you sell a rental property and use the proceeds to fund a larger property, the government waives taxation on the proceeds. Many investors take advantage of this as their portfolio grows. Swapping a smaller rental for a larger one is a great way to grow your investment portfolio.

MANAGE YOUR TENANTS AND BE CONSISTENT

With this baseline understanding of why tenant management is essential and what will happen if you don't do it well, let's cover the basics of tenant management. Managing tenants doesn't begin and end with signing the lease agreement. As a landlord, you must be consistent in managing your tenants to abide by the expectations previously established. Think of children. You tell them to do their homework before they can play with friends. This is the baseline expectation. If your child disobeys this expectation once and you don't enforce a penalty of any kind, the behavior will continue. If your child disobeys and you simply 'tell them' or 'remind them' of the expectation, chances are they will disobey again. Not following rules or expectations should come with a penalty or punishment. Though you wouldn't treat a tenant as if they were your child in terms of the penalty given, there are similarities. Be sure to hold them to the rules and expectations established or the behavior will continue, likely worsening over time.

What are the basic rules and expectations that you need to enforce? Let me name a few:

Rent collection. Enforce payment of rent, in full, every month. Enforce late fees for late payments. Post eviction notices promptly if rent remains unpaid. Make this a priority for tenants or they will not make it a priority themselves.

Clean & organized living. Your lease agreement should include the expectation that tenants treat your property with respect, while maintaining order and cleanliness. If they don't, enforce a penalty and move to evict if not rectified.

Move-in/move-out process. Set the expectation of tenants completing the move-in/move-out checklist. It is up to them to complete and return the move-in checklist. If they don't, they can't claim they didn't cause any damage found in the residence upon move-out. When moving out, they must follow your move-out checklist with precision or security deposit deductions will be made.

Repairs & maintenance. Tenants must notify you of the need for repairs or maintenance. *They* are living there, not you. It is their responsibility to make you aware through prompt and clear communication. If they don't, hold them accountable. This should be noted in your lease agreement. Be sure to also charge them a fee if you schedule maintenance and they either are not present or refuse to let the repair professional enter their residence.

Yard/property maintenance. Your lease agreement should also include yard/maintenance requirements. If you take care of the yard—great; no issue. If the tenant has any responsibility then be sure to enforce this via drive-by and formal inspections. Enforce maintenance and penalize tenants through fees for non-compliance.

Utility payments. If you pay utilities, move on. If the tenant has any responsibility for paying utilities, enforce this closely. Be sure they switch into their name promptly and then stay on top of their bills.

Inspections. Conduct inspections on the property with consistency. Your lease agreement should include a formal inspection agreement to periodically have the right to enter the residence and conduct an inspection. These are important to uphold because if the tenant isn't fulfilling their obligations and they know you conduct inspections; they may think twice before breaking the agreement. If you inspect frequently and enforce compliance, your tenants are more likely to behave accordingly.

Orderly conduct. It should go without saying, but your lease agreement should include an orderly conduct clause. It's the one where the tenant should not have raver parties at 1 AM that wake up the neighbors. The property is not theirs to act like crazy people at all hours of the day or night. They must be respectful of other tenants, if in a shared property, and be respectful to the neighbors. Believe me, this is needed. I've seen it all.

SAYING 'ADIOS' TO BAD TENANTS

You've followed the above guidelines and best practices, yet your tenant persists their poor, lease-breaking behavior streak. What to do next? Say *adios* or goodbye. Any lease agreement violation could merit eviction. Consistent, rebellious lease violations *require it*. Get rid of these damaging and headache tenants or they will ruin your day and potentially your business. Chapter Ten covers the eviction process: where we go into great detail in how to evict a tenant properly and lawfully. Consider Chapter Ten a comprehensive guide in how to evict nightmare tenants. Horrible, deadbeat tenants are not worth your time, energy and emotions! If merited and they are more painful to keep in place vs move on from, that's a clue to pursue eviction. You will be glad you did.

Your business should have clear expectations for tenants and associated penalties for non-compliance. Your property, your rules. *Enforce them*. Remember to check the law and ensure you are asking for legal compliance to your expectations. This will allow you to take legal action when required as a result of tenant disobedience and damaging behavior. Do your best to keep good tenants in place and happy. Also do your best to say adios to bad tenants and remove them quickly.

KEYS TO A HAPPY LANDLORD-TENANT RELATIONSHIP

We covered the challenges with managing tenants and some best practices for handling them. We also covered the approach to take with tenants to ensure they stay in line. The surface of positives has barely been scratched. Let's cover the keys to a happy landlord-tenant relationship.

Start off on positive footing. Before your tenant moves in, do what you can to build a positive rapport with them. This results in mutual trust over time. I am friendly with my tenants until they give me reason not to be. This doesn't mean we kick it at the burger joint, though I try and form a positive relationship with them that involves clear communication and mutual respect.

Replacing tenants is expensive! Be flexible with tenants when possible and listen to them. Replacing tenants is painful, time-consuming and expensive. It's best to build and keep a positive relationship. Don't be a scrooge or like so many other crappy landlords out there that give the rest of us a bad reputation. Do what you can to keep the good ones.

Tenants are your customer. Yes, it's true! Tenants pay for the service you are offering, renting them your property in exchange for monthly rent. Good business is treating your customers *right*. They are of extreme value to your business and, in turn, you. Leverage customer service skills by showing kindness, consideration and being responsive when they reach out with a maintenance request or concern. Consider it an opportunity to fine tune your customer service skills and continue building a strong rapport.

Stay in touch. Be sure your tenants know you are available to them when they *need* you. Not available for a random chat, though available if they need to make you aware of something. Try and touch base with them every few months to ensure continuity. Not doing so can also give the impression you are not attentive to your business and some tenants will take advantage of you and your property as a result. Be proactive as this can deescalate potential issues and build trust.

Understand your obligations as a landlord. You'd better know what is expected of you as a landlord and live up to those expectations. This is a *two-way* relationship. This chapter focuses on how to get your tenant to behave—that is because I am *expecting you* to know *your end* of the deal. Fulfill your duties as a landlord promptly and consistently. The quickest way to lose trust with tenants is to not take your end of the responsibilities seriously.

Flexibility is a value-add for tenants. Things happen, including pandemics as we've experienced. Show flexibility instead of being 100% tied to your lease. Unless your tenant is a problem child, try solving problems first before being aggressive in punishment. Flexibility creates a winning relationship that can last longer.

Tenants want to feel heard. Just like your significant other, tenants want to feel like *you hear them*. If something breaks and you respond quickly by resolving the issue without shaming them, that builds trust. Tenants deserve a landlord who is responsive and fulfils their duties. Sometimes the tenant's safety depends on it.

Address problems fast! If a tenant reports an issue, be sure to deal with it in short order. Show that you are responsive and care about their situation. Stick to your word and communicate if anything changes. I am sure to confirm when an issue is resolved or let them know right away if a delay is in the cards. In situations where something breaks, any delays or snide remarks from a landlord only hurts the tenant. Your goal should be to have tenants that *like* renting from you and don't feel put off.

Great tenants are worth more to you. Great tenants cost less over time, even if you don't charge them as much. A tenant who stays for extended periods of time, pays rent on time and doesn't raise hell is worth far more than a tenant who has higher rent but destroys your property. Your bottom line appreciates the value of a great tenant more than a few extra dollars upfront.

Put yourself in the shoes of your tenants. Don't lose touch with the human side of business. My wife's least favorite activity in life is moving. I'm guessing this is the same with many of you and your tenants. It is stressful and even more so for someone who lives paycheck to paycheck. Always be fair and don't be too emotional. Treat your tenants how you would hope to be treated. *Be human first*.

LET'S WRAP A BOW ON THIS CHAPTER

Congratulations, you've finished Chapter Seven and learned something new to improve your rental real estate business! The focus of this chapter is to teach you how to set and manage expectations with tenants from before you ever sign a lease with them. Your property, your rules. Ensure the expectations are clear and that your tenants follow them.

Setting expectations. The landlord-tenant relationship is a business relationship that requires setting expectations and creating very clear boundaries. Set mutual expectations upfront, during the application process and then emphasize them before lease signing.

You drive the relationship. Be the driver of the relationship: the alpha. Communicate and repeat what is important with clarity and kindness. Be consistent with your communication, engagement and expectations. Follow through with the expectations set.

Remember—it is *your* property. As owner, you make the rules and decide what changes are made to the property. When making upgrades, be sure you can answer 'yes' to the 3 criteria questions: Can I afford to make this upgrade? Is there a big enough return on investment? Will this provide a long-term benefit?

Manage your tenants and be consistent. Be consistent in managing your tenants to abide by the expectations you set with them. Enforce your rules around rent collection, proper maintenance, the move-in/move-out process and all other agreed upon criteria.

Saying 'adios' to bad tenants. Don't tolerate consistently poor behavior from tenants. If they violate your lease more than once, that is a pattern and they more than likely need to go.

Keys to a happy landlord-tenant relationship. Focus on building and maintaining a happy landlord-tenant relationship. It is worth every effort and penny. This should be a winning relationship for both sides. *Stay positive*. Remember that tenants are your customers and to put yourself in their shoes. *Be human first*.

EIGHT

YOU ARE ONLY AS GOOD AS YOUR SYSTEMS!

I n business and in life, systems can make a significant and positive difference. Any successful mother has systems setup in her household, such as the morning and evening routine, school drop-off and pickup, extracurricular activities, church worship and prayer time, dinner time, homework and more. The better the systems, the higher the chances of a low-stress, happy mama! In business, systems can boost productivity, reduce costs and increase revenues. Good systems for accounting, operations, tracking of inventory, staffing, human resources, education, and manufacturing are in many cases the key reasons for a company's ultimate success or failure. If a company has a great feedback intake system where they can quickly ingest and act upon customer feedback, this will result in higher customer satisfaction which produces more loyalty and sales. If a retailer has efficient logistics systems in place, they will be better able to ship customer orders, keep inventory at positive levels and better serve customer needs. This chapter will review the key systems used in rental real estate and provide ideas on how to leverage them in your business.

WHAT IS A SYSTEM AND WHY SHOULD I CARE?

The simplest definition of a system I found is from Oxford Dictionaries that states, "A set of things working together as parts of a mechanism or an interconnecting network." A good example of this is the railroad system. A system sounds boring and mechanical. The reality is that systems are liberating. Systems are the foundation of successful governments, companies and even *our lives*! What do you mean? Let's take the good ole' United States of America. The 'system' that governs this great country is The US Constitution, along with the supporting Bill of Rights. The US Constitution and Bill of Rights were crafted from learnings over thousands of years of history by studying successful and unsuccessful systems, i.e., communism and dictatorships. There are checks and balances, yes. However, the Constitution itself is a framework, or set of systems on how to successfully govern a country. As a result of the creation of a successful set of systems, known as the United States Constitution, this country has become the greatest and most successful country in the history of the world.

The goal here is not to setup our own country; yet, we need to learn how to be successful by studying what others have done. The industry, government or organization does not matter as much as the foundational principles, or systems they used. Having systems in your business is essential. Sure, you can find success without a consistent, reliable system. However, you will be wasting time and money along the way. You will also never be as successful as you could be if you had effective systems in place. Billionaire Investor and Founder of the Real Estate Empire Berkshire Hathaway, Warren Buffet, taught, "Risk comes from not knowing what you're doing." I believe this applies here with your rental real estate business. Having a set of systems that you follow is a sign that you know what you're doing. Systems, along with knowing what you are doing, reduce risk in your business.

OK—BUT WHAT SYSTEMS ARE YOU REFERRING TO?

Let's start with the most obvious: your rental lease agreement. This is the basis for how you will operate your business. It clearly articulates and outlines what you expect and what happens when expectations are not met, such as the payment of rent. We will break down some of the sections that are systems-related and then also discuss everything else that should have a system in order to be most effective, saving you both hassle and headaches. Here we go!

Marketing your property. Isn't this easy? Short answer, it can be. However, marketing your property is always time consuming and full of busy work. It is still one of my least favorite aspects of being a rental property investor. You must first decide on where you will post your listing. Will you simply put up a yard sign with a phone number that says 'For Rent'? If you do this, you increase the risk of someone breaking in and squatting; resulting in a nightmare scenario to follow because you are letting the world know that your property is vacant! The strangers who walk by may just decide to stay a while and call your place home, without ever paying you a dollar or getting permission to live there! I always recommend advertising online. This can be done via Facebook, Craigslist, Zillow, Trulia, HotPads, Cozy, Realtor.com, etc. Craigslist used to work for me, though beware of fraudsters just waiting to rip people off pretending to be you.

Once you decide where you will market your property, be sure to have a good understanding of who pays what. Are you paying some of the utilities or is the tenant paying? Are you allowing pets? If so, for how much and what is the additional deposit? You must price out your property. If you price too high; your place will sit unrented for a while. If you price too low; you attract low-quality tenants who aren't worth your time. Do your market research and choose a market price based on the condition of your property vs others in the same part of town with similar specifications. Be sure to track who is interested and reach out within 24 hours. If you don't, chances are they have reached out to 10 other landlords and someone else responded before you. I have lost prospective tenants by waiting too long. *Be proactive*. Track who you've reached out to, get basic information about them, such as: number of tenants, desired move-in date, if they have pets, how long they plan to stay, etc. Have this all written out in advance. Collect the same information for everyone. Make sure you post the best pictures possible for your property. Not posting pictures will be met with a lack of interest from serious candidates. Be sure to know when you plan to show the property and how. Will you be personally showing it? Are you taking appointments only? Are you scheduling an open house day?

This Happened to Me – The no-system 'headache'

When I listed my first property I went with Craigslist because it was what I knew. It was free and a bunch of people used it. I did get a ton of inquiries and quite a bit of interest during our open house. However, there was no tracking system. I was mixing up phone numbers, names and pertinent details about prospective tenants. I was so excited people were interested that I neglected to put together systems for how to market and rent my unit. As a result, it took me twice the amount of time it should have. I made calls on every application I received. I didn't charge enough for the application fee. I spent two full days of my time on-site trying to rent the property and the list goes on. Eventually we did find a young couple as tenants who were solid for the first 14 months or so. Then things got shady and a whole string of episodes ensued. I will share more on that later in the book!

Conducting repairs. You need a rolodex! Not literally, but in the same sense as when those were actually a thing. You need your repair personnel network in place. The following are highly recommended: a general handyman, an electrician, an appliance repairman, and a licensed plumber. You could also have a roofer, painter, tile specialist and more. Though your most important are those first four. Your general handyman is the most important of them all. Chapter Three delves into further detail on this one.

Part of the system beyond just having a person to call is the method of reporting issues and your timeframe for resolving them. This goes back to setting expectations. My tenants submit maintenance requests through our online rental management software or text/call me directly (for those that aren't as tech savvy). I have clarified in advance and set expectations of what constitutes an emergency. Is your building on fire? Ok yes emergency. How about water leaking through your roof? Yes, we are on it immediately. A gas line is leaking? EMERGENCY!! A light bulb went out? We will get to it within 72 hours. Refrigerator not cooling? We'll have it fixed within 24 hours. A breeze coming through your door because the weather stripping is peeling? We'll get to it within the next 72 hours. Do you see the point?

Level-set expectations with your tenants; but first, you need to clarify with *yourself* what your system and rules *within* that system are for maintenance requests. Consider charging a fee to tenants who do not make themselves available for repairs to be completed or miss the scheduled appointment. Expectations around communication are also important. For example, I don't answer non-emergency or non-urgent requests over the weekend. I simply don't reply or I remind them that normal business hours are Monday – Friday 9 AM – 5 PM. If you don't set these expectations, as we covered in Chapter Seven, you *will* be that Landlord getting 11 PM calls about a light bulb going out. FYI, I use the light bulb example as the most obvious and ridiculous one. It absolutely happens and proves that people will complain about almost anything. However, I do tell my tenants during the lease signing that they are responsible for replacing burned out light bulbs, not me. I also tell them not to ask me to replace those and guess what? I have never received a call asking me to replace a light bulb. Set expectations, have a system and most importantly abide by it.

Rent collection. Rent collection is by far the most important system you should have setup. This is a landlord's lifeblood. Without rent, you don't survive. It fuels your entire business and should be of utmost importance. A best practice is to use a rental management software. The software I use is TenantCloud.com. This is a free software (up to a certain number of doors) that charges fees for certain features such as online payments. I highly recommend that everyone use one. Record tracking is critical in this business, just like any other. This is especially true come tax time as discussed in Chapter Twelve.

Determine the due date for rent. I always default to the first of the month. If tenants move in on a different date of the month then pro-rate the next month's rent so you can stay on schedule with everyone. Having your rent come in on the same date and at the beginning of every month sets you up for success. I define a five-day grace period before rent is considered late. Some landlords prefer three days, others seven. Choose whatever you are comfortable with. I believe five is reasonable, so I went with that. If rent is not in on day five, I assess a one-time late fee. I typically charge $50. This amount is predefined in the lease. The rental management software I leverage notifies the tenant when rent is posted, when it is due, when it is late, and tracks the accounting of the lease for that tenant's lifecycle. It also assesses late fees if rent payment is not recorded by the assigned due date. I expect tenants to connect with me on the software, with some exceptions. It is very effective; providing a documented history of income, expenses, communications and maintenance. This is expedient come tax season or during legal pursuits. If my tenants don't pay on day six, I assess a recurring daily late fee of $20, on top of the $50 they already owe. This adds up quickly and is a solid motivator to get rent paid.

You must follow your own rules such as penalties for late rent. If you don't, tenants will walk all over you. I give one-time excuses in cases of emergency where the tenant communicated before rent was due. If a tenant doesn't show the courtesy to communicate, I don't give them a pass. If you give them a rent hall pass once, say goodbye to on-time rent for that tenant moving forward. If the tenant doesn't communicate, ghosts you, or has given you troubles in the past and you'd prefer to see them gone, this would be where you begin the eviction process. Posting an eviction notice on someone's door is a very bold reminder that they owe you rent and that rent is the most critical bill that tenant has. If you are lenient, it will hurt you. As I've stated before, be human first. However, be careful how gracious you are because tenants are really good pulling at the heart strings using fictitious reasons for the late or non-payment of rent. You are not a bad or unkind person by demanding rent be paid on-time and then taking swift consequential action when it is not. You are a smart business person and way more likely to be successful in this business than those that do not.

Another part of your system should be providing more than one rent collection method for tenant convenience. We pay $10 monthly to enable online payments for tenants. The more tech savvy tenants will take you up on this. The money transfers directly to your bank account each month when paid. I have seen on-time rent payments go up as a result of offering this feature. Well worth the $10/month. Plus, I can deduct this as a business expense each year. I call that a no-brainer. We also allow tenants to deposit rent directly into our bank account at one of two local banks where we hold business accounts. They are able to do this via ACH or direct mail. However, I *don't* collect rent in person. Nor do I give them my personal address for mailing rent. I prefer not to be another story of a landlord being stalked or murdered by a tenant. Be safe my friends. *Be safe*. If the tenant cannot pay rent in a reasonable fashion, either don't rent to them or evict them.

Eviction. Eviction is a bad word if you are the one being evicted. However, eviction can be a positive for landlords. If you are evicting someone you are in a precarious position and likely losing money. Without legal eviction, you could be stuck with a deadbeat tenant losing even more money for an extended period of time. If you have been a landlord for more than a year and have multiple properties, chances are you have had to evict a tenant. For me, it took one and a half years and I had five properties before it was my turn to evict a tenant. I learned from this experience and more until I became more proficient on how to get it done right the first time.

The system around eviction starts with being very clear in the lease about what rent is due, when it is due, where to pay and the consequences if left unpaid. This includes late fees and the possibility of eviction. Eviction *can* and *should* occur for many other reasons as we cover in Chapter Ten. For a system to be effective, you must understand the steps. If a tenant violates the lease, each state has specific eviction laws and steps that must be followed. In Colorado, you are required to post a ten-day notice on the door before any other legal steps can be taken. The law, when I first started, was just three days. It changed in 2019. Typically, eviction laws benefit the tenant, making evictions a challenge for landlords. However, knowing the steps will serve you well. If you don't follow the protocol, or miss a step, you may have to start back at step one, which delays the eviction process. This results in losing more money with each passing day. Understand the eviction laws in your state. Study them carefully. There are various resources online, though I find the most reliable is the State website itself. There are many websites and companies that offer to walk you through the process or carry it out for you in exchange for a hefty fee. Ignore those, unless of course you don't care about keeping your money. My business partner and I called around to a few local law firms that offer eviction services and found one that would conduct the entire process on our behalf for only around $400.

This service included the following:

- Posting the ten-day notice to pay
- Filing required paperwork with the court
- Setting a court date
- Delivering the court summons
- Appearing in court on our behalf
- Obtaining the eviction paperwork

From there, we have to work with the local Sherriff's office if a forceful eviction is required. Basically, if after the court has granted eviction the tenant refuses to leave the premises by the set date from the judge, we pay the Sherriff a small fee to forcefully remove them from the premises. I tried doing this entire process myself once and it was a nightmare. The $400 no headache process was a no-brainer for us and is now part of our eviction system.

Application process. The application process is another core component to rental property management that requires some focus and consistency. You need to establish your rental application process. If you don't, it will result in unnecessary pain, confusion and lost opportunities. Refer to Chapter Five for details. Each step in the application process is important. Missing one step can cause issues. Learn each step and follow them consistently. The steps are simple:

1. Receive a completed application
2. Collect application fee funds
3. Collect all necessary supporting documentation
4. Complete employment and income verification
5. Complete background and credit check
6. Complete rental history and reference verification
7. Complete social media review
8. Compare tenant qualifications amongst all applicants
9. Choose top applicant
10. Offer the property & agree on move-in date
11. Complete deposit to hold agreement & collect funds
12. Notify remaining applicants you have chosen another candidate

13. Agree to lease terms and complete rental lease agreement
14. Explain pre-move-in procedures, including utility transfer
15. Lease signing, collect remaining move-in funds, hand over keys

I did say "simple." This doesn't mean there aren't a lot of steps. Each are important to complete in the proper order. Sure, a few of these can be swapped around. Whatever your final order, make a decision and document it. Once documented, learn it and follow it every time. You should be able to share the application process with prospective tenants. Having the system is good. Following it each time is *best*.

Setting rental unit pricing. Each time you put a rental unit up for rent, you must price it. Just as if you were pricing your property for sale, you must be pricing your rental unit to attract the best and highest number of prospective tenants. Without demand, you cannot rent your unit. Pricing yourself out of the core demand zone will decrease your ability to rent the unit and make a decent return. Every day counts. Each passing day of vacancy is lost revenue for your business. Be sure to price your unit competitively. Understand your market. If you don't, study it. Search for a rental unit in your market as if you were the prospective tenant. What do you find? What do you see? What are rental units similar to yours renting for? Which part of town are those units in compared to yours? Is it comparable? Is more than one rental unit priced similarly to what you plan to market your unit for? Your system should involve market research. Once you feel comfortable with the price, it's time to market your property. If the unit isn't getting the attention you'd like or have gotten on other units, what do you do next? Your system should tell you! Do you wait three days? A week? Two weeks? Do you reduce the price? What does that look like? Will you take down your ad and repost a day or two later vs the same day? Whatever you choose, understand whether or not it is effective. Your system should include measurement of success and analysis of how far you've come.

Lease creation & signing. The creation of your lease and signing of this most important document is worth a repeat and perhaps more thorough detailing. Your leasing system should include a consistent and thorough agreement that protects you and your business, as discussed in more detail in Chapter Four. Be sure to include how and when move-in funds will be collected. As a rule of thumb, I highly recommend collecting 100% of move-in funds upfront prior to handing over the keys. Sometimes, there are circumstances where you collect a partial deposit with a signed commitment to pay the remainder within a certain period of time or at move-in. However, this is an exception to the rule and should not occur often. Back to the lease itself. You should have a standard lease with fillable sections that you adjust by tenant. Simply save a new lease for each tenant and fill in the proper information. Be sure to bring any applicable addendums or other related documentation (such as the lead paint advisory pamphlet in states that require it) with you to the lease signing.

Bookkeeping. It's not the most exciting topic, I know. However, you get this one wrong and you could be in a world of hurt with Uncle Sam and the law. Keeping an accurately documented history of your business books is critical. Again, I recommend a rental management software. There are many on the market; most of them at no cost to you. In fact, most of them allow you to have 100 or more units at no cost. What a deal! I researched and chose a software before I ever closed on my first deal. My mentor told me to use a tracking software. I listened and have benefited many times over from that decision. It allows me to enter all of my property, lease, tenant, income, expense, and other relevant information in an easy-to-use format. I can run on-demand reports, export into Excel, then save them to my computer. I have notifications enabled for maintenance requests, late rent, recurring expenses and more. I enter every single source and quantity of income as well as each and every business-related expense. Keeping accurate and detailed records can save you from a lawsuit, the evil tax man, and even from going to jail. Don't make the mistake of being naked (figuratively) when it comes to your business books.

Your system for bookkeeping should be fairly simple here:

- Find and select your rental management software.
- Enter all rental property information.
- Enter information for every tenant.
- Enter each and every rental lease agreement.
- Track all income and sources.
- Report every single expense and to which property it should be allocated.
- Repeat the above.

Turning over units. Unit turnover is another one of the components of a rental property business that can either help or hurt your margins. What determines your success here is speed. The shorter number of days to turn over a unit, the more income and cash flow you have. I recommend having a clause in your lease that states a tenant must notify you in writing 30 days in advance before moving out, even if the lease is set to expire. This is a standard clause that ensures you have enough time to turnover and re-market the property. Assuming you get the proper 30-day notice, there are two routes of reality here: the unit is rentable now or the unit requires rehab. The rentable option is obviously preferred, with the exception of the principle I teach in Chapter Eleven about upgrading a unit to increase rental income and cash flow. If there is opportunity and you have the capital, consider this option. However, sometimes cash flow is low along with available renovation capital. If this is the case, try to rent out the property ASAP. Your system should include coordinating with the existing tenant to allow prospective tenants the opportunity to enter and view the premises. By doing so, you also are likely to have a tidier unit. Even bad tenants will clean a unit if they know someone will be coming inside. Really bad tenants will never agree to let anyone inside to tour the place. This is a red flag and you should consider an immediate inspection to assess the condition of the unit.

For the second route, you know there are issues or 'opportunities' with the unit and will have to make some repairs/upgrades. Usually this is the case with smokers and pet owners if your unit has carpet. Not all pet owners are careless. I highly recommend in Chapter Six that you allow pets to increase your income and cash flow. There are other tenants who are just slimy, dirty and disrespectful. It is an unfortunate reality in the rental real estate business. People don't treat your property like they would treat their own. In these situations, be ready to have an immediate evaluation conducted to determine the extent of damages, required repairs and possible renovations. This walk-through should be conducted with your handyman. The agreed upon turnover work should happen day one of move-out. This allows for a shorter turnover time. Once the work required is agreed upon, do your best to have it completed in less than a week or two. During this time, begin marketing the property to attract prospective applicants. In some instances, if enough work is completed, you can show the property before the work is 100% finished. I have rented multiple units that were under construction as demand was high and the rental candidates could see the final potential of the unit. I recently renovated a unit and rented it on the day it was completed to a nice pair of people from out of state who were living in a motel for over a month. Their drive was high, they paid top dollar for rent and passed verification with flying colors. These are my favorite type of rental candidates. It doesn't go perfectly every time. There are unexpected bumps, repairs and candidate issues that arise. The truth here is that having a turnover system will benefit you every single time.

Marketing your property. The marketing of a rental property is not overly challenging, though it does take some level of concentration and intentionality to be most effective. Your system should be consistent. Know where you are going to list your property for rent. Know at what point in time you will market in common situations. For example, will you list on the day of move-out, two weeks before, or after move-out? Know if you plan to post a 'for rent' sign in the lawn or in a window. Know if you plan to leverage social media to market. Keep it simple, though be consistent. Know what to include in the marketing content. Include the right details, enough for the rental candidate to know what they are looking at. Highlight key features, including key lease details and showing information. Include photos and know when you will take those, along with which to showcase.

The application. Yes, there is even a system around the application process. Systems are what separate the *good* from the *great*. Having a system, even a simple one like the application process, is what will define your likelihood of success. You need a short, yet effective rental application. You should know who must complete it. The best practice is every single tenant that is 18 years or older, period. Define your application fee. Determine which payment methods are acceptable. Set a timeframe for communication and the method with which you will share updates with them. Be clear what supporting documentation you require at the time of application. Know what you will do if the application is not 100% complete. Each of these components is important to ensure you always receive a thorough application and consistent supporting documentation that allows for the next step, tenant screening. The screening will not be successful if you are unable to consistently collect the proper information and documentation.

Tenant screening. Tenant selection is the single largest determinant of your success or failure as a landlord. No pressure! It's true. Choosing your tenant will make or break your business. I compare tenant selection to the NFL draft. You have a certain number of draft picks to help your team improve. You conduct due diligence and do what is needed to make a decision and feel comfortable with it. Sometimes the draft pick becomes a star and other times they fail to meet expectations. Others become major flops. Be certain to conduct thorough due diligence! Consider yourself the General Manager of your very own business team. Follow the steps. Trust the data. Listen to your gut. Then make the draft pick. More often than not if you do this you will win. However, you *will* have tenant draft flops. It will happen because even a background check can't tell you if a person is going to become a deadbeat in the future or begin making poor decisions.

Your tenant screening system may be one of the more critical systems you have. I shared the system I created and use in Chapter Five. The inputs are what matters most. If you can't collect all of the inputs, you won't be able to produce an effective and reliable result. I leverage the 'Prospective Tenant Scorecard' for each and every tenant screening to ensure I don't just go with who I 'liked' the best. I learned the painful landlord lesson that it isn't about who you get along with or who seemed the best in person, though that is certainly a factor. It's about who is the *most qualified* based on the tenant-screening criteria. I created the scorecard to help me in the most important and challenging decision in rental real estate, finding the right tenant. The weighted averages also help during the tight decisions because someone that ranks high in financial stability vs the rest could very well be the deciding factor.

GET YOUR BUSINESS FINANCIALS IN ORDER

Warren Buffet provides some more sage advice for entrepreneurs seeking success when he said, "We don't have to be smarter than the rest. We have to be more *disciplined* than the rest." I believe that this quote has a direct correlation to the systems we do or don't leverage, both business process and financial oriented. I align closely with this statement from Mr. Buffet because I have never been the smartest kid in class or in the office. However, I *have* been disciplined in my focus and actions, which is a major factor in my life's success to-date. By no means do I compare myself to Warren Buffet, though I do believe in following the behaviors of successful people to find my own success.

An important yet not frequently discussed component of a rental real estate business is that of financial organization. The most successful business owners understand from where money is coming into the business and where it goes out of the business to. Accurate and consistent tracking of your rental real estate business' financials is essential for success. Why? Because you *have* to be in order to pay honest taxes and you need to know how your business is performing. Financial performance is a must-know. Let's cover some essentials with respect to the financial management of your business.

The importance of banking. Have a bank, or multiple, and use them for everything possible. Be sure your money flows in/out so it records a history for the IRS, the courts and yourself. Banking allows for safe and secure deposits, payments and other financial transactions such as ACH transfers or Cashier's Checks for closing. Having multiple bank accounts can help separate security deposits from operational cash. Some states require this, while others don't require separate bank accounts. Having multiple banking institutions allows more flexibility for your tenants and increased network opportunities for your business. Having more than one checking account also allows for cleaner financials once your door count is above 10 and tracking rent becomes more of a challenge.

Tracking software. Invest in or find a free tracking software for your business financials. Doing this by hand or in Microsoft Excel is asking for trouble. It is a *lot* of work and subject to human error. Most tracking software is now cloud-based and available on any device at any time. This allows for convenient tracking and a consistent understanding of your financials. Most rental management software includes financial tracking and is extremely user friendly. This is a *must* for your business. You can easily run reports and see charts or graphs that display your financial performance in the present and over time. I recommend consistent entry of transactions. The best practice is to enter them as they occur, in the very moment. Another best practice is to enter all transactions once per week. This allows for a quick audit to ensure everything is accounted for.

General accounting. Tracking the financial performance of your business is essential. Accounting software is easily and cheaply available in today's business market. If you have the time and are willing to commit to it, you can perform the accountant role for your business. Some prefer to hire an outside accountant or CPA as well. Accounting is simply the term to account for all the financial debits and credits of your business. Tracking the flow of money is important, especially come tax season.

Revenue, profit/loss & cash flow. Part of financial preparation is understanding where you are winning and losing in the income statement. If your business shows a loss, excluding depreciation, it's time to pivot. Understand if you are operating at a profit or loss each month, quarter and year. Know what are your largest expenditures, your highest revenue sources and everything in between. Use revenue, cash flow and profit/loss as key performance indicators (KPIs) in your rental real estate business. I am constantly measuring my business on these financial indicators of performance so I understand if I am winning or losing. Just understanding whether you are improving or not goes a long way. Accurate and consistent financial tracking is essential. I recommend tracking your Financial KPIs over time to truly evaluate the health of your business.

Financial capital. Be sure to understand your financial capital position at all times. Having capital on hand or knowing where you can quickly obtain capital is a differentiator for whether your business is able to grow. Have cash on hand for repairs, enhancements and acquisitions. If you have enough equity in some of your properties, consider taking out a line of credit that can be used as capital for new investments. Save enough capital from your cash flows to reinvest and expand when ready. Always understand how much capital is available, where your future capital will be derived and how to obtain more.

YOUR BUSINESS ORGANIZATION AND PERFORMANCE

Peter Drucker, the Austrian-born management consultant and author is famously quoted for saying, "What gets measured gets managed." Don't you want to successfully manage your business? Yes of course! Then be sure to measure every important KPI, such as: total revenue, cash flow, repair costs, turnover, occupancy and other expenses.

Rental management software. Bookkeeping and business organization are essential. Rental management software exists for this purpose. This can be the exact same software as I mention above for tracking of financials or it can be separate. I recommend using one system if possible, to house everything in one location. There are several great options on the market. Rental management software is widely available and of extremely high quality. The purpose is to effectively manage your rental real estate business finances and operations. Most rental management software is cloud-based and available on mobile devices, including your phone. This makes the management of your business very convenient. Rental management software is a two-way street in that tenants can be granted limited access. Though primarily for the benefit and use of landlords, tenants also have some features available to them which they appreciate. Here is a list of business activities a rental real estate business owner and their tenants can leverage with rental management software.

Landlord Benefits	Tenant Benefits
• Online payments & full accounting • Online rental applications & tenant screening • Contacts & team management • Online listings & vacancies marketing • Maintenance requests & tracking • Rental agreements, notices & e-signature • Lead generation & renter leads • On-demand printable reports	• Online payments • Online applications • Renter profile • Rental agreements & e-signature • Online maintenance requests • Renters insurance • Transaction history • Tenant screening profile

Documentation. Document everything in your rental real estate business! This is why I continue to reinforce leveraging a cloud-based tracking software. It simplifies the process for you. Better than keeping paper receipts around everywhere, take pictures and upload the images. Get email receipts and digital statements for all purchase and repair work. Rent collection, utility payments, supply purchases and a lot more are all in one place and can produce exportable reports for you in mere seconds. The best way to document is in an organized manner, it makes everything else easier downstream.

Taxes. Your business income is taxable. Similar to any other source of income, be sure to track everything and keep all documentation for tax season. Having the tracking available via the rental management software is a major benefit. Consistent documentation results in an easier tax season. Tracking your financial and other business activity should become habit, which will create more efficiencies and success. Having a system for your taxes is highly recommended. Decide now which software you will use to track everything, which software or accountant you will use to complete your taxes and plan ahead to maximize your tax benefits. Chapter Twelve goes into more extensive detail in how to maximize your rental business tax benefits. The takeaway here is to have systems for your taxes and plan ahead.

Property success. Leveraging the financial metrics and details we've reviewed, it's time to understand success or failure at the property level. Know which properties are most successful, either through revenue, cash flow or profit. Study your most and least effective rental properties to understand what determines their success or failure. Learn from your analysis and leverage best practices across your rental portfolio. If there is a property that is a loser (financially speaking) consider selling it and taking the sales proceeds to acquire another investment. You could even leverage the 1031 Exchange for real estate investors to sell the loser property and upgrade to a larger, more expensive property. Think of your business as a large corporation. Large corporations offer multiple products & services, which become multiple and diversified revenue streams. If a revenue stream or associated business unit is underperforming, a corporation will look to improve it or sell it. You are the corporation leadership in this analogy and each property is a different product/service that you are monetizing as a unique revenue stream. You want to build upon the high performers, improve the average performers into the high performer category and improve or eliminate your low performers.

LET'S WRAP A BOW ON THIS CHAPTER

Congratulations, you've finished Chapter Eight and learned something new to improve your rental real estate business! The focus of this chapter is to share how crucial business systems are for the overall success of your rental property business. Having systems can save you time, improve your financials, prevent disasters and more.

What is a system and why should I care? Systems are major differentiators in successful vs unsuccessful businesses. With rental properties, having systems in place for how you operate your business can separate you from the competition. Be consistent, be accurate and be more respected through systems.

OK—but what are the systems you are referring to? In rental real estate, there are quite a few business systems that could and should be created in order to run your business with higher levels of efficiency. Having a system for your application process, rent collection and screening tenants alone will save you time and effort.

Get your business financials in order. Financial performance has a lot to do with measuring your financial operations. All money in and money out needs to be accounted for. Leverage systems and people to get your financial house in order. This will help drive more favorable financial results for your business.

Your business organization and performance. To truly be a successful rental real estate business person, organization and performance tracking are essential. Be organized in order to maximize your time, money and effort. Leverage a rental management software! Track your business performance in order to identify where improvements can and should be made.

NINE

PROTECT YOURSELF AND YOUR INVESTMENT

I n business, like in life, health and safety are top concerns for most
people. Safety is all about protection from danger, whether that be
people, places or adverse risk. It is of critical importance to protect
ourselves. As a society, we pay lots of money to protect ourselves
through firearms, quality vehicles, home security systems and for
some even bodyguards. We also pay lots of money to protect our
possessions through storage units, car alarms, security systems, safes,
lock-boxes, safety-deposit boxes, our homes and more. Protection is a
basic human right. Another key area that we protect ourselves in is
our businesses. If we own a business, we do whatever we can to
protect it, whether through security, insurance or legal entity
protection. When you invest in rental real estate, you are now a
business owner that needs to protect yourself, your business and your
possessions. The proper protection can make all the difference in your
business. Disaster can strike at any moment via natural disaster, a
robbery, a fire, fraud or even a lawsuit. When it does, being prepared
and ready is what matters. This begins with ensuring you have the
proper protection setup and in place: ready to protect you, your assets
and your business. This chapter will take you through what forms of
protection are essential, how to cover your bases and how to prepare
for the worst should it show its ugly face.

THIS IS A PEOPLE BUSINESS—THAT PERSPECTIVE IS CRITICAL

Understanding business means one understands that business doesn't
always go as planned, despite your best efforts or good intentions.
Given the unavoidable fact that people are a core component to the
rental real estate business, there will always be the possibility of
dishonesty, violence, accidents, poor behavior and sometimes worse.
Yes, you are in a real estate business, but, the real estate business
is...a *people* business. Get used to the reality that you are in the
people business. People need a place to sleep at night. People need a
place to store their personal belongings. People pay rent. People
collect rent. People behave poorly. People evict other people. People
sue people. People treat people with respect and kindness or they
don't. The list goes on. I recommend approaching your rental real

estate business from the perspective that you, too, are 'people' to others. Therefore, treat them how you'd like to be treated (as I elaborate on in Chapter Seven). Take the people perspective *into* your business. It will go a long way in the mental game and allow you to not take things too personally when they go sour because sometimes, they just do—no matter how well you treat people.

A major component in understanding the people factor is that people can do unpredictable and unjust things. People are selfish by nature and many will do things to inflict physical and emotional harm onto other people. This is where protection comes into play. Every business owner must protect themselves, their families and their assets. This means that you, as a business owner, must realize that people can and will bring harm to you and your business. It is not a matter of if, though a matter of when. Then you must prepare for how often and the amount of harm that can be inflicted. If another person decides to bring forward a lawsuit, this can and will have a serious impact on you and your business. If another person decides to hurt your business by not paying rent and subsequently destroying your property, that can and will have a serious impact on you and your business. If someone decides to try and harm you physically, that can and will have a serious impact on you and your business because *you* are your business! Before you go thinking that I see the worst in people, I assure you that I believe deep down that people are good. I am an optimist by nature and overly positive in my approach to life, including the trust I give to others. Though I believe it is *my duty* to prepare you for the worst. The worst has happened to me, even when I've given tenants the benefit of the doubt. It's best to be prepared for what *could* happen, even though I hope it *never* does happen to you.

COVERING YOUR BASES AND WHY IT'S IMPORTANT

It's important to understand that your business is vulnerable (as is your personal financial situation) if you don't cover your bases. No need to stress out; this applies to everyone who jumps into this game. However, having knowledge of why legal protection is essential and how to attain it is a good start. In essence, when you own a property and rent that property to another person, there is a chance something will go awry. Your tenant may accuse you of mistreating them, neglecting your duties as a landlord or even breaking the law. The tenant may also have an accident on the premises, which may or may not have been more likely to occur due to something you did or did not do. For example, you left a low hanging electrical wire that snapped and caught the yard on fire. Another scenario may be uneven cement, such as a walkway or sidewalk. This is very common where I purchase properties as the earth shifts a little each year. As a result, constant maintenance of this is required.

This section isn't intended to scare you, but to *prepare* you. It's always best to be prepared when less than ideal scenarios occur. It's best to know how to evict a tenant vs not. When the time comes it will save you money, time and lots of stress. The same applies here with legal protection. It's best to be prepared for something bad to happen so that if it does, you are ready to handle it. I like the analogy of knowing how to swim. Most days of your life this skill isn't essential. However, if you happen to be boating with a friend, fall off and don't have a life jacket or the boat capsizes, your likelihood of survival increases significantly *if* you know how to swim.

Landlording is similar. You want to survive should a dangerous situation arise. If you weren't properly covered and a tenant sued you, your personal assets and wealth would be at risk. If it were serious and you lost the lawsuit, you could potentially lose everything. Think about the impacts not just to you and your business, but your family and loved ones. Your financial future could be wrecked. I'm here to help make certain that this never happens to my readers, to *you*. It goes without saying that you should run a good, honest business and do what's essential to prevent a lawsuit from the onset, such as: treat people with kindness and decency, don't harass or abuse people, don't be racist, sexist, or exhibit prejudice of any kind, fix what's broken promptly, keep your word, fulfill your legal obligations as a landlord and don't be a jackass just because you own the property. Stick to that and people will be far less likely to even have the thought of bringing a lawsuit against you.

I've been a landlord for five years and have not once had a tenant bring a lawsuit against me, my business partner or our business. I have had a couple of tenants threaten it, but the threat was more during a discussion around the tenant not fulfilling their part of the rental lease agreement and threatening me with baseless claims to try and skirt responsibility. I prefer to end tenant relationships amenably and have even agreed to end a lease term early with no adverse consequences to the tenant because the headache just wasn't worth it. Each landlord must decide for themselves what is worth it vs what is not. The truth is most people who rent from you are not financially well off. Studies have shown the vast wealth disparity between those who own homes and those who do not. As recently as 2015 a renter in the United States was barely worth $5,000. A homeowner was worth on average 44x that number. In other words, if you sue your tenants or take them to small claims court to collect a debt, there won't be much to collect. The court may award you a judgment against them, but rarely do they enforce payment and it's more likely you pay more in legal fees than you will ever see in return as payment from your ex-tenant. Be smart. Protect yourself, your investment and your family. The rest of the chapter will cover what forms of protection you should carry, why you need them and how to go about attaining them.

GET THE RIGHT INSURANCE COVERAGE

Buying insurance is a requirement for purchasing a home when you borrow money from a financial institution. In other words, if you have a note, you have to prove that the property is insured before the bank will loan you money to close. It is highly recommended to have insurance on a home regardless of whether you paid in cash or borrowed funds. Not all insurance is created equal. Not all insurance agents are created equal, either. I recommend getting multiple quotes for insurance when you acquire a property and to check back every year to ensure you have the right coverage at a fair price.

Be certain the coverage is sufficient in case of emergency or unexpected damages. The realities of weather damage are different in each and every area. Some deal with hurricanes, others tornadoes, others hail and snow storms, earthquakes, then fire and extensive rains. Whatever risks are highest in your area, be sure you have the proper coverage! Some areas even require separate insurance for floods, fires and hurricanes. Know what is covered under your insurance and what isn't in order to prevent a potential financial disaster should a natural disaster hit. Believe me, they will. Just assume for the worst when deciding what to cover for insurance. Also remember, insurance costs are a *tax-deductible* business expense, so an additional $10/month isn't going to break the bank.

This Happened to Me – Heavy hail and a leaky roof

I purchased a property in 2018 that had the roof replaced within the previous five years. Typically, a roof will last 20-50 years. Where I live, hail storms are common, especially in the summer. The hot summer days tend to make way for late afternoon and evening thunderstorms that are sometimes accompanied by hail.

The hail can be small and inconsequential or it can be the size of golf balls or larger. At times, storms come in 2-3 times in a single week. Even the highest quality roof can be damaged. I received notice from a tenant that there was water damage to the ceiling in the living room because they noticed a small hole forming in the drywall. I sent my repairman out the next day to take a look. From the time the tenant notified me the hole had doubled in size and it appeared to be a result of water damage. My repairman got onto the roof and quickly identified a leak. To his and my surprise, he noticed a significant amount of hail damage to the roof shingles and took some pictures for me to send to the insurance company.

As luck would have it, this was all happening in the middle of the COVID-19 pandemic and insurance companies were contracting out the actual visits to properties when conducting damage assessments. I opened a claim immediately and couldn't make any repairs until the assessor came out to conduct the formal assessment. If I began repairs right away, I wouldn't have received the proper payout from insurance. The third-party contracting assessor took *three days* to get to the property! In the meantime, another storm had blown through and the ceiling began to cave down to the floor causing debris to spread everywhere resulting in further damage. I had no choice but to tarp the roof at this point. We also tarped the inside ceiling so nothing else would fall inside the residence. Once the exterior roofing damage was confirmed and assessed, I contracted the roofing company to begin work. Unfortunately, the assessor from the third-party company refused to go *inside* the property, blaming COVID. I couldn't believe it. I had to go back and call my primary insurer to explain the situation and demand an immediate interior assessment. Another three days go by before a new third-party contractor goes to the property to assess the interior damage. At this point, I'm hearing it every day from my tenant (and rightfully so)! Believe me, the insurance company was hearing it every day from me! In the meantime, the exterior roofing work began. Three more days go by before the assessment from the third-party contractor makes it to my primary insurer. Total worst-case scenario here. Out of my control, I do everything I can to appease my frustrated tenant and get the proper help from my insurance company. Finally, that assessment was delivered, and I immediately conducted the repairs to my property. The total process took around two and a half weeks when it could have been seven to ten days.

BE CAREFUL—PROTECT YOURSELF

I'd be remiss if I didn't include a section about protecting yourself from physical harm. The ugly truth is that there are bad people out there who are willing to inflict harm on others with very little regard for anything. I came across a news story where a landlord went to collect rent from a tenant and was subsequently kidnapped, then shot dead. Another similar though more gruesome news story where a landlord went to collect rent from a tenant and the tenant, with a samurai sword, decapitated the landlord! I couldn't make this stuff up. It's real and it happens. I will share with you a few pointers on how to stay physically safe as a landlord. Pay attention because it could literally save your life!

Just like you wouldn't walk in a dark, downtown alley at night, you shouldn't conduct an inspection or an open house alone. Safety should always be your top priority. Preparedness is critical. Some of you may be uncomfortable with this topic and decide to hire a property management company as a result. This is your choice. My objective is to best prepare you for success, which in this case means your physical safety. Remember these next tips, write them down and take the appropriate precautions to keep yourself, your business partners and your family safe from danger. You'll be grateful you did and so will your significant other, business partner or kids!

Know your applicant. Be sure to conduct a background check of all applicants. When you go to meet them at the property, you'll want to at least have basic information on them as a person. Always collect a government-issued form of photo identification for documentation. Meet people in public and refer to the buddy system below for prospective tenants and more.

Don't collect rent in person. *Never* collect rent in person. This is the year 2021; there is zero need. Between online payments, direct deposit, ACH transfers and cash payments into a local bank branch, tenants have a myriad of methods for payment of rent. Plus, collecting rent in person is a colossal waste of your time. Outline the rent payment requirements before signing a lease to ensure a tenant agrees with their rent payment options.

Don't try and evict someone yourself. This is just a *hard no*. First, legally, you can't. Second, it's stupid to try! Your life is not worth evicting a deadbeat a few days or weeks early. Your best bet here is to post and/or deliver the 'notice to comply with lease' or eviction notice punctually and safely. We pay a local lawyer to physically post eviction notices on our behalf.

Be on alert at all times. Trust nobody. Not because you don't want to think the best of people, but because your life could depend on it. Be vigilant and alert at all times while conducting rental business. Be sure to conduct business during the daylight, in public, with a buddy and/or with a self-defense weapon. It's not being paranoid; it's caring about your life enough to take the necessary precautions. Other people cannot and should not be trusted. It's sad to say it, but assume the worst so that you come prepared.

Use the buddy system. Take someone with you to conduct rental real estate business if it must be conducted in person. For inspections, I never go alone. I also never conduct open houses alone. The rule of thumb is to have someone with you because criminals are much less likely to commit a crime when multiple people are present. It becomes more challenging and is a natural deterrent. Most commonly, I conduct business with my business partner, with my real estate agent, with my contractor or with my wife. I even am known to bring my German Shepherd defender dogs Louie and Indy along with me.

Carry a self-defense weapon. Where possible and where legal, carry a weapon of self-defense with you when conducting rental business. Hopefully you never need to use it. However, if you do, you'll be glad you came prepared. As mentioned above, I've taken my German Shepherd Dogs with me to open houses and move-ins. They are fierce, intimidating weapons. Recently, I became a handgun owner for the first time and obtained my Concealed Handgun Permit primarily because of the rental real estate business I conduct and the inherent risks that are associated with it. I carry my firearm with me each time I conduct rental business because it's better safe than sorry, as the saying goes. Other reliable options for self-defense weapons are knives, a taser, pepper spray or a stun gun.

Never give out your home address. This one may seem obvious these days, though it is still important to mention. *Never* give a tenant your personal address, period. If you or your tenant are old school and prefer to pay via check, either have them send the rent check to a PO box or have them direct deposit the check to a local bank branch. Never send a piece of business mail with your personal address as the return address either. The last thing you want is someone seeking revenge on you. If they know your personal address, *watch out*. Please be careful!

When it comes to protecting yourself, *preparedness* and *awareness* are key. It's essential you practice these guidelines or you could become the next headline news story caught up in a tragic disaster.

This Happened to Me – The 'porch gangsta' neighbor

My business partner and I had just purchased our second investment property. We were still so very excited to be running our own business and were still learning. We learned a bit from the first time around, though were definitely still very 'green' in our approach. We had marketed the property and decided to hold two full days of open houses to find rental candidates. We opened the door, posted a 'for rent' sign and eagerly awaited the arrival of our numerous rental candidates! As we were waiting, listening to some punk rock music on a mini-speaker, we noticed some yelling and agitation coming from across the street. We still didn't know the entire town too well and soon came to the realization that this may be a bit rougher part of town. The altercation wasn't singular in nature. Over the two days, we witnessed around five of these. Each time, a rough-looking couple of guys, most likely gangsters, were arguing with the neighbor, who appeared to be one of them, (though more specifically a drug dealer). He had many visitors. He was exchanging something for cash and his visitors would drive away. This neighbor was rough looking, as was his house. On numerous occasions, as we went to observe the raucous, the neighbor gave us the death stare. Once, he even yelled over, "You interested in something over here, punks?!" To which we replied, "No, Sir! Nothing at all." We then proceeded back inside.

There was a small bakery and sandwich shop across the street, next to this unfriendly neighbor. We visited each day for lunch and made quick friends with the owners. The business had been around for over 100 years and the owners knew the neighborhood well. We inquired about the neighbor and they provided quite a bit of interesting information. They confirmed that they were indeed affiliated with a local gang and were definitely dealing drugs. In fact, the police had visited the residence frequently and were consistently on alert. They told us to stay away from the house and we obliged. The neighbor seemed to still be a teenager, 18 or 19 years old, and proved to be a very real danger. We stayed clear from that point on, though his presence and behavior proved difficult in renting that particular property. We were sorely disappointed that the numbers were so low in attendance to our open houses. We maybe had 10 people total over a two-day period and only had two submitted applications. It became obvious as to why! Even to this day the rents are lower than we could get just a half mile down the road. Our lesson learned was to do more research on the area before buying and also understanding how to avoid this type of danger.

BE LAWFUL AND ETHICAL

This should go without saying, though if it didn't need to be said I wouldn't have included this section in the book. Be *lawful* and be *ethical*. Being lawful as a landlord isn't as cut and dry as being a normal citizen. As a citizen, we generally know the laws of the land. You know...don't steal, don't break into someone's home, don't punch someone in the face. As a landlord, the law can vary greatly state by state. For example, certain states require 60 days minimum before you can evict someone. States differ in the quantity of late fees a landlord can assess, the number of days before a security deposit must be returned and when personal property of an evicted tenant is legally considered possession of the landlord. In short, learn the landlord-tenant laws of the state(s) in which you conduct business.

As discussed in Chapter Ten, knowing and following the law becomes a major advantage as a landlord. Not knowing it can be equally disadvantageous. Missing a step in the eviction process, for example, results in starting over or at minimum returning to the previous step in the process. This undoubtedly delays the process and results in lost revenues and profits for your rental business. Assessing reasonable late fees can be a positive revenue add for your business. In contrast, charging late fees in excess of what your state considers to be reasonable can result in a lawsuit and serious losses. I will repeat it once again: *learn the laws* in each state which you conduct rental real estate business. Trust me, it's worth the time spent.

The ethical side of the house is a bit less clear. Chapter Thirteen goes into more detail around operating ethically and being a good person. Remember, *people* are your customers and your business needs people to be successful. Treat people fairly, with kindness and respect, and live by your word. Your word may not be the law or even legally binding, however, it should mean everything to you as a landlord. Be honest and do what you say you will do. Yes, things will slip through the cracks. Make up for it. Own your actions— even the mistakes. Doing this will create enduring tenant relationships through loyalty and mutual respect. Every landlord wants sticky tenants. You know, the ones that stay for long periods of time and don't want to leave because they like renting from you. The key to creating sticky tenants is acting ethically and doing what you say you will. This is also a great strategy for protecting your investment because legal fees can damage or even take away your rental real estate investment.

This Happened to Me – The crumbling porch steps

At one of my rental properties, an elderly couple that has health struggles, including physical limitations, struggled with the outside stairs leading to the front porch because they had shifted over time as the ground moved. The stairs didn't completely align with the porch anymore. It wasn't significant enough to where it needed immediate replacement, though we acknowledged the condition and mentioned should it become an issue, that we'd get it fixed. Fast forward a year, we get a call from the husband that mentions his wife had tripped and hit her bad knee due to the deteriorating condition of the stairs. Once this came to our attention, we had the damage assessed and within two days contracted for the entire stairway to be demolished and replaced with fresh concrete.

We also identified some wear and tear in the path leading from the sidewalk to the stairs and decided to correct that all at once vs waiting for another accident to occur. We could have just done a patch job. We could have left it and done nothing. Instead, we went above and beyond for tenants that had paid on time each month and never asked for much or demanded anything unreasonable. I take this responsibility seriously and do my best to provide a safe and clean home for each and every tenant. As a result, our tenants are stickier than most. Our average tenant stays 3-4 years. These particular tenants plan to stay for an extended period of time. That is not only good for business, it is good for the *soul*. Be good to others. *Everyone wins*. End of story.

LEGAL ENTITIES AND REAL ESTATE

Now to the meat of this chapter, legal entities and real estate! A basic rule of thumb when choosing a legal entity is to protect yourself and limit your personal liability. This is a business, and without a separate legal entity, the owner(s) of the business would be held fully liable against legal proceedings of any kind. Given this fact, choosing and establishing a legal entity for liability protection is extremely prudent. If an owner chooses not to, they could be held liable for defaulted loans, legal liability from accidents on the property or even a tenant bringing legal action against them. In short, understanding what legal entity options are available to you as a real estate investor is important and equally as important is knowing which one benefits you most! The rest of this section will cover each of the legal entity options available to you along with some of the advantages and disadvantages of each one.

Sole Proprietorship. A sole proprietorship is owned by a single individual and has no separate legal existence from that owner. No formation of a legal entity is required. This type of legal entity may hire employees or individual contractors, though all decisions are run through the sole proprietor. This holds the owner completely liable for all business-related debts and they are also exposed to lawsuits. This legal entity is not ideal or recommended for rental real estate because of the lack of personal or asset protection offered.

Tenants in Common. Tenants in Common is the ownership of real estate by more than one individual, where each owner retains an undivided interest in the property. No legal entity is actually formed here either. Similar to the sole proprietorship, this holds the owners completely liable for all business-related debts and exposed to lawsuits. This legal entity is not ideal or recommended for rental real estate because of the lack of personal or asset protection offered.

General Partnership. A general partnership is an association of two or more people to carry on a business as co-owners. No written agreement is necessary. Each partner can participate in the management of the business. One primary benefit is that no taxable event happens with a general partnership, it is a pass-through entity and the tax burden is split amongst the partners according to their percent share of ownership, i.e., profits and losses. Similar to the Sole Proprietorship and Tenants in Common, this legal entity holds the general partners completely liable for all business-related debts and exposed to lawsuits. This legal entity is not ideal or recommended for rental real estate because of the lack of personal or asset protection offered.

Limited Partnership. A limited partnership is an association of two or more people where the entity has one or more general partners and one or more limited partners. This type of partnership allows for a passive investor, not active in the day-to-day operations or management decisions, to participate in the investment. The liability of each partner is limited to the amount of capital that the investor has agreed to put 'at-risk'. One major disadvantage of a limited partnership is that the limited partners must rely on the ability and expertise of the general partner or else they risk losing their limited liability. This legal entity has more use within real estate investments and is more common among larger investment groups.

C Corporations (C-corp). C corporations have a separate legal existence from the entities listed above. The corporate structure isolates debt from shareholders and is able to hold property in its own name. The board of directors and officers of the corporation provide the management and business operations of the corporation. C corporations mitigate both the tax liability of self-employment taxes and the inherent liability of having contractors and other third parties working on a piece of property. All business conducted with this legal entity type is conducted in the name of the corporation. Your personal assets are protected as a result. C corporations are double taxed, in that the income from the corporation itself is taxed, and then owners are taxed again for dividends or capital gains. This type of legal entity is not commonly used for rental real estate; it is more targeted for flipping businesses and standard real estate conglomerates.

S Corporations (S-corp). S corporations are very similar to C corporations, though have a few major differences. First, they allow investors to avoid the double taxation of the corporation's profit. Second, its income tax losses and credits are passed onto the shareholders while still providing the primary investors with limited liability. An S corporation is limited to 100 total owners. S corporations do offer pass-through taxation, similar to a Limited Liability Company (LLC), without the above-mentioned corporate income tax. One disadvantage of this legal entity is the difficulty in transferring real estate and other property held by the corporation due to the limitation of the number of investors.

Limited Liability Company (LLC). Buying a property in the name of a Limited Liability Company (LLC) is common business practice for real estate. LLCs are by far the most popular choice of legal entity for rental real estate because of the inherent flexibility in most state statutes that enhances the ability of the entity to adopt features that best service its objectives. LLCs are pass-through entities, which means the entity itself doesn't pay taxes. The taxes flow to the owner's personal financial statements. There is no limit to the number of owners with an LLC. There can even be assignment of more limited partners with this legal entity. An LLC can hold a single property or multiple. An LLC can also be leveraged for investments where other investors are required. There is no need for a board of directors because the LLC members manage the entity and can write up an operating agreement should they choose to formalize responsibilities.

Trusts. Trusts are worth a mention because they do offer unique features that the other legal entities do not. A trust does keep the property ownership out of someone's personal name altogether. This puts a cloak of secrecy over the ownership of the property because nobody could find the property being owned under the individual's name. Some states have property ownership as public record, where anyone can search the ownership database and find out who owns the property. Putting a lid on this is attractive and worth looking into. A trust can also hold other legal entities within itself, such as an LLC. This legal structure is typically recommended for family estate planning, though is also used for investors. A major challenge with using a trust is that most lenders won't lend on a property when the deed is in the name of the trust. Trusts are also a very expensive legal entity to setup and require an attorney to complete the process (5).

To summarize, the type of legal entity real estate investors and owners should use to hold real estate largely depends on the specifics of their situation. Some of the factors to consider are the type of property, location of the property, the purpose or intended use of the property, taxation factors and preferences, distributions of cash, management of the property and the overall business strategy or reason for buying the property in the first place. Most real estate investors that buy and rent long-term real estate do so within the legal entity structure of an LLC. The advantages are many and most people benefit from this legal entity more than any other with rental real estate. Before making your final decision, I do recommend consulting with a real estate attorney.

LET'S WRAP A BOW ON THIS CHAPTER

Congratulations, you've finished Chapter Nine and learned something new to improve your rental real estate business! The focus of this chapter is to learn about protecting yourself, your business and your assets. Your life can depend on your attention to these critical factors of protection.

This is a people business—that perspective is important. Your business exists because of people. People are unpredictable, so be careful who you trust. Understand that people are the lifeblood of your business; treat them accordingly. People are your customers regardless of your personal opinions of them. Learn to be good with people and your business will succeed as a result.

Covering your bases and why it's important. Covering your bases means to be prepared for anything. Be prepared for a lawsuit. Be prepared for a natural disaster. Be prepared to protect yourself physically. Be prepared for someone to do wrong against you. It will happen at some point, so be prepared.

Get the right insurance coverage. Having the right insurance coverage matters. Be sure what you purchase is sufficient in case of emergency or the unexpected. Shop for the best price, though don't skimp on coverage amounts. In the end, that could cost you big time.

Be careful—Protect yourself. Your physical protection is worthy of a section in this book so I hope you paid attention! Knowing how to protect yourself is vital. Be aware of your surroundings and be smart about how you conduct your business. Don't put yourself in a dangerous situation. Don't trust people. Your life could depend on it!

Be lawful and ethical. Being lawful and ethical as a landlord isn't as cut and dry as being a normal citizen. Landlord and tenant laws vary by state. Be sure to study yours and operate your business within those laws. Be a good person. Be a good landlord. Be good to people. This means show them consideration, fairness and respect in everything you do.

Legal entities and real estate. Legal entities exist as a form of financial protection. They are intended to protect you from personal liability, which is a major factor when you own rental real estate. Be sure to study which legal entity is right for your business and consult a local attorney before deciding how to proceed.

TEN

TIME TO GO! THE EVICTION PROCESS & SAYING BYE TO DEADBEATS

O wning rental real estate is business that is made up of people. This was established earlier in the book. I don't just mean that people keep it going. I mean it is one of the most direct people businesses in existence. As a landlord, you are providing an individual or a family, with a place to *live*. They aren't patrons that just come and go once in a while like if you owned a restaurant. You aren't simply offering them a storage unit for their personal belongings. This business provides real people with a place to lay their head at night after a long day's work or caring for children. Your rental property is where someone invites family and friends over for holidays and other special occasions. Your rental property is where some children may grow up and other adults grow old. It may even be the place where life ends for some of your tenants, as it has some of mine. Your rental property is *home* to your tenants. Home is a sacred place for many, a sanctuary in fact. For some it is quite the opposite. It's a place where bad behavior takes place and carelessness presides. Home in 2020, during the pandemic, took on a whole new set of realities. The focus of this chapter is around what to do when someone doesn't respect your rental property as a home and instead treats it like a dartboard for their negligent and irresponsible behavior. Let's dive right into the scary topic of eviction.

HOW EVICTION REALLY WORKS AND WHY IT IS YOUR FRIEND

Eviction is a terrifying word. I think whoever created the word intended for it to be so. Like murder. That's a terrifying word! Eviction in the real estate game is a scary word yes, but it can also be a landlord's best friend. This chapter will detail the eviction process and why I am convinced it is actually your friend. One you can rely on time and time again.

As a new landlord, I too was terrified of the word eviction. My personality is non-confrontational. I prefer to avoid even the likes of confrontation. Anything dealing with confrontation makes me anxious, nervous and speeds up my heart rate. I struggle to handle confrontation or cope well afterward. The thought of someone not paying rent, abusing my property or being evicted evokes those anxious and heavy feelings for me. My first year in the rental real estate game was very fortunate. I didn't have any tenants choosing to not pay rent or doing anything worthy of being evicted. This was a major bonus! I had heard the stories, especially the nightmares. I realized that it was only a matter of time before I had to deal with one of those myself. The mere thought of it made me anxious. I wanted to continue to build my real estate portfolio, but wasn't certain how I would manage something like that when it came up. I had only read about eviction in books. I had never actually taken the steps required to evict someone. Once I was faced with having to, it wasn't as bad as expected. The eviction process, just like any other process, system or skill, requires doing it to become more comfortable. Let's talk more about that and what it means for your rental business.

When you market your rental, the basic expectations are that you will be seeking a responsible tenant pay rent every month and take care of the property. There is so much that is baked into those three expectations and what each of them truly means. The basis of the expectations is understood by anyone who has ever rented and those who are landlords. Chapter Four goes into more extraneous details around what those expectations are. The sad reality is that many renters do not live up to those basic rental expectations. Compound that reality with the likelihood that you have never met your rental applicants and don't know their past, which adds up to a general consensus that you shouldn't trust anyone you rent to. Unfortunately, often times a landlord rents to family or friends that are worse than the average tenant. You're probably thinking, "Who are these guy's family and friends?! He needs some new ones!" You'd be shocked that yours are likely similar to many others out there.

Always hope for the best, though *trust nobody*. This is why a rental lease agreement exists. The basic expectations of human behavior are outside the realm of reality for many tenants. Not trusting the people you rent to has nothing to do with your goodness as a person or the kindness of your heart. It has everything to do with protecting yourself, being a good landlord and running a successful rental real estate business.

The eviction process is a safety net for landlords. The requirements for the eviction process vary from state to state as does the effectiveness of the process as a result. We will review this detail later in the chapter. Knowing the process in your state is the first place to start, even before you have to pull the trigger on evicting someone. The rest of this chapter will explore when you should evict someone, how that process works in detail and how to move on to the next tenant successfully.

WHEN TO SAY GOODBYE TO DEADBEATS

What is a deadbeat? Let's start there. In the rental real estate world, a deadbeat can be defined as someone (a tenant) who knowingly and willingly breaks the duties outlined in the rental lease agreement to the extent they must be evicted. Having a well-constructed and lawful lease agreement is extremely important as it pertains to getting rid of deadbeats. A deadbeat is someone who is hurting your business. They are either impacting your finances, your reputation, your sanity, or a combination of the three!

From a financial standpoint, they are likely not paying all or any of rent. The easiest and most expedited way to evict someone is proving they haven't paid rent. This is fairly simple to do considering the readily available bank statements and rental management software. It is also the fastest way for a court to rule in your favor for eviction. The tenant stands little to no chance of remaining in your property past the state-allowed timing requirements for eviction proceedings. Even if a tenant pays partial rent with a promise to pay the remainder, they can be evicted. Now, if we are talking $50, that may be tricky. However, $500, pretty easy case. Also, if there is a history of late or partial payments, the case is rock solid.

You should only pursue eviction if the tenant is unlikely to pay. That doesn't mean, however, that you don't begin the process. For example, if a tenant's rent is due on the first of the month, with a grace period through the fifth of the month and they haven't paid by the sixth, you can technically begin the eviction process. You are within your legal rights to do so. The first step in most states is the positing of a 'Notice to Vacate Form', which is typically associated with a time period, i.e., 3 days, 5 days, 10 days, 14 days, etc. The period is dependent upon state law. Again, reference the law in which your rental unit exists. If a tenant reaches out to you on the first of the month, or even the fifth and states that rent will be late due to a seemingly valid reason, you should be the type of landlord you would expect to have and show them sympathy. Unless it is a repeat offender. Perhaps you can grant them an additional day or two depending on the situation. I have even allowed late rent for weeks at a time if the tenant has a solid on-time payment history and the excuse is valid and sensible. Sometimes, an emergency arises. We've all had them. Sometimes, a family member passes away and you have to pay funeral costs unexpectedly. Sometimes, you lose your job and can't pay full rent immediately. There are a myriad of reasons why rent can be late and as the landlord, you must decide whether you will let the tenant pass. I assess late fees for late rent. Typically, the first occasion I give a 'free late rent pass', meaning I don't assess the fee. However, it is case by case and if I view the tenant as trouble or someone I may have to evict down the road, I will assess the fee. The fee must be reasonable according to your state laws. However, if they don't pay or acknowledge the late rent, this also may be grounds for eviction. This may be true even if they pay the full rent late. It just makes it more challenging if the eviction goes all the way to court. Understand that full and on-time rent payments are the single biggest key to your business success. Be sure to always maintain proper awareness of this fact.

From a reputation standpoint, you need to be a landlord that enforces your own rules. If not, people will learn they can walk all over you. Be consistent and enforce behavior requirements for all tenants. Inconsistency can damage your business and your reputation. You want to have kind and respectful tenants in your properties so that neighbors, local business owners and government officials come to respect you and can be of help to you. Respectful and appreciative neighbors can share news with you about your tenant's behavior or other activity in the area. Local business owners can be of great help to you when you build a solid reputation with them and around town. Government officials can help or ruin your day, so be respectful and create relationships where possible. Represent yourself and your business well. If you are a landlord to a multi-family property, the importance of this amplifies as now other tenants in the building will form opinions about you and how you operate your business. If they disapprove, they may file complaints against you, vacate your property or even take you to court if you violate a landlord-tenant law. In short, be a reputable business person. Give your best efforts in being a good landlord that respects people and your business rules.

THE MEAN 'OLE EVICITION PROCESS

The mean 'ole eviction process in real estate is kind of like the big, bad wolf of this business. It's scary, yes. It can be very intimidating as we've discussed. But in the end, just like the big, bad wolf, the eviction process becomes a delicious dinner plate for your rental business. Perhaps this isn't the best analogy, though I'm alright with that in order to prove a point. The eviction process shouldn't be feared. It should be viewed as a necessary step to accomplish eventual good in your business. Yes, the process can be painful, frustrating and long-winded. However, if understood and used properly, it can and should be an asset.

As another reminder, each state has different laws that pertain to landlords, evictions, tenants and the entire real estate process. Be sure to check with your state's laws prior to making an assumption about the eviction process that could end up setting you back instead of helping you move on from the bad relationship at hand. I will outline the standard eviction process and then share some insights into how things are currently handled in the State of Colorado.

Legal notification. The first step in the eviction process is a legal notification to the tenant that you are planning to evict them. In the state of Colorado, as well as many others, this step is called the '10-Day Notice to Vacate Form'. This one-page document is typically posted to the front door and delivered or served to the tenant. In Colorado, the notice period used to be three days. In 2019 the law changed to ten days. This step is both a formal notice to the tenant that they have violated the rental lease agreement and they will be evicted if they refuse to comply. Most of these notices come with default language around the next steps, which include a court date and potential judgement.

File eviction paperwork. Once the notification period on the notice has passed, the next step is to file eviction paperwork with the court. Now this assumes the tenant has not complied or vacated the property on their own at this point. The eviction paperwork covers the reasons for filing eviction, along with a specific request for the court to proceed with setting a hearing date.

Court date scheduled. Once the court has reviewed the filed paperwork and deemed it acceptable to proceed, they will assign a hearing date. The tenant is advised of the request to make a court appearance and the landlord either needs to show or have representation in court for them. At this juncture, the tenant is very close to eviction and may choose to leave on their own before a judgement is formally filed. Once it is, this judgment becomes permanent on their record and will appear on future background and credit checks.

Court hearing. This is the step where a judge will formally review the case. They will ask for testimony from both parties. The tenant will be given the opportunity to plead their case, assuming they appear in person. If they are guilty, which they should be if you've gotten this far, they likely won't show. If they don't show, the judge will most likely grant the eviction request and move on. If required, the landlord or their representation can provide any supporting testimony or evidence. Most times, this is not required. However, if the tenant does appear, it may be needed.

Judge decision. Once the judge finishes reviewing the documentation, testimony and other supporting evidence, they make a final decision. If the judge rules in favor of the tenant, this will prove very challenging for a landlord. If they rule in favor of the landlord, the tenant will be given a short amount of time to vacate the property and remove their personal belongings. The judgement becomes permanent and a black mark on any tenant's history and credit report. Nobody should get to this point if they are intelligent and understand the long-term consequences of this being on their record. The judge may also award a financial judgment (if the landlord wins) that states the tenant must pay the landlord the missing rent or other damages. When getting to this point, if the eviction was filed properly and the tenant was in clear violation of their lease agreement, it's hard to see the judge ruling in favor of a delinquent and lease-violating tenant.

Order to vacate premises. Assuming the judge ruled in favor of the landlord, further paperwork will be filed for the tenant to vacate the premises within a specified time period. This occurs within a few days. At this point, depending on your state, this process could have been two weeks or six weeks, potentially longer. The tenant has zero recourse at this point and must comply.

Sheriff's Office. This step is not necessary in every state. It is also only necessary if the tenant refuses to vacate the property after receiving the judge's order. If this is the case, the landlord must contact the local sheriff's office, who will forcefully remove the tenant from the property. This is a hassle and no landlord wants to have to go this far; though this step is there to ensure the safety of all parties. As a landlord, you need to be careful and safe in these situations. There have been too many horrible stories of landlords attempting to collect rent or enforce evictions on their own and the tenant inflicting harm upon them, even death. Take care of yourself; be *cautious* and be *smart*.

Eviction wrap-up. Based on personal experience and assuming you want the most efficient, least stressful eviction process possible, I highly recommend hiring an attorney or law firm to represent you and complete the steps in the eviction process on your behalf. If you do this alone, you are required to personally post the notice, file the paperwork, appear in court and so on. By hiring a law firm, for a modest fee, they have this process on autopilot and will handle everything for you, ensuring 100% accuracy of each step. Most landlords, like myself, have a full-time job that requires their physical presence and attention. This makes it very challenging to conduct the required steps yourself. Also, if you don't live close to the property, this makes it even more challenging. Finally, hiring legal representation will ensure all the steps of the process are handled properly, without mistake. If you take this responsibility on yourself, and you miss a step, the process starts over and you are left as the losing party.

Does that seem scary? It really isn't that bad. The most daunting component is knowing the law and following the proper sequence of steps in your state. At first, I posted the eviction notices myself. The process never reached the courts. The tenants moved out and moved on due to the forthcoming reality. Once deadbeat tenants know you are serious, they will most likely figure it out and either pay up or get out. This doesn't always happen and in many instances going through the entire eviction process is essential. When it is required, be prepared to either represent yourself in court or hire an attorney. Personally, I don't have time to attend court and represent myself. I prefer to have an attorney manage the entire process is followed to ensure there are no eviction process mistakes, resulting in delays. I am able to hire a local real estate attorney that specializes in evictions and landlord rights, to complete the entire eviction process on my behalf for around $400. This includes creating the legal notice, posting it to the door or serving the tenant, filing the court summons, representing me in court, obtaining the final judgment and paperwork to take to the local sheriff's office. Truly, it is a lot of work for $400 from an attorney in my opinion! My educated guess is that if I can find an affordable local attorney to complete the process for me, so can you. Do some research and contact some law firms to inquire. This is a fail-proof way to conduct your evictions and ensure your business can return to normal, profitable operations as quickly as possible!

This Happened to Me – The one that went 'all the way'

Most people who face eviction aren't dumb enough to delay the inevitable and have a permanent judgment on their file or wait around for the Sheriff's deputies to come to the property and force them and all their personal belongings to the curb in embarrassment. *Most people*, that is. Most people I have threatened with eviction usually take off in short order. I have had a few get to court where we have won 100% of the time. In each of those instances, the tenant vacated the unit without too much further resistance. Until recently, when one particular tenant took us down the entire legal process to the very end of the yellow brick road.

This tenant was a complete and utter nightmare. She lived in our eight-unit apartment building and would scream until all hours of the night, scare our tenants and constantly act as if she was on drugs or out of her mind. Both of which were likely true. She posted scribble notes with threats toward other tenants in the building and the police on the outside of her apartment door. She would replace one crazy note with another about every other day. She would knock on other tenant's doors to bum cigarettes and reportedly helped herself to one of our elderly tenant's cigarettes when she was away because her door was left unlocked! Due to the COVID pandemic, all eviction proceedings were on a delay. This added over 30 days to the eviction process and a whole slew of headaches along the way. The other tenants in the building were livid and suffering from this lady's inability to peacefully reside and leave people alone. Instead, she did everything possible to make other's lives miserable. I was getting calls and texts early every morning with video evidence of her erratic and alarming behavior. Let's just say she didn't come as advertised from the placement program we coordinated with.

After two months of this hell, the court finally granted us the eviction paperwork. Unfortunately, she didn't acknowledge anything throughout the process. Her plan was to ride it out to the end, which she very much did. On top of all this, the Sheriff's office took nearly ten days to set an appointment for her forceful removal. We had to line up six guys to be there when the Sheriff's deputies arrived to remove her personal belongings. She moved in with next to nothing. Somehow with no job, she managed to accumulate quite a few things, most of which was junk. It took them about 45 minutes to remove everything and literally throw it to the curb. She wasn't home at the time. We locked up the door so she couldn't make her way back in when she returned. When she did, she just sat outside the building for a while. Then she propped her mattress on the patio and *slept outside* that night! I found out because the tenants notified me the next morning. They left for work and about had heart attacks as they walked by her asleep on the patio.

I called the police department and they had her taken to the local precinct. I didn't hear of her again. She never did come and collect her belongings, so after the legally allotted timeframe we hauled it away to the dump and pay for that as well. Alas, she was gone and to this day is the only tenant who went the full eviction distance.

TENANT MOVE-OUT AND TURNOVER

If you have had to suffer through the entire eviction process, or at least start the process to remove a deadbeat tenant, you are excited about the steps that follow! The next steps are three-fold: inspect the property to assess any damage or rehab required, complete the appropriate repairs and/or rehab, market the property and find your next tenant! Let's cover each step in further detail.

Inspect the property to assess any damage or rehab. Just like any tenant turnover process, a good landlord conducts a proper move-out assessment to determine what level of damages have occurred, looking through any items left behind to see what's worth keeping vs dumping, then finally any other improvement opportunities that could result in additional rental income. Normally, you are looking for items to deduct from the security deposit. In the case of eviction, the security deposit has long been forfeited to cover missed rent, legal fees, damages and repairs. The list could be very long. What is left behind with an eviction is typically rough, though you may find some surprise items worth keeping or selling. I have found tools, a brand-new outdoor folding chair, an awesome longhorn skull with horns, and a brand-new Christmas train set. It is important to be thorough during the damage assessment to know exactly which repairs need completed and in which priority. Next, do an assessment of improvements that would be made to the property that could attract better tenants and higher gross rents. I recommend always doing this step, especially if you haven't done it before with this particular property. Most times, there will be an opportunity to enhance the property and subsequently increase the rent as a result. Typically, when I purchase a rent-ready property or one with inherited tenants, I don't enhance those right away. I get them rented ASAP or keep them rented to ensure immediate cash flow and profitability during the first year plus of ownership. Once the existing tenants move out, this is where I take the opportunity to upgrade. By this time, you should have acquired sufficient capital from cash flow to cover the upgrades that will result in higher rents, cash flow and capital. Did you notice the cycle? Upgrade for higher rents that provide more cash flow resulting in increased capital to build your rental real estate business.

This Happened to Me - Stuffed animal heaven

The very first rental property I purchased was a dream first rental. The young couple with a child we rented to seemed wonderful when we first rented to them. In fact, they were wonderful for well over a year and a half's time. It wasn't until later in that second year we had a late rent payment, then another, then a missed payment all together. Upon further investigation, we discovered the happy couple had separated and just the man was living in the property. They were splitting time with the child. Rent did come in once employment stabilized, but not for long. He went missing and so did the rent. After no communication for five weeks, we went into the property and found it abandoned. There were still some personal belongings, but nobody was living there. In talking with the neighbors, we heard some stories about him splitting in a hurry one day and never returning. I spoke with his employer who said he had been fired several weeks back. The stories included drug use and dealer issues. I did find some drug paraphernalia in the home during inspection to corroborate that story.

As we did a thorough review of the property, we noticed an extreme number of stuffed animals present throughout the home. In the child's room, they were everywhere. When I searched the basement, I found full boxes of them! Most of these stuffed animals were brand new and never played with. It was very unusual. I bet there were somewhere close to 400 of them inside the home. Now, each state requires a certain amount of time pass with ample opportunity for people to take their personal belongings before you can discard, keep or sell them. Yes, this even applies to deadbeats who don't pay rent. The time had passed in our state before we discarded his belongings. When it did, my kids naturally wanted a few stuffed animals, though we kept it very limited. All the extra, we donated to a local charity after giving some to the neighbor kids. A very peculiar finding, in this instance, and surely not our only story of interesting finds from evicted tenants.

Complete the appropriate repairs and/or rehab. Once you have identified the extent of the damage and prioritized repairs, it is time to get to work. The quicker you can complete the repairs, the quicker you can generate income by renting your property again. Repairs should be done to the extent necessary for your particular rental. For example, patching a drywall hole or paint section on a wall vs making a significant repair. Do what is necessary, safe and proper. Don't go overboard if it doesn't add value or provide a financial return. Another example: the toilet is broken. Replace it with the lower-priced $100 or on-sale $85 toilet vs buying a designer toilet worth $249. It's a toilet. It works. It's new. That's all you need. Don't go out of your way to add something you think is cool or that you'd want to have in your own home. This is a rental; remember that. Also remember that your tenants will never treat your property or care for it the way you would. You own it, not them. Think of it this way, they are borrowing it, in exchange for money. Most times when your kid 'borrows' something, you don't get it back in the same or better condition than when they borrowed said item. The same applies here, so keep it in mind. You are running a business, not a charity. Run your business well to ensure the most value out of the efforts put in. To summarize repairs, make those you need to make to confirm the property is safe and functions properly. There is no need to spend money or waste time on unnecessary repairs.

Next, complete whatever upgrades or rehabilitation you decided at the beginning would help drive additional rental revenues. Do not make upgrades that have no likely financial return. Just don't do it. For example, don't tear down a wall just because you think it will 'look better'. If 'look better' doesn't increase your financial return, just say no. If by upgrading the flooring, bathroom and kitchen will bring an additional $150-300 monthly rent, you are making a smart business decision. I often look for highly noticeable and mostly cosmetic improvements to drive up rental revenue. Look at finishes, paint, kitchen cabinetry and counters, flooring, bathroom vanity and sink, appliances, and perhaps adding a ceiling fan. Every tenant wants a nicer place to live. Most are willing to pay more to get it. So why not offer it to them and reap the benefits? In the end, you are aiming to make your financials 'look better' than just the unit itself.

Market the property and find your next tenant. I have already discussed much of this topic throughout the book and in most detail in Chapter Six. However, repetition and action are the keys to effective learning, so allow me to share those things with you again. The difference between marketing your property for rent post-eviction is that you have the opportunity to queue up your next potential tenant and draw interest in your property. A very worthwhile and successful method for future tenant prospecting is to build and develop relationships with existing tenants, ex-tenants, business owners, real estate professionals and housing organizations. This is essentially the equivalent of building a network, which it is, just for a different reason than most build networks. Business networks in the traditional sense can be made for various reasons, such as to find a new job opportunity, to find your next gig (music, comedy, clown, etc.), find your next real estate deal or even a significant other. In this particular instance, you are searching for your next tenant. The standard tenant search process is cumbersome and lengthy. It is my least favorite component to my rental real estate business, however, the most critical of them all! As explained in Chapter Five, finding a quality tenant that is willing to stay longer than a year is crucial to your success as a landlord. The marketing of a property to a wide audience, the subsequent filtering down of candidates, then ultimately completing the due diligence on your next tenant is challenging and unfun work.

When searching for new tenants after eviction, make sure to not make the same mistake twice. Evicting someone often translates into a bad business decision on your end. Not always true, though to some extent always a *little* true. The tenant you chose to live in your residence didn't work out. You as the business owner bear the responsibility of this decision. Learn from the poor decision and the situation in general and don't repeat the same mistake(s). In my time as a landlord, I've made my fair share of mistakes with tenant selection and being a bit too lax with my own standards. Trusting other people with this critical responsibility has proven to be a terribly poor business decision. Be sure you either have direct oversight of or take great responsibility of tenant selection in your business. If not, the next story could be yours!

What I learned from this awful situation was that regardless of program affiliation or promises given by said program representatives, I must not trust anyone to conduct thorough due diligence on my prospective tenants. I also learned to trust my gut and not offer any of my residences to anyone who does not qualify to my high standards of rental criteria. I have been burned enough times from this that I will never make that mistake again. The quality of tenants matters, so choose wisely. To summarize this section, find quality tenants, don't cut corners with due diligence and be sure to choose only the tenants that meet your rental criteria standards.

LET'S WRAP A BOW ON THIS CHAPTER

Congratulations, you've finished Chapter Ten and learned something new to improve your rental real estate business! The focus of this chapter is to realize when to cut your losses as a landlord. This means saying bye to deadbeat tenants who violate your lease agreement and give you headaches. Your job is not to babysit other adults and tolerate childish, unlawful behavior. Your job is to run an efficient and profitable business.

How eviction works and why it is your friend. Don't be scared of eviction. As a landlord, the eviction process can be your best friend when you need it. The eviction process is a safety net for landlords. It varies by state and it's important to know the process, then follow it sequentially to ensure a smooth process without delays.

When to say goodbye to deadbeats. There is absolutely no need to tolerate having deadbeats as tenants. No landlord is perfect, though when you make a poor tenant selection, or your once solid tenant takes a turn for the worse, say goodbye quickly.

The mean 'ole eviction process. The eviction process should be viewed as a necessary step to accomplish eventual good. The standard eviction process should be followed thoroughly to ensure the courts award you with the eviction paperwork and authority to remove the deadbeat tenant from your rental property!

Tenant move-out and turnover. You've successfully made it through the eviction process; now what? First, inspect the property to assess any damage or rehab required. Second, complete the appropriate repairs and/or rehab. Finally, market the property and find your next tenant. Learn from your mistakes in tenant selection and don't repeat those mistakes again.

ELEVEN

TO REPAIR, REPLACE OR LEAVE ALONE

I nvestopedia defines a business as "an organization or enterprising entity engaged in commercial, industrial, or professional activities." The term 'business' also refers to the organized efforts and activities of individuals to produce and sell goods and services for profit. The good that you provide in rental real estate is a place to live and/or store belongings. You offer this good in exchange for currency. Businesses don't magically operate and perform on their own. They require time, focused attention and real effort to succeed. If not, they likely will fail or never reach their potential. This chapter focuses on decisions you'll need to make that will help you sustain and grow your rental real estate business. Understanding what to repair, replace or leave alone can make significant and positive impacts in your business.

YOUR BUSINESS IS SUPPOSED TO GENERATE NET INCOME

Let's start this chapter with a reminder. You are doing this to make *money*! Chapter Six covered this critical point is detail. You are running a business and a business needs to have positive margins that generate *actual* income to you as the business owner. Otherwise, it's not a business, it's a hobby. Or if it is a business, you are not good at business! Keep this in mind as we progress through this chapter.

When analyzing repairs, think like a business owner. Creating a successful business often depends on your approach to managing expenses. In the rental business, the largest expense item is repairs. Most repairs are unavoidable and require attention. We'll cover that in a bit. However, think about it this way. When you go to purchase a new vehicle for your family, do you need the Porsche? Or, could you do just fine with the Toyota? We all know the answer. You don't *need* the Porsche. But it's so cool! I can show off to my friends! It's a dream of mine! That's all fine and great, but it's by no means considered an investment. It is a big, expensive toy. It's a very expensive decision that does not generate income for you. It is purely an expense. Let's apply this concept to your rental real estate business.

Be very cost-conscious when deciding how to address repairs and property improvements in general. The ultimate goal should be *net income* (profit). Ask yourself this question: What is the best return on investment for this repair or improvement? If the repair is simply fixing what's broken, that is likely to be your best return on investment. If you have a 20-year-old refrigerator that's on its last leg, replacement is likely the answer. However, should you buy the $500 model or the $850 model? Ask yourself the following question to determine the answer before proceeding:

- Will the more expensive option bring me more rent, more tenant loyalty or attract higher quality tenants?

If the answer is no, go with the cheaper option. Why? Because as the business owner, there is *zero* benefit to purchasing the more expensive model. Buying more expensive stuff because of quality could be a consideration in certain circumstances, but not here. Go with the cheaper option that keeps more money in your pocket and still brings in the same tangible benefits as the more expensive option. It also solves the existing problem and is likely to satisfy your tenants. I will put a disclaimer on this statement though. If you rent higher-end units, you have a different business model with a different target market of prospective tenants. In each case, assess your business model and make decisions that apply best.

Let's do a quick return on investment (ROI) analysis for a repair and an improvement.

Repair Scenario ROI: 10-year-old refrigerator

Repair Description	Repair Costs
Appliance repair visit	$75
Parts	$80
Labor	$150
Total	$305
Cost of new refrigerator	$600
Savings	$295

In this scenario, the repair is cheaper than the replacement. However, if a second repair is required within one to two years, the return on investment is now negative. Conduct a quick assessment of repair vs replace. If you have to hire an appliance repairman more than once for an appliance, you are likely better off replacing the appliance. Also, it's a hassle fixing broken appliances! Generally, if an appliance is over 10 years old, I will opt to replace it because the likelihood of additional repairs is high.

Improvement Scenario ROI: New flooring, bathroom & kitchen upgrades

Upgrade Description	Upgrade Costs	Current Monthly Rent	Monthly Upgrade Rent
New laminate flooring	$1,750	$900	$1,050
New kitchen sink/faucet	$250	Current Annual Rent	Annual Upgrade Rent
New bathroom vanity/sink	$250	$10,800	$12,600
New bathroom mirror	$50	One Year ROI	Two Year ROI
Refresh paint	$500	$1,800	$3,600
Total	$2,800		
Break-Even Timeframe			19 months

In this scenario, you are completing some upgrades that cost money upfront with the expectation that you will recoup those costs over time and then improve net income over time. The rent before upgrades is $900 and the rent after upgrades will be $1,050. The total upgrade costs are $2,800. With the new after-upgrade rents of $1,050, the monthly cash flow increase is $150. After one year, the ROI is $1,800, which is still negative $1,000 from the total upgrade cost. After two years, the ROI is $3,600, which is $800 in surplus net income. The break-even timeframe of the upgrades is 19 months. Each dollar of additional revenue after 19 months goes straight to the bottom line! I would pull the trigger on this upgrade without hesitation.

WHAT TO REPAIR OR REPLACE IN EVERY RENTAL PROPERTY

If somebody would have magically shared this section of best practices with me at the beginning of my real estate journey, I would have been much better off. Most everything I studied was about finding and acquiring rental properties, sprinkling in a little about tenant management. There wasn't much about repairs and best practices for how to go about fixing stuff! This is why I am sharing my learnings with you in this book, so you can avoid the same situations I dealt with, forcing me to scratch and claw my way through. It's important to start with the general best practice rules for repairs. I'll cover them in the following order: leave alone, repair and replace.

Leave alone. If something doesn't need to be repaired or replaced, then leave it alone. Well, what does that mean? It means, if something isn't broken, the tenants aren't complaining or repairing/replacing it won't help your business, then you leave it alone! I have this problem in my personal home with replacing things that are in perfectly fine order and look good as-is. I will add shiplap, repaint the walls or build a new custom built-in. Yes, they are great to have and certainly look better, but they don't truly add much value to my home. It's more for me and my preferences. With a rental property, resist the same urges. You will spend money that will never return anything for you.

This Happened to Me – Our first rental upgrade

I mentioned my business partner earlier in the book. We share ownership and management responsibility with most of my rental portfolio. He and I are quite different when it comes to money. I am more aggressive, while he tends to be more conservative. We balance each other out quite well. While I am more eager to repair and replace things, he is quick to remind me that minimal improvements and fixes are sometimes best.

With the purchase of our first rental property, I got really excited and with very little money in the bank, decided to make some landscape upgrades outside. They weren't extravagant, though I did want to do more than what we ended up doing. I bought some border wall blocks, plants, mulch and a few other things. We spent a day doing the work, which included ripping out a tree that was way too close to the foundation. My business partner helped me see that minimal upgrades were the way to go and that renters likely wouldn't A) care about these minor upgrades, B) wouldn't take care of them or C) both! I convinced him to do some minor upgrades anyways and he reluctantly agreed. It cost maybe $250 in total but an entire day of labor and wasted time when we could have been finding our first tenants!

Ultimately, the upgrades didn't make much of a difference. Nobody even noticed (to be honest) except me. It didn't garner any extra rent. It was a waste of time and resources. Now the good news is we didn't spend a fortune in this scenario, though I did learn quite a bit. Not everything needs to be fixed, replaced or upgraded. In fact, most times a quick clean up job is all that's required.

Repair. With rental properties, I recommend repairing before replacing in *most* circumstances. If it is salvageable, go for the repair first. Definitely repair broken doors, windows and flooring vs leaving it in a dilapidated state. Tenants don't want to live in a property where things are broken and dirty. This should be your rule of thumb: if it's broken and fixable, repair it! However, if the repair is close to the same price as the replacement cost, or the repair will only get you another six months before you'll have to replace it anyways, consider the upgrade.

This Happened to Me – The holey doors

Somehow, someway, many of my tenants have put holes in interior doors. Use your imagination to come up with how that may happen. One tenant left holes in four different doors throughout the house. These were interior doors to bedrooms and bathrooms. The cost to replace each broken door was $150, including materials, installation and paint. The cost to repair the holes was just $50. Our repairman would patch the door and then repaint it. To replace them all it was $600. To repair them all it was $200. The upside for replacement? Zero. We decided to repair the doors and save $400 to the bottom line. The reason for zero upside on the replacement is that rooms *should* have doors and doors are not something tenants will pay extra rent for having. In many cases, it is best to just repair what's broken.

Replace. As mentioned above, if it is salvageable, go for the repair first. Let's talk replacement for the times when it doesn't make sense to repair. Replacement comes in two forms: like for like or an upgrade. If the replacement of equal or lesser value is appropriate, go for it. If an upgrade will allow you to charge more rent and the return on investment is solid, go for it. I prefer to upgrade on items that will bring in more revenue and attract better tenants. I don't care as much about the top-of-the-line water heater. A new, quality water heater is sufficient. A refrigerator or countertop may be a different story. The rule of thumb here is replace/upgrade if it is similar in pricing to the repair or will allow you to bring in more rental revenue. Replacing a dinky, old refrigerator with a new one can help attract better tenants and also justify charging more in rent. However, refrigerators can cost anywhere from $500 - $5,000. Choose wisely based on the overall quality of your rental property and the market of tenants available. The other component to this worth remembering is long-term valuation. If the upgrade improves the long-term valuation of the property, it should also be a factor in your decision-making criteria.

This Happened to Me – The new window treatments & doors

Once upon a time, one of our rental properties was left in disarray by a tenant. Oh wait, this isn't a fairy tale, it happens often! The window treatments, or blinds, were all broken and the doors, both exterior and interior were beat to hell with holes in many of them. We had planned all along to complete some upgrades in the kitchen and bathroom when this tenant vacated. Since we were upgrading the property, we decided to make sure the whole place appeared new and fresh vs just here and there. That can be a turn off to prospective tenants willing to pay more in rent for a higher quality, newer-looking unit. So, we pulled the trigger and replaced the doors with a uniform look. Then we upgraded all the window blinds with a faux white wood finish that was appealing and not easily breakable. In this case, it made sense. It also paid off. We turned the unit and charged an additional $200 in monthly rent, which is $2,400 additional revenue each year!

It's important to understand the options before you find yourself in a repair/replace situation. Following the above best practices will allow you to make more sage decisions in your rental real estate business. Now we will cover some of the most common items that require a decision to repair, replace or leave alone.

Flooring. If the floor can be repaired, repair it. Flooring is a major expense. Carpets can many times be cleaned professionally. Hardwood floors can be refinished vs a complete replacement, which can be a quality and significantly cheaper expense. When you must replace flooring, I highly recommend laminate faux-wood (vinyl) flooring material. The reasons are fair pricing, good quality and long-term durability. They are great for protection against kids and pets. Finally, they look great!

Walls. Most walls can and should be patched, cleaned or painted. If the walls are filthy and haven't had a fresh coat of paint in some time, go for the fresh paint. This makes a significant difference to prospective tenants. Most holes in walls can be patched if caused by the tenants. Wall damage from water and fire will require more serious repairs.

Doors. Quality, functioning doors are important to any property. Holes in doors can usually be patched and painted. If the door is still fully functional, go for the repair first. If the door is falling off its hinges and a repair isn't going to last long, replace it. If the door casing is busted, repair it quickly to save the door from becoming damaged as well.

Kitchen countertops. The kitchen is an area worth investing in. Countertops take up significant real estate in a kitchen and are a point of attraction or a deterrent depending on looks and quality. If your kitchen countertops are dilapidated, consider replacing them. Countertops can be refinished, though long-term viability for a refinish isn't great. Consider an upgrade to a newer, more aesthetically pleasing finish. There is no need to go marble here, but a nice faux granite countertop or even a less expensive granite option could attract more tenants and allow you to increase rents.

Cabinets. Cabinets are typically in the kitchen, bathroom and laundry spaces of a property. The area worth focusing is the kitchen. As stated above, the kitchen in general should be an area of focus for upgrades because they can improve rents and long-term equity. Kitchen cabinets can be an easy upgrade. Replacing them is expensive, so only do this if necessary. Some other options are fresh paint, adding pulls/knobs to the doors and drawers or replacing the cabinet doors vs the entire cabinet. Quality and attractive kitchen cabinets along with countertops will only help your rental real estate business.

Bathroom vanity. Bathrooms are the other area of focus where investment often pays for itself. Bathroom vanities can go a long way in refreshing a bathroom's overall condition. An existing vanity can be refreshed by replacing the sink/faucet and adding some fresh paint. Many times, there are discounts on bathroom vanities at big-box hardware stores. This is an upgrade of choice because it is very inexpensive and adds to the overall value of the property for both tenant attraction and property value.

Windows. If a window is cracked or broken, it needs to be fixed promptly. Most windows cannot be repaired in the typical sense; they are usually replaced with a new window. Once the glass is damaged, it is challenging to match, though can be done. My handyman knows a local glass specialist who has been able to fix broken windows for me, which has saved money on the repairs. If the lock or seal is the issue, that can likely be repaired. Go for the best option that provides a quality finished product.

Faucets. New, clean faucets are attractive and will attract better tenants. Faucets, in general, are not overly expensive. If the faucet is in good aesthetic condition and can be repaired, fix it. If the faucet is older and dilapidated, go for the replacement. There isn't a need to buy a top-of-the-line model. Go for a new model that is of good quality and average price.

Roof. Replacing a roof is a major expense. Repairing a roof can also be a significant hassle. Most insurance plans cover the repair or complete replacement of a roof once the deductible is covered if the roof was damaged from hail or high winds. I recommend consulting your insurance agent before making a decision here. Also, if there is roof damage of any kind, address it immediately as any delay could result in further damages to the property (which can be very costly).

Electrical. When fixing electrical, be sure to use a licensed electrician who knows what they are doing. A cheap or faulty repair can not only be damaging, but in extreme cases, deadly! Many electrical issues, such as outlets not working, can be fixed rather easily and at little expense. Larger issues, such as breaker boxes, 220-volt additions and general wire problems require a more focused effort to be completed by a licensed electrician.

This Happened to Me – The wires could ignite at any time!

One of my single-family home rentals was going through a turnover transition. I had cleaners in and did some minor repairs. Once the new tenant moved in, she reported some flickering of a few lights throughout the house. I sent my repairman over to assess the situation and he was unable to identify the core problem. He assumed it was more than a minor repair, so we called a licensed electrician to conduct a more thorough assessment. He got back to me the same day with some scary news. He said the entire house was full of exposed, faulty wiring that could result in the house catching on fire! He actually said he was surprised there hadn't been an accident yet. I was mortified. This was shocking news and a first for me. I figured the repair damage would be significant, though I had no idea just how significant. I was quoted over $10,000 with the final cost being $11,000. The *entire house* had to be rewired. New GFCI outlets had to be added. A new breaker box was installed and all of the faulty wiring removed. The result was a major financial loss on that property for the year. The positive news is that the electrical is safe and updated for the long-term. Oh, and I don't have to fear the place will catch fire anymore!

Foundation. Foundation repairs are major, regardless of condition. Additional support can be on the lower end of expense and still cost $5,000. I've recently had to do two significant foundation repairs totaling $17,000 and $24,000. Rarely are they inexpensive. Though they are always essential. Not repairing a damaged and shifting foundation can result in catastrophic consequences. It will not improve your home value or attract better tenants, but it is still a must-do due to safety concerns and to prevent further damage to the property.

Exterior stucco/siding/brick. Most exterior siding can be repaired when damaged. Replacing the exterior of a property can be very expensive. Siding can be replaced. Stucco can be patched. Brick can be replaced and reinforced. I recommend repair first. Full replacement should only be required if the property is truly in remodel shape.

Water Heater. A water heater won't bring any additional value to your property. That being said, the first option should always be to repair it. Most repairs will be less than $200. A new unit plus installation is likely going to cost around $1,000. I recently replaced a water heater that needed a $300 repair and was also eleven years old. It wasn't going to last much longer and could have required another repair within a year, so I opted to replace it.

Furnace. Similar to the water heater, a furnace needs to function, though it will not attract better tenants. A non-functioning furnace will *detract* tenants though! Furnaces are known to last 20 or more years. Conduct proper maintenance and go for the repair first. Furnace replacements are expensive, and can surpass $10,000 in overall expense.

Toilet. Toilets need to function, bottom (no pun intended!) line. Most toilet issues can be found inside the tank where the valve assembly is located. Repairs here should be done first and are inexpensive. A toilet that is old, crusty, missing its finish, etc. should be replaced. Toilets are not a major expense. Most people can manage this repair themselves in limited time. They are also a nice little upgrade for tenants and an inexpensive way to improve the look of your bathroom(s).

Plumbing. This area is of utmost importance. Plumbing issues can ruin your business. Address them speedily and *don't* go cheap. Yes, repair existing lines where a repair can fix the issue. Replace everything else. Be sure the plumbing used is of high material quality and completed by a licensed professional. Poor plumbing repairs can be detrimental and result in worse long-term issues that could displace a tenant and cause foundation damage.

Kitchen appliance. Kitchen appliances are not cheap, yet they are of importance to all people. If your refrigerator is 20 years old and needs a repair, go for the new one. Prospective and existing tenants will be much more receptive than if you opt to fix a dumpy fridge or range. I never buy a top-tier appliance for my properties, though I do like to buy a new, functional and solid quality appliance that both looks good and functions well. Kitchen appliances also contribute to the overall property value.

Bathtub. Bathtubs are fairly durable and last many years. If a bathtub has a chip or has faded over time, there are repair solutions. A bathtub can be resurfaced for less than $200 in most cases and look nearly new. Go the repair route first on bathtubs, because replacing them is expensive and unlikely to return much for you. Consult a professional to determine your options, though I have resurfaced more than one bathtub successfully without having to replace it.

Exterior fencing. Exterior fencing should be repaired first. A few new fence boards or a replacement post can salvage an existing fence. New stain and protectant can prolong the life of your fence. A fence may be worth replacing if it is destroyed in several sections and the material is unsightly (without a reasonable option for reparation). When replacing a fence and building a new one, I recommend a low-maintenance material. Cheap, cedar planks require maintenance over time.

Concrete. I face this issue often in Colorado, where we have snowy, cold temperatures in the winter. This often creates shifts in the soil, which is mostly made up of clay. Sidewalks, patios, walkways and stairs all deteriorate over time. If the problem area is small, a patch is doable. A pothole can be filled. However, when stairs and walkways begin to crumble, the best practice is to rip out the old and replace with the new. Safety is the first priority with concrete. Be sure your property is safe and secure above all else.

Railings. Another safety concern are railings. Primarily the handrails that go up and down stairs. If a railing is loose or broken, this is a safety hazard. Most times, a repair is plausible. If the railing is beyond reasonable repair, be sure to act quickly and replace the railing to avoid more serious safety concerns.

This list covers most everything within a rental property that you'll need to repair, replace or leave alone. However, it is not all inclusive. Consider the above recommendations as guidelines vs gospel. Each and every repair situation is unique. Consult a professional and leverage your own personal experience in making repair, replace or leave-alone decisions in your rental real estate business. Repair expenses can add up and can be a major detriment to your business. The next section reviews what you can do to avoid some of those costly repairs.

AVOIDING CATASTROPHIC REPAIRS

Repair costs are typically the largest single expense in a rental real estate business. Eliminating or minimizing them where possible can be a major boon to your bottom line. It can also reduce stress and headaches. Many repairs are essential, though not every repair must happen immediately. Major repairs can be forecasted, planned for and even completely avoided with some attention to detail. If it reaches the point of 'catastrophic', there is a decent chance it was avoidable. Knowing what to look for and how to go about looking are important details this section will cover. Each of the following are proven methods to reduce, delay or completely avoid costly repairs.

Complete a pre-purchase home inspection. I always recommend having a home inspection done before you purchase a property, regardless of whether or not you purchase the home 'as-is'. A home inspection completed by a certified home inspector will help you understand whether you will have likely repairs and the extent of those repairs. Some of them may be worth walking away from the deal and that's alright. In other cases, an inspection can identify the likelihood of other repairs down the line, near or long-term. For example, an older furnace that has a higher probability of being replaced within a couple of years could cost you between $2,000 and $10,000. A weathered roof that is recommended for replacement could be $7,500 - $15,000. Damage or severe wear to a main sewer line could cost between $4,000 and $10,000. The bottom line here, get an inspection to save on costly repairs or at least understand what repairs to expect in the future.

Perform regular inspections. Performing regular inspections will be informative and help you understand what condition your rental property is in. Ongoing inspections can help prevent repairs altogether by identifying areas of concern or notify you of something that, if not addressed quickly, *could* result in a major repair. You may be asking how often inspections should be done. The answer is: it depends. Routine inspections are recommended. As a general practice, twice a year is sufficient. However, quarterly may be warranted if that makes you feel more comfortable. I say it depends because some trouble tenants may require a more frequent inspection cadence. Regular inspections let tenants know that you care about your property and that they should abide by the rental lease agreement. It also keeps them on their toes because you could show up at any time. Twenty-four-hour notice is typically required before you can inspect a property, per law. However, if there is an emergency repair or other extreme concern, you may possibly enter the residence with less notice or no notice. Be sure to check local landlord laws to ensure you are in compliance. Routine inspections are also a great excuse to 'checkup' on tenants that concern you. The chances of tenants totally destroying your property decrease by implementing these routine inspections in your business.

Preventative maintenance. Similar to an automobile, preventative maintenance prevents major repairs in the future. Yes, it is an additional cost. Though the cost is minor and worth it in terms of long-term viability. Preventative maintenance can also help to prolong the lifetime of appliances, fixtures and other things, which significantly reduces necessary repair costs. The simplest and most basic example of this is replacing the furnace filter in each property when expected to. The cost is minimal and the benefits lasting.

Here is a list of preventative maintenance recommendations for landlords to follow:

- Check for leaks.
- Repaint your property.
- Replace filters in the air conditioner and furnace.
- Patch cracks in ceilings or drywall.
- Test smoke and carbon monoxide detectors.
- Look for mold.
- Keep your electrical system updated.
- Check for leaks or other water damage.
- Refresh shower caulk and grout.
- Spray for pests.
- Inspect roof and clean gutters.

- Check for other activity that violates the lease agreement.

Ideally, landlords should create a system or checklist to conduct an inspection on each property and check to see where preventative maintenance may be necessary. Once per-year per-door is typically sufficient, though some items require more frequent attention (such as replacing the furnace filter). Make this a regular part of your rental business. The last item on the list is more generalized, though applies here too. It's best to identify proactively when a tenant is violating the lease agreement than to have the FBI busting down your front door because your tenant has been running an illegal operation from your property. Something similar *might* have happened to me...

This Happened to Me – The FBI raid

Our first property as a partnership has served as a lesson in do's and don'ts in rental real estate. One of those is around tenant selection. We had limited initial interest from prospective tenants in the property, primarily due to the time of year. Given the fact that we were super anxious about renting out the property, we extended the property to an older, rougher, unmarried couple. For a while, things went just fine. In fact, including the additional monthly rent coming in for two pets, we were cash flowing quite well. This lasted about a year, then a few small issues arose here and there. Strange amounts of "beware of dog" signs were posted on the property, including most windows. The yard was less cared for. More junk began appearing out back and they became a bit less responsive. Despite these issues, the rent always came in. Then something changed. Rent was late, so we contacted them to inquire why. No response. This lasted for over a week before we finally heard from a neighbor across the street. There was an incident at the property and our tenant was going to jail for a long time. Well, *that's news!* Apparently, this guy had been under FBI surveillance for a year.

The story goes: when the stepfather of our tenant passed away, our tenant buried his body in the guy's own backyard in the state he previously resided, instead of reporting his death. He did this to collect veteran's and social security checks as if his stepfather was still alive! And yep, he was absolutely paying us rent with that money. We had verified the money coming into his bank account and the source. What he didn't disclose was this wasn't his money. It was his stepfather's. We would have no way of knowing this and he didn't have a criminal record. Smooth...or so he thought. In the end, the FBI raided the property one morning, gaining access to the home by breaking the kitchen window and eventually hauling our tenant off to jail. He *did* go to prison for a very long time. Though, the girlfriend eventually convinced us she could cover rent ongoing. This lasted three months before money started drying up and, in the end, we had to remove her from the property along with a thousand lies and headaches. Part of her plan to pay rent was to sell her boyfriend's gun collection to random strangers. She even tried to sell me a handgun! Oh my, the crazy things tenants do to get by.

Respond quickly to repairs. When a tenant requests maintenance or repairs, get them done as quickly as possible. This prevents issues from escalating into catastrophes (which of course saves money). If a tenant calls or sends a message notifying you of a repair that sounds like it has any possibility of escalating, act immediately. For example, if they mention the ceiling looks damp, this could indicate a roof leak and there is likely damage caused over time that could rot out joists, bring the ceiling down, and even cause mold growth. The first sign of a water issue, wood rot or decay, discolored walls or ceilings or backed up drains could be a sign of something much worse.

Avoidance of costly repairs is simply staying on top of property maintenance and keeping tenants in line. Keeping track of the little things in order to avoid costly repairs down the road is a worthy exercise. Create a maintenance schedule, like those built into most cars these days, to ensure you aren't negligent.

KEEPING REPAIR COSTS LOW

Whether you are on a tight budget or not, keeping repair costs low should be a focus in your rental real estate business. Each and every dollar spent toward a repair is then removed from your bottom-line profit. Many repairs are essential and often they are expensive, however they don't need to be detrimental to your business. I'll share with you some tips for keeping repair costs low to maximize your bottom-line profit.

Shop around for repairs. If you have to hire a tradesman, such as a plumber or electrician, and you call one of the generalized repair chain companies, expect a higher bill. The tradesman are affiliates of the company that are paid hourly and the rest of the money goes to the 'owner'. I recommend finding a local repairman who works for themselves. You are much more likely to find a more reasonably-priced tradesman who operates their own shop. I have saved over 60% on the exact same repair by doing this.

Use a discount credit card or rewards card. Some home improvement stores and other retailers offer a discount for credit card holders. If this is an option for you, it's a great way to both build credit and save on each purchase, for example 5%. There are often other times when that can be 10% for cardholders only. This can add up to significant savings over time. There are also reward credit cards that give 1-5% cash back on everyday purchases. Using the rewards cards to purchase repair supplies, just as the discount credit cards can add up to good cash back over time.

Buy second-hand materials. I'd bet every reader of this book has seen the popular HGTV television show, "Fixer Upper", based in Waco, TX. Chip and Joanna Gaines are well known for their ability to find and purchase second-hand materials and finishes that they use for their home renovations. Buying new is expensive, yet many times unavoidable. Where possible, shop around. There are in-person and online options for finding second-hand materials and finishes. Flea markets, antique shops and Facebook marketplace are a few options. The Habitat for Humanity is also a fantastic place to search.

Restore antiques or relics. New doesn't have to be *brand new*. Restoring antiques and relics is a major business in today's design world. Antiques and relics in many cases provide something most modern pieces don't...character! These pieces, when restored, can make a major difference in both appeal and cost. In a rental property, the extent to which you take this route is up to your discretion and should be economical. Some antiques and relics to look for in a rental property are doors, light fixtures, knobs, handles, shelving, furniture (if furnished), counter tops, vanities, kitchen and bathroom décor.

Buy from salvage yards. Salvage yards are a great place to find usable materials and furniture at basement prices. Expect to have some rehab work to complete on much of what you buy from a salvage yard, though the finished product could be more than worth the effort. I also recommend encouraging your handyman to find parts from salvage yards. We've had some luck finding fence pieces, doors and more.

Do it yourself. Everyone is watching HGTV or the DIY Network these days. My wife and I are both huge fans of several of their programs. We like to think we are as cute and funny as Chip and Joanna from Fixer Upper! There are countless shows about doing it yourself and saving lots of money. Keep in mind, those people are professionals. Are you? It's possible. I would determine whether you have the skills and the time to do the job before you commit to doing it yourself. If it makes sense, by all means, this is a great way to save money and get the job done quickly. However, if you don't have the skills, tools or time, it's best to hire the work out to someone that does.

Have a go-to handyman you trust. I saved the best for last here. The handyman is part of your 'core four'. Having a reliable and trustworthy individual who can fix almost everything is a significant advantage. This person should be able to either get the work done themselves or be connected with those specialists who can. This takes a huge amount of stress off your plate. Our handyman goes above and beyond, saving us on each repair because of his connections in town. These connections have almost always saved us money! They have also saved us a spot in the front of the line for roll-away dumpsters, materials, discounts and more. Invest here, you'll thank me later.

HOW TO UPGRADE ON THE CHEAP AND STILL INCREASE RENT

Upgrading your property doesn't necessarily mean you must spend many thousands of dollars to get the job done. There are various inexpensive upgrades you can make to do this successfully. Keeping more of your hard-earned money is the objective. Let's talk about a few upgrades you can do on the cheap together.

Paint. Painting is an affordable and very effective home improvement opportunity. There is no need to purchase the premium paints for your rental property. Most paint brands will do just fine. Go with neutral-tone colors to remain in style longer. It is preferred to go with lighter colors to make the space feel larger. Stay away from dark or splashy colors in your rental. Go with a semi-gloss sheen so the walls can be easily cleaned. Paint is something that can be done yourself or hired out. I don't pay top of the line painters for my properties, unless the job is a big one. This doesn't mean I hire just anybody. A low-quality paint job has the opposite effect you are targeting. Be sure the paint job itself is of good quality, regardless of who you hire to do the actual work.

This Happened to Me – The handyman paint job

My primary handyman can do most everything. *Most* is the key word in that phrase. He can replace a roof, excavate and fix/replace a broken sewer line, upgrade flooring, replace a water heater and so many more challenging repairs. Painting, however, is a challenge for him. I've used him for paint several times because he is a one-stop shop for most everything. Though I was never happy with the quality of his paint work. He did a satisfactory job with walls until it came to lines, corners and ceilings. He would not use paint tape and it was obvious. He would paint the wall color onto the ceiling about a solid inch around each side, with no sharp line, and he thought this looked good! He clearly didn't have very steady painting hands either. As someone who has painted many walls and pieces of furniture in my own homes and has OCD tendencies with labor finishes, this was not acceptable to me. I called it out on numerous occasions and he would justify his approach with random reasons that I did not agree with. I dealt with it for a while, though I was overpaying for his paint work and was not happy with it.

Over the past year, I've tested out other painters. I even used a couple that are tenants of mine who were out of work and in need of odd jobs. I gave them a shot and they did a great job with paint. In fact, they did a better job than my handyman, for about 60% of the price tag. I have used them a few times after and now believe they could be my new interior paint crew, at least in the short term. My lesson learned here was to not accept below standard paint work and to find someone that is reliable, affordable and of quality.

Make minor repairs. Minor repairs may seem insignificant, but they can make a *big* difference. A prospective tenant will look at these things when they are deciding whether to choose your place as a potential rental. The following repairs do make a difference and don't cost much:

- Leaky faucets or tubs
- Old window blinds
- Outdated lightbulbs
- Damaged light fixtures
- Worn out cabinet hardware

- Running toilets
- Paint touch up
- Fix/replace broken toilet lever
- Fix a leaky kitchen/bathroom pipe
- Patch small holes in drywall
- Fix a broken light switch
- Dirty carpets

These inexpensive repairs will make your tenant feel more comfortable renting from you. Depending on the extent of the repairs, potential costs can range from $10 - $250.

Deep clean. Want to scare prospective tenants away from your rental property? Leave it dirty. It's amazing what a deep clean can do. Hire a professional cleaning service to turn your rental property. Be sure to clean the floors, walls, baseboards, refrigerator, oven (inside and out), other appliances, toilets, inside cabinetry, window tracks, bathtub, shower, doors, handles, light covers, etc. Conduct a deep clean and impress prospective tenants.

This Happened to Me – Dirty walls and dusty floors!

I had a tenant that was moving out who assured me that the property would be totally clean and cleared out. I had posted the property for rent earlier in the week and had scheduled appointments for Saturday morning. When I arrived for the move-out walk-through, I was disappointed with what I discovered. The place was mostly clear, however, there was still an old couch in the living room, dust everywhere and nothing was cleaned well. In fact, the walls were smudged an unsightly color in various spots, a few lightbulbs were missing and some blinds were broken/missing. I literally had 15 minutes to transition before prospective tenants were arriving. Unfortunately, this was one of my better properties that I'd hoped to increase the rent on. The applications I received that day were not my favorite and there were several people who walked away without applying because of the condition of the property who could have been great fits.

I hired a professional cleaning service and had the place cleaned up real nice the very next day. I showed the property one more time and attracted great prospective tenants, had three times the paid applications submitted and found a great tenant for the property!

I learned several lessons from this experience. Always have the property inspected and cleaned *before* the day of showings. Don't trust your tenants. Not trying to be mean, but in the end, *you*, as a landlord, are responsible for your own property's condition. There is nobody to blame but yourself. Finally, I learned to be more intentional and proactive with move-out expectations and procedures from that point on. It has served me very well. Let's continue with the cheap upgrade options.

Install a backsplash. A backsplash in kitchens and bathrooms is not only aesthetically pleasing, it also protects your walls! This upgrade is very inexpensive, but goes a long way in attracting the best tenants. Keep the color and style neutral so it will be attractive for longer. Keep the backsplash simple. There is no need to go all the way to the ceiling when 10-12 inches will have the same effect on prospective tenants.

Replace doors. Consider replacing interior doors, which are inexpensive, to a more attractive style that is durable and safe. I like to keep my interior doors uniform. The front door should also be in good shape. It is the first thing a prospective tenant will see when they come to view your rental property. The appearance of doors can add to or take away from the overall look and feel of the premise and even make it more difficult to get the rent you deserve.

Upgrade finish hardware. If you replace doors, hardware upgrades must follow. Finish hardware can be door hinges, cabinet knobs/pulls, door handles, towel racks and more. Go for a neutral finish here. Satin/nickel is typically safe. Upgrading finish hardware has a major aesthetic impact and the expense is not outrageous.

Replace the trim. Another large square footage item is the interior trim of a property. A clean, modern and well-constructed trim is appealing to prospective tenants. Given that interior trim is present in every room of your property, prospective tenants will take notice. If the trim is modern and well-constructed, try cleaning it first. If this doesn't get it done, a fresh coat or two of paint is a great option. Lastly, if the trim is a liability, go for the replacement. The cost is minimal with a high level of impact.

These are just a few of the upgrades you can make that are both inexpensive and return actual results in rental revenue. There are other options available. Do what makes sense in each property.

WHERE UPGRADES ARE WORTH SPENDING THE MONEY

Not all upgrades are created equal. There are an infinite number of things you can upgrade in your rental property. Not all of them matter to most people. In fact, most of them don't matter to most people. I believe there are four key areas to focus improvement dollars on to get the highest and best return on investment: paint, kitchen, bathrooms and flooring. In every circumstance, high quality finishes in each of these areas will have a positive impact in your business.

Paint. Having a nice paint job can be the sole differentiator between someone wanting to rent your property or not. Paint is in every room of the property, so if it's ugly, it will remind people in every room. If the current paint job looks messy and unprofessional, this sends a negative signal to your tenants about how you maintain your properties. Is every room painted a different, uncoordinated color? This also sends a poor signal. Do the colors of paint chosen scare people away or invite them into the home to relax? This makes a major difference. Paint is all about the *feeling* it gives people when they walk in the door. It shouldn't be the focal point, but it also shouldn't be a reason people look elsewhere. This is the simplest of the four fixes and definitely worth the money. Now, this doesn't mean you have to pay a fancy paint guy or buy the most expensive paint for sale at Sherwin Williams. Think like a business owner and go for affordable quality every time. If your painter can't paint edges or paint a wall evenly, you need to replace them. Middle-grade paint is more than suitable for a rental property. Don't waste your time paying extra for the highest-graded paint that won't be more than marginally better and adds no extra value to rent.

Kitchen. Everybody likes a clean, attractive and stylish kitchen! This doesn't mean you rip everything up and start over. Rehab where possible before replacing something. Create a fresh, clean and appealing kitchen. Paint the kitchen walls a neutral, yet welcoming color. Paint the cabinets white (where possible) to open the space up. Add a backsplash. As I mentioned before, this upgrade is relatively inexpensive, yet adds quite an appeal. Replace the kitchen finish hardware, such as the cabinet pulls and knobs. Consider replacing the faucet and light fixtures to add to the ambiance. Update the kitchen flooring. Add a roll-away kitchen island for additional counter and storage space. Upgrade the appliances if needed. These are all places to start looking. Not all of them must be done in every kitchen. Inspect carefully and upgrade where it makes sense. If you can achieve by having a clean, attractive and stylish kitchen, you've been successful.

Bathrooms. Similar to wanting a clean and attractive kitchen, people want the same for their bathrooms. Much less expensive than upgrading a kitchen, bathroom improvements can go a long way in attracting the best tenants and top dollar for your rental property. The areas to focus on are wall paint, flooring, vanity, shower tile, toilet, sink, faucet and shower head. Choose lighter-toned paint as this will help the space feel larger and more inviting. Consider lighter-colored flooring and shower tile as well for the same effect. Shower heads, sinks, faucets and vanities are not expensive upgrades, though they can make a big impact. Most bathroom tiles and flooring can be inexpensive. There is no need to choose a top-quality, expensive finish when the cheaper model still looks great and is serviceable.

Flooring. The floors people walk on matter more than most other areas of the home. The reason? It takes up the entire livable square footage of a property. It's everywhere and is unavoidable. If your unavoidable flooring is unavoidably terrible to look at, it will turn people away. There is no need to get crazy here and lay marble tile or the most expensive hardwood flooring down. If an upgrade is required or badly needed, upgrade your flooring. The return on investment is immediate and long-lasting. Laminate wood floors are extremely popular amongst landlords because of the clean/stylish look, the quality, the durability and the price. They are also very pet and child resistant!

Remember: this isn't the home you live in. It is a rental property. As such it's important to remember it won't be treated with the same respect as if you lived there. This means that as a landlord, you shouldn't overdo upgrades or renovations. Expect damage and poor treatment of your properties. Further reasons to collect a higher security deposit and protect your investment (literally).

Here are some low-budget renovations for your rental property that attract quality tenants and top-dollar in rent:

1. Replace cabinet doors
2. A fresh coat of paint
3. Bathroom vanity
4. Fix the holes yourself
5. Hiring low-cost painters
6. New cabinet handles

7. Resurface cabinets
8. Replace appliances
9. Add a rolling kitchen island
10. Attractive faucets
11. Finish the garage
12. Electrical switches/plates
13. Upgrade flooring
14. Modern light fixtures
15. Landscape
16. Granite countertops
17. Replace doors
18. Pressure wash
19. Add backsplashes
20. Crown molding
21. Pay off your renovation with increased cash flow
22. Shop around

Each rental property is unique and requires a property-specific analysis to determine what upgrades or repairs should be made and when. Conduct the necessary analysis, determine what is needed and then take action!

LET'S WRAP A BOW ON THIS CHAPTER

Congratulations, you've finished Chapter Eleven and learned something new to improve your rental real estate business! The focus of this chapter is understanding whether to repair something, replace it or leave it alone. The answer varies according to the situation.

Your business is supposed to generate net income. Remember, this is a business, not a hobby. Your objective is to make money. When analyzing repairs, it's important to remember you are operating a business and businesses are supposed to make money.

What to repair or replace in every rental property. Avoid the situations where you lose money unnecessarily on repairs. Follow the guidance of what you should repair, replace or leave alone.

Avoiding catastrophic repairs. Repair costs are typically the largest single expense in a rental property business. Eliminating or minimizing them where possible can be a major boon to your bottom line. Some proven methods to avoid costly repairs are: complete a pre-purchase home inspection, perform regular inspections, preventative maintenance and respond quickly to repairs.

Keeping repair costs low. Keeping repair costs low should be a focus in your rental property business. Each and every dollar goes to or away from your bottom line. Follow the tips in this section: use a discount credit card or rewards card, buy second-hand materials, restore antiques or relics, buy from salvage yards and do it yourself.

How to upgrade on the cheap and still increase rent. Upgrading your property doesn't necessarily mean you must spend extreme amounts of money. There are inexpensive upgrades you can make to increase your rental revenue, some of them are: paint, minor repairs, deep clean, install a backsplash and replace doors.

Where upgrades are worth spending the money. Not all upgrades are created equal. Choose the upgrades that are worth the money and matter to most people.

TWELVE

HOW TO MAKE UNCLE SAM YOUR FRIEND!

I don't know about you, but I don't like paying taxes. Does anyone really? Nobody I've met. I understand that taxes are essential to fund the government which operates our country. However, after seeing how the government spends my hard-earned tax dollars into oblivion and then comes back for an even larger piece of the pie, my entire appetite towards taxes is beyond spoiled. The one instance where the government still has even a little good business sense left in them is around the topic of real estate. The government is wasteful, but not stupid. Our government leaders understand that real estate drives the economy. When real estate is churning positive, the economy is likely positive. Therefore, the taxes are rolling into Uncle Sam's giant bank account. The government has incentive to make real estate attractive as an investment because of the positive waves of economic impact it rains on the country.

Due to my disdain for paying a larger share than I have to in taxes to a wasteful government, this chapter focuses on how you can *save* even more of your hard-earned money instead of watching it disappear into the endless government coffers. Follow this chapter closely to learn the most common best practices for doing just that. Here we go!

UNCLE SAM LOVES REAL ESTATE

Let me reiterate, Uncle Sam *loves* real estate! No really, he does. The United States Government wants us, the people, to buy and sell real estate. There are many reasons for this. The bottom line is: it helps the economy grow. Every politician can agree on one thing. That being—economic growth is a good thing. As a result, the United States Tax Code is incredibly real estate friendly.

The tax code is nothing close to simple, however, for your benefit I will simplify real estate taxation and its associated advantages into the following three major categories: (1) Depreciation, (2) Property-related expenses and (3) Business-related write-offs.

This chapter does not do a deep dive into the tax code. I will briefly touch on the most important factors to be aware of. My focus is on showing you the incredible tax benefits of having your own rental real estate business. If you want a deeper dive into the subject of tax and real estate, I highly recommend doing some online research or purchasing another book that focuses on this subject specifically.

Marshall Field was an American entrepreneur and the founder of Marshall Field and Company, the Chicago-based department stores. He amassed a fortune of $66 billion during his lifetime. His department store empire was acquired by Macy's in 2005. Marshall shared this perspective about real estate investing, "Buying real estate is not only the best way, it is the quickest way and the safest way to become wealthy." I'm sure Marshall understood the benefits of real estate investing and how favorable the investment was on taxation from the United States Government. The government wants you to invest in real estate, hold those investments, or move onto bigger ones. They are investing *with you* because it benefits both parties. Every real estate investor should be taking advantage of the vast number of freebies the government is willing to give up so that we continue to invest into growing the economy via real estate.

LEVERAGING UNCLE SAM IN YOUR RENTAL REAL ESTATE BUSINESS

Tax season recently began and it is time to put my real estate business to work in my favor. Taxes are never a sexy, fun or positive topic. Not even my eternal optimism can change that stark reality. However, tax season can be much less painful when you know *how* to maximize your real estate business toward favorable taxation. The truth is the US Government gives real estate investors tax breaks and the ability to reduce their overall taxation because they want to drive economic investment and encourage spending on real estate vs sticking your money in a bank somewhere. Your investment dollars, at work in the economy, is a benefit for the government. In turn, they make it a benefit for *you*.

I recently heard of a couple that purchased a second home solely for the purpose of taxation benefits. I thought this was a little crazy at first. Then I realized it wasn't at all. Sure, they rented it out and about broke even from an 'investment' standpoint. However, owning just the *one* rental property allowed them to take advantage of *many* tax benefits not available to the average citizen. I will break those down for you below and share briefly how each of them work. To be clear though, you can't just buy property and sit on it. You must actively rent out the property in order for these tax benefits to be applicable for you.

Here are the new deductions you can use in your favor as a real estate investor that a standard salaried or employed worker cannot. I cover each of these in more detail later in the chapter.

Depreciation deduction. This one is likely the largest single benefit associated with owning a rental property portfolio. The Internal Revenue Service (IRS) allows you to deduct over a 27.5-year period from the time you close on your rental property the depreciation value calculated with your property itself.

Cell phone deduction. Yes, you can deduct your entire cell phone bill from your taxable income. The reason? It's simple really. You can't operate your rental real estate business without a phone or a service plan to use the phone.

Mileage deduction. If you have a car and you use said car to conduct business for your rental real estate business, you can deduct the miles driven for that business purpose. The IRS calculates a price-per-mile deduction that it applies to each mile driven for business purposes. It was most recently at $0.56 per mile.

Home office deduction. Do you have a home office in your home that is used to manage your rental real estate business? You'd better! If you didn't, you do now. It doesn't have to be a designated 'office'. Though it has to be a dedicated *space* within your home where business is conducted. This could be a spare bedroom, a loft, a third of your bedroom, etc.

Investment mortgage interest deduction. This one is obvious. Any debt interest associated with the note held by a financial institution for your rental property portfolio is fully tax deductible. Most people who own a home and qualify for this deduction are already leveraging this one for their personal home.

General expense deduction. This deduction buckets several other expense categories together to ensure all expenses associated with the management of your rental real estate are deducted from your allowable taxable income.

THE POWER OF DEPRECIATION

Depreciation in rental real estate is a benefit that investors take advantage of to deduct the costs associated with purchasing and improving an investment property over time. Depreciation of rental real estate occurs over the course of the property's useful life in accordance with IRS depreciation method. As of today, that timeframe is 27.5 years for residential real estate and 39 for commercial property. In this case, the 27.5-year timeframe applies because we are renting property for someone to live in as a residence vs operate a business. Depreciation is truly awesome and proves my point in this chapter that Uncle Sam loves real estate and actually encourages people to invest. It is a major tax savings offered year after year.

To qualify for depreciation, you must meet the following requirements:

You own the property. If you purchased the property, whether in cash or borrowing funds from a financial institution, you qualify. If you have partial ownership, the IRS will allow for depreciation on your ownership share. If you own 50%, then you can depreciate 50% in your taxes.

The property is expected to last for more than one year. You plan to keep the property longer than one year. If not, the depreciation will reverse if you tried to claim it in a previous year.

You use the property in your business or as an income-producing activity. You are reading this book because you own rental real estate, therefore your property qualifies for depreciation. Allowing someone to occupy your rental property in exchange for the payment of rent is considered an income-producing activity. The same would be the case for a commercial real estate property.

The property has a determinable useful life. If your property is useful, though loses value over time through decay, becomes obsolete, or from natural causes it is considered to have a useful life. Now, the property is obviously expected to last longer than 27.5 years and the government knows this. It is just how they define useful life and allow for this tax savings to be implemented.

Real estate depreciation begins the moment you place it in service, which means you've rented it out to someone. Depreciation ends when you sell the property or take it out of service. For example, if you kept the property but decided to live there as your primary residence you can no longer claim depreciation and the property is considered out of service. You can still depreciate during vacancy periods as you transition from one tenant to the next or conduct a property improvement. Land itself is not depreciable because it doesn't meet the above requirements.

Depreciation is used to deduct the costs of purchasing and improving your rental property. Depreciation equally distributes the deduction across the 27.5-year useful life of the property, whether or not you keep it for 27.5 years. The amount that is depreciated is calculated through the 'basis of the property' or the amount you paid to acquire it, including closing costs and some other legal fees as applicable. You are required to separate the cost of land and the buildings on the land since only the structures are depreciable. You can determine this value by the fair market value of the land and structure of when you purchased the property or by using the most recent real estate tax assessment. The tax assessment can be found on your state's website through a simple lookup.

Not just the structure is depreciable in rental real estate. You are also allowed to depreciate larger improvements made to the property, such as: appliances, flooring, furniture, equipment, plumbing systems, HVAC systems, a roof, fences and even roads. Each of these follow a different depreciation timeline, see below:

- Appliances, flooring & furniture: 5 years
- Office furniture & equipment: 7 years
- Fences & roads: 15 years
- Residential buildings, other structures, HVAC systems, roof, electrical systems, plumbing systems: 27.5 years

Repairs are not considered depreciable, though improvements are. You can either classify something as a repair and deduct the entire expense in the year you incur the cost or you can depreciate it over time. One example is a roof replacement. Let's say the replacement cost was $10,000. The depreciation timeline as stated above for a roof is 27.5 years. You can either classify this as a repair and deduct the entire $10,000 this year or you can depreciate it over 27.5 years, which means you'll only get a $350 deduction this year. Consult a tax advisor for the best practice here and to remain compliant with IRS rules. I highly recommend using a certified tax software or a tax advisor to help you calculate depreciation correctly. Since this is a major tax savings, typically in the thousands of dollars, it's important to get it right.

PROPERTY-SPECIFIC DEDUCTIBLE EXPENSES

Property-specific expenses are anything associated with operating your rental real estate business. For the purpose of taxes and accounting, expenses are specific to each particular property vs your portfolio as a whole. Each property is considered its own business for tax purposes. Ultimately, they are all accumulated together to determine your final tax savings or bill. The below are the most common property-specific expenses that you can deduct from your tax bill.

Advertising. Chances are, you spent money to market or advertise your property for rent. Every dollar spent here is tax deductible. I used to be able to post my properties for rent on Zillow.com for free. Now, they charge a $9.99 per week listing fee. This fee is tax deductible. If you purchase a 'for rent' sign and post it on a window or in a front yard, this is tax deductible. If you take out an advertisement in the local newspaper, which most don't today, this would also be tax deductible. You get the point.

Travel. Do you travel to visit a rental property? This is not the standard vehicle expenses that I discuss further on. This is more applicable to plane travel. For example, you live in Washington State yet half of your portfolio is in Indiana. If you purchase a plane ticket, take a ride share to the airport, rent a car, stay at a hotel, eat food to stay alive and then fly back, this is all tax deductible for your rental real estate business. In my case, my business partner lives in a different state. Each time he travels here to conduct business, we expense his travel costs and then deduct the expenses per this allowable deduction each year in our taxes. I also became a multi-state investor and started traveling out of state to conduct business in the other state. This will all be tax deductible travel expenses for me going forward.

Cleaning & maintenance. You likely pay for your rental to be cleaned upon acquisition or tenant turnover. If you do, deduct the expense in this category. The same goes for maintenance, i.e., snow removal, yard work, sprinkler winterization, gutter cleanout, furnace filter replacement, watering plants, mowing the yard, etc.

Interest. Unless you paid cash for each rental property you own and operate, you likely have interest paid on debt service that you can deduct from your taxable income related to your rental business. The amount of interest paid in that calendar year is tax deductible for that year only. If you have a sizeable amount of interest paid this deduction can yield high returns for you.

Insurance. Every property should be insured, no questions asked! Simply deduct the total insurance premium paid per property to take advantage of this deduction.

Professional fees. These are more of the professional services fees you would pay a lawyer for evictions or lawsuits. Tax or accounting services would also apply in this category. If you paid someone to create a lease agreement, that would apply here.

Management fees. If you have a property manager, what you pay them is counted in this category. Also, if you pay someone to conduct showings or something along these lines, that would be accounted for here as well.

Repairs. Any expense you make toward a property repair of any kind, is tax deductible. Every dollar you spend on repairs is essentially a dollar off your revenue to the IRS, just like the rest of this expense list. Account for every repair, no matter how small, to ensure you aren't paying tax money you don't owe. The primary expense in this category is labor. This is where you pay a plumber, handyman, electrician, landscaper, or any hired help for the repair labor they perform.

Materials. This category is the actual physical things you purchase for the property. Some examples are a new water heater, wood for a repair, paint, fencing, a new toilet, blinds, a faucet, etc. This is separate from the repair itself, though counts the exact same. The categorization is important though because if you enter all of your expenses in a single category it will look suspicious to the IRS. And nobody wants the IRS to look suspiciously because an audit is the last thing anybody wants. If it comes, however, this guidance and those from a CPA or tax accountant will help you avoid that by filing correctly.

Supplies. Supplies are different than repair materials. Supplies are more in the realm of cleaning supplies, paper towels, marketing signage, keys or garbage bags. These are tax deductible dollar for dollar similar to the other categories.

Real estate taxes. Just like insurance, you have to pay property taxes for your rental property. These property taxes are fully tax deductible in the year they are paid.

Utilities. Any dollar spent on utilities for your unit, i.e., water, sewer, trash, gas, and electric is tax deductible. Sometimes you pay partial utilities for a unit, sometimes you pay 100%. For others, you pay nothing at all. However, when a unit turns over, you are likely covering utility costs temporarily until a new tenant moves in and assumes that expense. All of those dollars spent are tax deductible.

Refinancing fees. If you refinance your property, you are allowed to deduct any costs associated with the refinance, such as the appraisal and related closing costs.

BUSINESS-SPECIFIC DEDUCTIBLE EXPENSES

Business-related expenses differ from property-specific expenses in that they are not specific to a particular rental property. They are expenses associated with running your entire rental real estate business. These expenses are sometimes overlooked by investors. Be sure that isn't you!

Mobile phone. The government allows you to write-off your mobile phone and related service costs? I will answer that with a question, "Do you need your mobile phone to run your real estate business?" Why yes of course you do! Therefore, it can be written off. Your mobile phone, which you likely couldn't live without, now becomes a tax benefit of your rental real estate business. You use your phone to communicate with potential and existing tenants. You use it to field maintenance requests and contract repair services. You use it to communicate with lenders, real estate agents, your insurance agent and much more. You also use it to post and respond to advertisements. Therefore, the government allows you to write it off as a business expense even though you also use it for many other reasons. I call that a bonus!

Internet service. The same rules apply with internet service as the mobile phone write-off. You leverage the internet service in your home to manage your real estate business. You use it to search for properties, pay taxes, find agents, conduct market analysis, pay bills and much more. Yes, you also use it to power your streaming service, but hey, let's not complain about this one!

Home office. This is a deduction that can easily land you a few thousand-dollar deduction from your taxes. Shockingly, many people do not take advantage of this tax benefit because of an ancient fear of being an audit trigger. True, years back, when this deduction was less common, the IRS did flag this as a higher-risk audit deduction should it be taken. However, this was also the result of it not being common in American households for people to work remotely or have a part-time gig or hustle that would require a home office. Today it is extremely common for people to have and use a home office for a personal business or a qualified side hustle. Having a rental real estate business as a side hustle absolutely qualifies you to take this deduction. Your office for use of your day job does not qualify, unless you are a small business owner. Rental real estate is a small business, which qualifies for this annual deduction. Using a reliable tax software, such as TurboTax, the 'guide-me' walk through is straight forward. I do strongly recommend taking the time to ensure you have the proper information, such as the square footage of your home vs the square footage of your office space, the cost of utilities, any office furniture expenses, etc.

Business equipment. Any equipment purchased to manage your rental real estate business is tax deductible. Most investors own a laptop computer that is used to operate their rental real estate business. I use mine for property management, creating and posting property advertisements, analyzing deals, signing contracts and more. What you pay for this is fully deductible, including an extra monitor and other related equipment such as a printer.

Business supplies. Business supplies are essential to run any business. For rental real estate, it is common to require supplies such as: printer paper, printer ink, sticky notes, pens, rental signs, folders, envelopes, stamps and more. Be sure to deduct all of these expenses in the year you incur them. I purchased a foldable table from Costco that I use for showings and I deducted that the year I purchased it!

Learning & education. Anything you purchase that contributes to your learning & education as it pertains to rental real estate is 100% tax deductible. If you pay to attend a real estate seminar or conference, this is deductible, as well as any associated travel expenses. Any books that you purchase that help with your business or real estate education are deductible. Essentially any learning and education that contributes to your rental real estate business qualifies for this deduction.

Vehicle expenses. There is a high probability that if you have rental properties, you will require a vehicle to conduct business related to each property in your portfolio. Each time you use your vehicle to conduct business related to a rental property you can deduct the associated expense from your tax bill. Here's how it works. The IRS allows you to deduct the percent of total vehicle expenses where your vehicle was used for rental property business. Let's say the normal usage of your vehicle is 70% personal and 30% business (related to real estate). If your total expenses for the year were $10,000 then you could deduct $3,000 of that from your tax bill. Let's review a scenario together for clarification.

Your total vehicle expense breakdown for the year is as follows:

- You drove 12,000 total miles on the year
- 4,200 of those miles driven were related to your business
- 35% of your expenses for the year can be deducted

Expense Category	Total
Fuel	$1,750
Oil changes & other service	$850
Repairs	$2,200
Tires	$800
Insurance	$1,200
Loan interest	$400
Other, i.e., car wash	$200
Total	$7,400

In this scenario, your total expenses were $7,400. This is going to be higher than if you were to take the standard vehicle deduction. Therefore, you would itemize your vehicle expenses for the year, which would be $2,590 that is deductible for your vehicle expenses.

We've covered quite a few expense categories related to your rental real estate business that reduce your overall tax burden. I highly recommend taking advantage of each one of these. In order to do so you must keep records of your purchases, including dates, category and total expense amount. Purchasing via a credit card vs cash helps here because you can print your entire expense report for the year. I use a business-specific credit card for taxation purposes to ensure I don't mingle personal expenses with business expenses. It creates a much more expedited tax season by doing so.

KEEP YOUR PROFITS FROM A SALE VIA THE 1031 EXCHANGE

To round out the chapter on taxation I'd be remiss if I didn't mention the amazing tax benefits associated with the 1031 Exchange. The 1031 Exchange is a tax deferral system the United States Government has setup to make it more attractive for rental real estate investors to leverage proceeds from the sale of a rental real estate property into the purchase of a larger one without being taxed on those proceeds. The purchase or sale has to be completed within six months or 180 days of each other and the proper paperwork must be completed, though beyond that the requirements are not overly strict. This tax-free method of exchange from one asset to another can produce massive results for rental real estate investors. To ensure adherence to the tax code, it is recommended you hire a professional, specifically a 1031 Qualified Intermediary to help guide you through the process.

To be more specific around the timeline, you have 45 days from the date of sale of the existing property to identify a new property. You have 180 days *in total* to have closed on that new property for it to be a qualified 1031 Exchange. Taking advantage of the 1031 Exchange allows you to continue purchasing larger and more expensive properties without having to pay any capital gains taxes to the government on any properties you sell within the exchange formula. This is a strongly recommended method to propel growth within your rental real estate business. If you want to transition from single-family properties to multi-family properties or even apartment buildings, this is a great way to get access to tax-free capital!

LET'S WRAP A BOW ON THIS CHAPTER

Congratulations, you've finished Chapter Twelve and learned something new to improve your rental real estate business! The focus of this chapter is to help you keep more of your hard-earned dollars to fund your rental real estate business and your life.

Uncle Sam loves real estate. The US Government encourages people to purchase real estate, especially rental real estate. The tax code is favorable to rental real estate investors.

Leveraging Uncle Sam in your rental real estate business. Take advantage of the tax benefits afforded to you in the tax code. Owners of rental real estate have access to many more tax deductions than a standard employee does.

The power of depreciation. Depreciation is a major tax-savings afforded to rental real estate investors that is important to both understand and leverage when finalizing taxes.

Property-specific deductible expenses. Each expense associated with a rental property is deductible. Be sure to track every expense, including the type of expense, date, amount and vendor.

Busines-specific deductible expenses. The expenses you incur to operate your rental real estate business are tax deductible. Understand them and leverage them to your advantage.

Keep your profits from a sale via the 1031 Exchange. If you are looking to grow or expand your rental real estate business, the 1031 Exchange may be your tax-free ticket to more capital!

THIRTEEN

BE THE LANDLORD YOU WOULD LOVE TO RENT FROM

A s a landlord, you carry a heavy burden of responsibility. A responsibility of providing other human beings with a place to call home. A responsibility of ensuring that your tenants have access to clean water, a comfortable environment and a safe place to reside. It doesn't stop there. As a landlord, you have the choice to be someone that is kind, compassionate and responsible, or you have the choice to be rude, inconsiderate and irresponsible. I'll tell you that the first option results in better success and less headaches for you. I also believe in karma. It pays to be a good person first and also a good person of business. Being a good person is the human side of it, meaning you show kindness and compassion toward other people. Being a good business person is about being responsible and intelligent. Both are essential for long-term success. This chapter will dive into specific strategies and steps you can take to be the landlord you would love to rent from.

FIX IT FAST AND KEEP IT MAINTAINED

As the owner of your property, you are expected to care for it from top to bottom. There are certain responsibilities that lie with the tenant, sure. However, the majority of the burden for fixing and maintaining the property is on the landlord. When you pay rent to live somewhere, the expectation is that the landlord will fix what breaks and keep the property in good, functioning order. Every single tenant should have electricity, running water, hot water, a working fridge, heat, and a functioning toilet. These are essentially basic rights and are also mandated by landlord-tenant laws. Make sure at all times that each one of these is properly accounted for. This list is likely the reason some landlords get 2 AM calls. A pipe bursts and water is leaking everywhere. The hot water isn't hot for a shower in the morning. A toilet is backed up and it's the only one available. If these things happen, you will be getting a phone call with the expectation you will address the matter immediately.

The lessons learned from the nightmare repair experiences we've been through are numerous. We learned to properly diagnose a repair quickly, choose a qualified professional for the job, improve communication with our tenants and repairman throughout the repair process, along with verifying all information directly. When a tenant reports an issue, be quick to address it. Otherwise, you could end up in a nightmare scenario yourself. It's important to understand how vital having the right network is. Your professional contractors are a critical component of that network. Having these relationships established when a big repair comes around goes a long way in ensuring your repair experience doesn't become a nightmare experience for both you and your tenants. Proper repairs and maintenance are a major factor in doing what you say you will do. This is where you build trust with tenants. Be on top of your property and be certain that your tenants have what they need, when they need it. It is the landlord's obligation to maintain the property and to respond quickly when issues do occur.

HAVE A REPAIR SYSTEM AND FOLLOW IT

One important lesson I've learned both in my personal and professional life is the importance of consistency. Consistent actions produce positive results. A lack of consistency leads to disappointment and failure. How I show up for my family each day matters. How I show up for my team and employer each day matters. How I show up in my rental business for tenants, repairmen and my business partner matters. Inconsistent behaviors lead to inconsistent results. Don't confuse consistency for monotonous. Consistency is *how* you show up more than what you actually do. For the past four years, I have woken up each morning and done the following: exercised, prayed, listened to the Word of God, walked/jogged my dogs, had a protein shake and meditated/reflected before attacking the rest of the day. What matters is not that I exercise, walk the dogs, pray, etc. It is that I *have* a morning routine that works for me. I am intentional about what I choose to do in the morning so I can feel a certain way and become the most productive version of myself each day.

The long introduction had a purpose; I promise! When it comes to being a landlord and managing your rental real estate business, consistency is of utmost importance. Being consistent in managing repairs is a top tenant priority. I briefly covered my repair process in Chapter Eight, though this is a more detailed explanation.

Set expectations upfront. Repetition is a major key to learning, so let's repeat it again. Setting expectations upfront with your tenants on when to contact you, for what reasons to contact you and how to contact you are essential if you hope to establish a dual process of success. Set these expectations before and during the signing of the rental lease agreement.

Inform tenants how to report a repair. Be clear with your tenants how to report a repair. Make it clear that repairs must be reported, especially those that are urgent in nature. Define whether you'd prefer tenants to email, text or call your personal phone. I also give my tenants the option to report issues or submit maintenance requests through the rental management software I use. The benefit here is it is centralized and gives me the ability to update the status of repairs from pending to working to complete. It's also a great record keeper.

Have office hours. Defining office hours for your tenant communication is recommended. For example, you can say that you will answer inquiries between Monday – Friday from 9:00 AM – 5:00 PM. Anything outside of this will not be addressed until the following business day during business hours, with the exception of emergencies. This will help prevent the random weekend, 11 PM (and worse) tenant calls.

Define emergency. Be sure to define what consists of an emergency, which would warrant communication and a response outside of predefined office hours. Some examples of emergencies are a fire, a significant leak, roof damage, gas leak or a break-in. If a tenant contacts you outside of office hours for a burned-out light bulb you have permission from landlords everywhere to ignore this!

Identify repair severity & timeframe for completion. Each repair is unique and could be categorized for level of severity, which in turn determines the level of attention required. In the corporate world we call this a 'Service Level Agreement' or SLA. Let's classify these as emergency, urgent and non-urgent.

- **Emergency.** Examples: fire, flood, major leak, roof damage, gas leak. Repair timeframe: 3 hours.
- **Urgent.** Examples: broken refrigerator, water heater issue, furnace malfunction. Repair timeframe: 24 hours.
- **Non-Urgent.** Examples: minor sink leak, broken interior door, broken window glass. Repair timeframe: 48 to 72 hours.

Having a classification and repair schedule provides comfort for your tenants and a guideline to follow for you. I recommend communicating this with your tenants as part of setting expectations.

Tenant Notice & Scheduling. Most states require a landlord give notice to tenants 24 or 48 hours before entry to their unit. However, in the case of repairs, simply coordinate the repair with the tenant. A best practice I have used, so as to not be a middleman, is to have the repairman communicate directly with the tenant to coordinate. In the case of true emergencies, most states allow entry without permission.

Follow-Up. Once a repair is completed, be sure to confirm with the tenant that everything is in working order. Just like a customer, you want to be sure they are satisfied. Also, this is a great way to double check the quality of the work completed by the service man or woman.

DON'T BE THE REASON A GREAT TENANT LEAVES

Keeping your rental units occupied is the most important factor in your success or failure. Constant turnover is a margin killer for a rental real estate business. Your obligation as a landlord should be to operate your business ethically. You are providing other human beings with a place to call home. Your unit, however big or small, fancy or meek, is going to be where these tenants rest their heads at night. When you find a great tenant, hold onto them for as long as you can. This means be reasonable, responsive, kind and generally good to them. Tenants already have plenty of reasons to leave your property. Tenants leave for a myriad of reasons, such as:

- Needing more space
- Needing less space
- Job relocation or change
- Don't get along with neighbors
- Want to buy a home
- Change of neighborhood
- Can't afford rent
- Separation, divorce or marriage

What then, are you to do as a landlord to keep the best tenants?! Why must good things come to an end? Trust me that as a landlord, losing a great tenant almost compares to a personal heartbreak. There is no magic key to retention because life happens, however, there are several areas you can focus on to keep great tenants in your property longer. Let's review several of these together.

Communicate with your tenant. Communication is important at work, with children, with spouses, and yes with tenants as well! Tenants like to be in the know. Keep them updated on home repairs. Ask them how things are going every now and then. Give them a heads up about potential rent increases. Ask for their feedback and opinions. Be available when they need you. Be responsive when they reach out. Be sure to encourage two-way communication; your tenants will be appreciative.

Update your property or unit. People want to live well. *Well* doesn't mean extravagant or lavish. It simply means having a clean, organized space that feels safe and secure. Make sure your faucets aren't leaking, cabinets are screwed in properly, countertops are secured, toilets are tight and doors all lock completely. Keep the paint fresh and do your best to maintain a clean, organized rental. Light bulbs and fixtures shouldn't be broken. Don't leave holes in walls. Make sure all electrical outlets function and there are no loose wires around the property. With extra focus and some elbow grease, you can make this part of your business systems without breaking the bank.

Be reasonable with rent increases. The number one reason landlords lose money? Tenant turnover. The number one challenging aspect in rental real estate? Tenant turnover. How do you avoid losing money and avoiding key challenges in rental real estate? Low tenant turnover! The quickest way to lose a great tenant is to jack up the rent more than is reasonable or to increase rent too frequently. Raising rent annually is a solid plan. This is an expected cadence for tenants. You can also set this expectation upfront. When you do raise rent, do it reasonably. Be sure to understand the rental market you are in and be prepared to justify the increase. The message here isn't to not raise rent. This is an essential business practice. The lesson is when you do raise the rent, do it judiciously. If you purchase a property with inherited tenants and inherited rents, this doesn't apply the same. If you inherit a unit with extremely low rents, be quick to get rents up to the fair market value.

Do what you say you will do. Whether you believe it or not, trust is a core component of an effective landlord-tenant relationship. Trust is gained by doing what you say you will do. If you say you will fix something, fix it. If you say you will spray the property to kill cockroaches, do it. If you promise an upgrade in the future, make sure it happens and provide an estimated timeline. As stated above, communicate clearly and be responsive. Be a person of your word. Most people don't like to reach out to their landlord, and when they do it means they need something from you. Get back to them quickly and help resolve the issue(s) at hand. If tenants don't trust you—especially the best quality tenants—they will leave.

Personally, *home* is a sacred place for my family and I. I have constantly strived to have a very comfortable and personalized space to call home. Do your best as a landlord to provide such a place for your tenants. Keep this in mind. It should drive your behavior. Be sure your unit is safe, comfortable and clean. Do what you say you will do. Update and fix what needs to be updated and fixed. Don't raise rents too often or at an unreasonable rate. Speak *kindly* to your tenants. Have compassion for others and be likeable. Don't mistake this counsel with not being a good business person. That is reckless and will lead to failure in this business. Operate ethically and be a good person. Yes, this is the real estate business and it doesn't operate without people. People are your customers. People are to be treated with kindness and respect as we go into further in the next section.

TREAT PEOPLE WITH KINDNESS AND RESPECT

You are the property owner. You are the landlord. You did enough things right to be fortunate enough to own a rental property. Congratulations for your efforts! This does *not* make you better than anyone else, especially your tenants. So, *don't* act like it! I have met far too many individuals that have a better situation or circumstance in life than others and as a result they posture themselves up as if they are the greatest thing walking while everyone else is inferior to them. If not everyone, then certain people in certain groups or situations, certain towns, certain work teams or certain neighborhoods.

Alison Levine, Author of "On the Edge: The Art of High-Impact Leadership" shares, "How we treat people is always our choice, and if we choose not to be respectful, it can come back to bite us." Yes, you are the landlord. Yes, you are in charge. This is clear without you having to act better than your tenant or like they 'work' for you. Face the facts: without your tenant your property is worth very little! Your tenants pay the rent, which in turn pays the mortgage, insurance, taxes, repairs, upgrades, etc. Need I go on? *Stay grounded*. Show kindness, respect and appreciation for each and every tenant. Follow this counsel until they commit eviction-worthy mistakes. That changes the landscape entirely. Remember though, how you treat people is always *your* choice. Be respectful or karma may not be so nice to you.

This Happened to Me – The angry 'teenage-girl' mama

I had a tenant who portrayed themselves to be a very kind and loving single mother of four. I had compassion on her because of her situation and discounted the rent slightly to accommodate her finances. The first month was okay. She paid everything as expected. However, from that point forward things became more difficult. During a drive-by, I noticed there was a couch on the front patio and some garbage on the property. I politely reminded her that this was not permitted. She replied with clear annoyance of my reminder. The next month she didn't pay rent on time. I followed up and reminded her of our late fee policy, to which she became frustrated and spoke unkindly to me. I was planning to waive the late fee for the first offense. After the attitude she replied with, I decided to enforce it. She paid it, though gave me flack in the process. I received a letter from the local police code enforcement office of a fine for an infraction of excessive weeds. I shared this with the tenant and reminded her of her responsibility to maintain the grounds of the property as described in the lease agreement. She became bitter and tried to argue with me about the cleanup plus the fee charged that I passed along to her. The relationship went south and never returned.

A month later, she demanded a plumber come to the property because the toilet was backing up. I sent over my plumber immediately. Upon snaking the tube, it was discovered that feminine products, girl hair and *socks* had been flushed down the toilet! Upon this discovery, I mentioned the $120 service fee I was charged would need to be paid by her as a result of the backup being caused by them. As I explained this to her, she started shouting at me and I lost it. I was at my wit's end with this particular tenant. I was doing right by her and she was making my life miserable to the best of her ability. I lost my temper a bit during that conversation.

Month ten came and she hadn't paid rent. I reached out to inquire. She replied after repeatedly ignoring my communication attempts and rudely stated, "WE MOVED OUT!" At this point, it wasn't worth taking her to court. I was *glad* she left! She displayed contempt time after time without true cause. Her cats and daughters badly damaged one of the bedroom floors that was carpet. Another reason why I never replace carpet with carpet.

The damage plus missed rents resulted in the loss of her entire security deposit. For damages and missed rent I was out around $2,500 even after the deposit. I didn't mind. On to the next! We marketed the property and got it rented to a couple that moved from the Paradise, California fires after losing employment due to the devastation. They have now been there for over two years and are paying fair market rent. No headaches, no back talk, on-time rent and no damages. I consider that a lesson learned and a win!

This story is a reminder that being kind and treating tenants with respect doesn't always translate into the tenant reciprocating the behavior. That is just a reality you must accept. You can't control other's behavior, though you *can* certainly control your own. Your reputation matters, with tenants, repair personnel, contractors, lenders, lawyers, bankers, etc. Show kindness and respect and it will pay dividends in your business.

HAVE A HEART AND THE GOLDEN RULE

Let me begin this section of the book by saying that every single person on earth will at some point or another in their life go through something very challenging, painful and sometimes downright devastating. It is at these moments where people need to be offered a lifeline, a second chance, a helping hand or just a friendly gesture. I am not condoning the non-payment of rent, or the forgiveness of a security deposit where someone destroyed your property, or allowing illegal behavior to persist on your property once you become aware of it. That is poor judgment and irresponsible. What I am saying is that you should have a heart. You should treat others the way that you would like to be treated as it states in scripture. Believe it or not, there can be a mutual respect between tenants and landlords. I've experienced it personally and believe it comes down to the points discussed throughout this chapter. I will share with you some examples of what I mean from my experience as a Landlord.

This Happened to Me – The pandemic hits

The COVID-19 pandemic that struck the world in 2020 was completely unexpected. It put a halt on the global economy, forced people to remain at home on government orders for extended periods of time and resulted in massive and immediate unemployment for millions. For many, family members and friends lost their lives and funerals could not even be held. Never in my lifetime has anything like this happened, nor will it likely happen again. However, people across the globe suffered and this is exactly the time that landlords should have a heart and put themselves in the shoes of many of their tenants who are likely going through these unimaginable events.

One of our tenants recently moved into a unit in our triplex building. He still owed some of the security deposit. We were working with him as an exception to the rule on providing all of the funds upfront. This was due to another unrelated event in his life. He is a single father with shares custody of his son. He also works at the local dispensary in town. He was notified that his business was non-essential and his employer would be mandating employees remain at home without pay for a minimum period of two weeks. He immediately reached out to us and shared the situation, then asked that we work with him on rent payments. We replied that we absolutely would work with him and appreciated his honesty to come to us and ask for assistance after sharing the situation. Chris has since caught up on rent and is a solid tenant.

Another tenant of ours pays $1,150 in rent on a property that cash flows over $600 per month. She is a wonderful tenant and had been with us over a year. She reached out before the end of the month asking if she could pay $500 on time and the rest later in the month as a result of the COVID-19 impact on her employment schedule. We replied that absolutely she could and we'd work with her as needed until she was able to get back to the regular cadence of work and rent. She was grateful. Less than three months later she was back on track and she is very happy with us.

Our rental lease agreement states that tenants must pay rent in full each month; we do not accept partial payments. Of course, this is the letter of the law and going by this 100% of the time without consideration for each circumstance could backfire. Given the pandemic affected everybody worldwide in one way or another, it would show a landlord's true colors if they didn't show compassion and understanding for tenants impacted financially. We decided to do our part and work with people who experienced setbacks and difficulties.

The result? 75% on-time payments and 25% that paid in installments for one to four months. If you did the quick and easy math, you'll see we received 100% of rental payments during the pandemic months. Even I was surprised! We also didn't lose a single one of those tenants that we worked with and have built a trust and positive relationship with them for being flexible, accommodating and merciful.

This Happened to Me – COVID-19 rent realities

I had several tenants during the COVID-19 pandemic that had their employment impacted in one way or another. They needed rent support to get through the tough time. I offered to reduce a particular tenant's rent by $375 per month for two months. The reduced amount would be taken from her security deposit total and allow her to continue living in the property without any negative repercussions. I also allowed her to pay the remaining rent in two installments vs being due in full on the first of the month as is required by the lease. She was very grateful for the offer and expressed her appreciation for the hand of support. It didn't take much, but for this tenant, it meant everything!

This was another COVID-impacted tenant that needed some flexibility. Behind the scenes, this was a tenant I didn't particularly care for. She was demanding, ungrateful and often rude in our interactions. However, I decided to be the better version of myself and extend her the same flexibility and compassion. It was the right thing to do. It was also a bit unconventional in the offering. I didn't want to discount rent because this impacts my overall business. However, I allowed this tenant to deduct from her security deposit for a couple of months. I wrote up a quick agreement that we both signed/dated to ensure there were no conflicts when she moved out. I felt as if I acted ethically and I could live comfortably with that decision.

This Happened to Me - Death in the family

We had a tenant that signed our lease agreement with her oldest daughters and her elderly mother. They were late on rent and we had been working with them on a payment program. Sadly, the tenant (the mother) became ill and passed away within just a few days, leaving her daughters alone and in a very difficult situation. According to our lease agreement, we could technically evict them and search for another tenant. Instead, we gave them a few days to figure out the situation and get back to us. They got together with their father, who wasn't much involved in their lives before. He stepped up to help with rent payments. He agreed to contribute ongoing and they are very grateful for the patience, understanding and compassion we showed them. Since that time, they have held up to their end of the agreement and so have we.

Though the situation isn't ideal, we feel we are doing our part in being kind, considerate and respectful of others. I've never been a fan of people with power and in positions of authority who look down on others and don't show mercy for them. Certain government leaders come quickly to mind. I have also dealt with far too many in the corporate world. I would never want to be considered similar to them in how I treat others. As a landlord, I am in a position of power and authority. I choose not to abuse my position of authority simply because I can. As a man of faith, I believe in mercy, compassion and the golden rule. I can't expect to be shown mercy and compassion if I am unwilling to do the same, even if it costs me a few dollars here and there. I am also a sound and savvy businessman, which means there is a healthy balance. Showing mercy and compassion doesn't mean you let people run all over you or take advantage of you. There is a difference. However, ultimately, I believe in my heart that people are good and being in the journey of life together, I must do my best to be good to others. As a result, I can operate my business each day knowing that my business practices are ethical and good, and that I have done right by people. Do unto others as you would have them do unto you. The golden rule.

LET'S WRAP A BOW ON THIS CHAPTER

Congratulations, you've finished Chapter Thirteen and learned something new to improve your rental real estate business! The focus of this chapter is to remind you that though you may be a landlord, you are a human being first. Be kind, considerate, compassionate and respectful.

Fix it fast and keep it maintained. Good landlords fix issues with attention and speed. Don't leave issues lingering that result in frustrated tenants or could result in a more serious issue down the road.

Have a repair system and follow it. Consistency with your repair system is important to your tenants. Have a repair system outlined— defining expectations and severity of repairs, then follow it. Your tenants will be grateful and so will you.

Don't be the reason a great tenant leaves. Tenants leave for a myriad of reasons; you shouldn't be one of them. There are exceptions, such as if they don't like you because you enforce your lease agreement or expect them to pay rent. Be a landlord of your word and uphold your obligations to provide a comfortable and safe residence.

Treat people with kindness and respect. This should go without saying; don't be a jerk. Show kindness, respect and consideration for your tenants. No, don't let them break all the rules and not pay rent. Landlords are not better than their tenants, so don't act like you are.

Have a heart & the golden rule. The golden rule summarizes this entire chapter. Treat others (your tenants) the way you would like to be treated. Have a reasonable blend of enforcing the rental lease agreement while having a good heart.

FOURTEEN

KEEP GOING—THEN WATCH YOUR NET WORTH SOAR

W e've already established that rental real estate is not a hobby for you. It is a bona fide business that requires focus, business acumen, discipline and entrepreneurship. A major component of business is the principle of income, which ultimately determines your overall success in rental real estate. Income in your rental business is similar to net worth in your personal life. Your net worth is essentially your life's worth in terms of a single financial metric. No, it does not make your actual life worth more or less. However, it is a measure of your financial health or success. Financial health is a component of your life's success. Some people don't place any credence on net worth, discarding it as unimportant. Those are typically people who don't have very much money and are rationalizing why they don't have any by saying that money isn't important to them. The truth, whether you like it or not, is that having more money improves the quality of your life. Money is a major stressor in most families and marriages. The lack thereof is a cause for many terrible situations, choices and tragedies. It can be a significant burden that crushes you or a liberator that frees you.

Money is *not* the root of all evil. The love of money *can* be. Neither of those are a focus in this book. Having a positive and pragmatic outlook on money is important. Money is good. *Having* money is important. Using money wisely is of the essence. Money can have such a positive impact in one's life. Money allows for humans to provide a better life for themselves and their family. Money allows for people to do good and benefit others with it. It's truly challenging to have major influence without money to back it up. This is a true statement in your personal life and in your business. Your business needs money to survive and likewise more money to thrive. Your net worth is a financial metric that tells the story of your relationship with money combined with your business acumen. This chapter will cover the importance of net worth and how real estate will contribute to *yours*.

WHAT IS NET WORTH AND WHY DOES IT MATTER?

Net worth is a financial calculation. In other words, the answer to a math problem. This math problem defines your monetary worth. The calculation is quite simple:

Assets ($ cumulative dollar value) – Liabilities (all outstanding debts) = Net Worth

In essence, net worth is the amount of money remaining if you were to sell every asset you own and then pay off 100% of your debts. The cash remaining is considered your net worth. Net is just like on your paycheck where you have your 'net pay' or 'take-home pay' after taxes and other deductions have been accounted for. Net worth is the cash remaining after all your debts, including credit cards, mortgages, student and car loans are paid off. There are other calculations and versions of net worth, such as those that exclude your personal residence in the asset calculation. These are more considered 'working net worth' figures to show that the money is available for investing or more liquid in nature. Most people can't leverage their home to invest elsewhere. It is risky and sometimes there is nothing to leverage. This is why planning and consistency are so crucial to building your net worth or overall wealth.

The net worth metric is a critical measurement of your personal or family wealth. Tracking net worth is essential; every person should do this. This is the true barometer to your financial success. Income is a leading indicator of your wealth picture, though it only tells a fraction of your wealth story. When you apply for a mortgage, they ask for a full accounting of your assets and liabilities. They want to know your true financial picture, not just your current earnings. Your financial burdens are equally as important to be aware of as your financial assets. If your liabilities are less than or equal to your assets, you are not wealthy at all. In fact, you are barely getting by! In the next section, we cover how and where to focus so you can build your net worth exponentially.

HOW TO BUILD YOUR NET WORTH AND IMPROVE YOUR FINANCIAL HEALTH

Robert Kiyosaki, famed Author of the book "Rich Dad, Poor Dad" shared the following about real estate and wealth, "Real estate investing, even on a very small scale, remains a tried-and-true means of building an individual's cash flow and wealth." A primary focus of mine in writing this book is to help you reach new financial heights through tried-and-true rental real estate investment strategies. I truly believe that every reader of this book who applies the principles and best practices shared within these pages will build greater wealth and achieve more financial freedom in their personal lives than they would have otherwise. Building long-term wealth should be a personal goal of yours, because abundant living opens the pathway to increased happiness and the ability to bless the lives of many.

Continuing upon the theme of tried-and-true, your focus in building your net worth and watching it soar is summarized in these three areas of focus:

1. Increase your income
2. Build up your assets
3. Pay down your debts

Let's dig into each of these areas to understand why they are the most important areas of focus for your overall wealth picture.

Increase your income. It should be a primary focus of yours to earn as much money as possible within your scope of capacity and talents. Earning potential is one thing; *actual income* is what matters. Each person should be turning their earning potential into actual income if they want to become wealthy and financially independent. This requires discipline, sacrifice and a focused effort. If your primary source of income is stagnant, say a yearly salary, and you only expect a raise annually of 2% to 3%, you are likely going to creep along the financial net worth game. Unless your salary is $500,000 or more. For most of us, that is not the case. How can you change this? It's simple, though not easy. You must do whatever you can to drive up your income! Here are some examples of things you can do in this regard:

- Ask for a raise.
- Work more hours & overtime.
- Get a second job.
- Seek a higher-paying job.
- Start a side hustle.
- Earn a promotion.
- Further your education.
- Buy income-producing assets.

I will elaborate on two of these as I believe they are the most critical for you. First, seek a *higher-paying job*. If you have been in the same position for more than two years without a significant pay increase, you should be either getting a quick promotion or you are stuck on the road to always being an average income earner. Seek a new role. Earn a promotion. Develop new skills. Leave your company for a new one in the same capacity to get a 10%+ raise. Don't sit at your current company for 5, 10, 20, 30 years because you 'like it there' or 'are comfortable' or 'like your colleagues' or 'they have great benefits'. That is called being complacent. You are allowing yourself to excuse yourself out of real income growth and wealth. Focus on it. Do what it takes. *Be proactive*!

Second, buy *income-producing assets*. This is a book on steps to success in rental real estate. Therefore, the assumption is you are already doing this, whether one door in or one hundred. Congratulations! You aren't settling. You are pursuing wealth through a proven method. Income-producing assets bring additional income and support your overall net worth. Real estate isn't the only income-producing asset. You could buy a snow cone trailer and sell shave ice out of it. However, I am biased to rental real estate and it has created many millionaires over. Studies have shown that millionaires, on average, have seven different streams of income. How many do you have? Technically I have 38. 37 of them are from rental real estate and one of them is the salary and bonus from my full-time job. Throw in my wife's income and we have 39 total streams of income as a family. I am not a millionaire in the sense that I bring in at least a million dollars per year in income, though I am striving to reach that pinnacle. I am however, a net worth millionaire primarily because of my rental real estate portfolio.

This Happened to Me – My net worth & real estate

I started my corporate career in the business field. Eleven months into my entry-level role I was offered a promotion because of my drive, hard work and excellent work product. I was given an 8% pay increase. Fourteen months later, I asked for a promotion to become a manager of people. Two weeks later, my Vice President got back to me and said, "We'd like to let one of our managers go who isn't a great performer and offer you the position. Are you interested?" Well, of course I was interested! I just asked for that two weeks prior and she believed I was ready, which allowed her to move on from the other manager. That move came with increased responsibilities and a 12% pay increase. When I left this company three and a half years from when I started, I was making 35% more than when I started. I decided to leave the company because I was offered a 21% salary raise plus 30% overall raise including bonus by a competitor. It was my first time 'jumping ship' as they say in the corporate world. The majority of pay increases worth sharing (or considered significant) happen when you leave your current employer. The system is rigged to only increase your salary by 2-5% annually, which is barely keeping up with inflation. You will not become wealthy this way.

After two years of service at this new company, I was only making 7% more than when I started. I had completed a Master's program, obtaining an M.B.A. in Strategic Management during my tenure there. I was not offered a pay increase for my new education accomplishment even though I was promised it would happen. I was also passed over on two promotions. Naturally, I decided to go somewhere that recognized and valued my skillset.

As I was seeking a new opportunity, my old employer reached out and offered me a 20% pay increase above my new salary to return. In short, just five and a half years after I started working, I was offered a 117% income increase. This would *not* have been possible had I not forged my own path. This would *not* have been the reality had I stayed at the company and accepted the measly 2-5% annual pay increase. Not me. What about you? I actually turned down their offer because of a competing company's offer that I found to be more advantageous in the long-term. This new company offered a slightly lower salary, though with a 15% annual bonus. Overall, the compensation jump was 33% and put me into six-figures for the first time. I found myself a new path that paid a lot more, where my value was recognized and appreciated. I don't just talk the talk, I *live* it.

Just 10 months into this role, I was offered a promotion with a different department and a hefty 24% compensation package increase. Another 14 months after that I was promoted and my earnings increased another 14% plus new equity grants. Fast forward another 18 months and I was promoted once again with a whopping 28% overall compensation increase. Three years prior to this latest promotion, I began investing in real estate. I will share how real estate dramatically impacted my income and net worth in the following section of this chapter. Another two years passed and I found my current position, where I am now a Vice President in a major real estate company. I received a 48% total compensation package increase over where I was before. To put this into perspective, in a 12-year period, my annual income rose an astronomical 701%!!

I don't share this with you to boast. I share it because if *I* did it, *so can you.* The lesson here is that I was proactive, worked hard, excelled in my field, increased my education, sought out promotions, found better situations and as a result was rewarded. Nobody gave this to me. It didn't just fall into my lap. I had to earn it every step of the way, so can you. Now, *go do it.*

Build up your assets. The financial term asset is interesting because not all assets are created equal. The short and sweet definition of an asset is a resource with economic value. That means anything you own that is worth at least one penny is considered an asset. Homes, cars, toys, sports equipment, boats, bicycles, furniture and much more are all assets. Assets themselves will not boost your net worth. In fact, most assets we purchase lose value either immediately or over time. Therefore, the cash you spent to purchase the asset is now gone and the asset has decreased in value. In short, so did your net worth! Now I'm sure it wasn't by much, unless you bought that brand new Corvette your spouse told you not to! Assets either increase in value or decrease in value. Assets also either produce income or they don't. That is the area I will focus on while we center the conversation around your net worth: *income-producing assets.*

Income-producing assets are assets that generate income for you. Many of those assets also increase in value over time. Here is a list, though not fully exhaustive, of income-producing assets:

1. Savings account
2. Money market account
3. Certificates of Deposits (CDs)
4. Interest-yielding Bonds
5. Dividend-yielding Stocks
6. Peer to Peer lending
7. Single-family rental houses
8. Multi-family rental properties
9. Apartment buildings

10. Trailer parks
11. Short-term rentals
12. Vacation rentals
13. Real Estate Investment Trusts (REITs)
14. Farmland
15. Small business
16. Timberland
17. Race horses
18. Franchises
19. Websites
20. Royalties
21. Selling a product
22. Royalties
23. Storage rentals
24. Publish e-Books
25. Online business
26. Land you rent

Now you may not be able to afford a race horse, but you *can* certainly start a savings account that earns interest! Take note above that this list includes many options for real estate assets that produce income: land, apartments, single-family homes, multi-family properties, storage units, vacation rentals, trailer parks, farmland, etc.! Real estate is the primary reason that 90% of millionaires in the United States became millionaires. Income-producing real estate is an incredible asset class to choose for improving your net worth. The primary focus of this book is to help rental real estate investors grow their net worth through creating an effective, efficient and profitable rental real estate business. Income-producing assets are the way to get there and you are in the right place because readers of this book have already taken the plunge into this asset class.

Pay down your debts. Just like the previous section around assets, all debt is not created equal. I would not own a home today or have a growing rental real estate portfolio without debt. I am a firm believer in the power of *leverage*. I am able to buy a rental property with a loan from a bank that affords me the opportunity to pay down the debt service while generating income on the property through rent. All the while enjoying the market appreciation of the property if the market increases. I have also been able to grow my rental portfolio through the refinancing of old notes, the consolidation of notes and the opening of a home equity line of credit. Each of these are forms of debt, though it is debt that is being used for my advantage to acquire and manage income-producing assets.

Back to the conversation around debt and how it impacts your net worth. Bad debt, for example: credit cards, high auto loans and other high-interest loans, is a net worth destroyer. Address those bad debts right away. I will briefly share the areas of debt to focus on eliminating to build your net worth steadily over time.

Credit cards. Never carry credit card debt unless absolutely necessary. When possible, pay it down (or off) immediately. Credit cards are great to build credit and take advantage of the rewards programs; they are terrible for consumer debt and carrying debt over month to month. Pay them off immediately!

Auto loans. Car loans are great because they are shorter in term, typically 3-5 years, and because you need a car. Don't hold them longer than necessary if they have an interest rate above zero. With good credit, new car loans can be at no interest, though they still come with the heavy burden of a new car price tag that will lose value once you drive it off the lot. Pay these off early where possible.

Clothes, consumables, other goods and services. Going into debt to purchase non-essentials is just not wise money management. Unless the clothes you purchase are the only ones on your back or are essential for a big job interview, it can likely wait. What we buy mostly is non-essential, but in the USA, we have a consumer culture that overspends on the latest trends, toys and other non-essentials. This is reality because of the easy access to credit and the desire to appear we have money. This is unwise. The money could be better spent in sage investments or starting a business.

The way one looks at debt has a lot to do with how they make decisions when it comes to money, business and risk-taking. As mentioned earlier, not all debt is bad. In fact, some debt is actually good! The simple rule to follow is if the debt increases your net worth or has future value, it's good debt. Good debt is taking advantage of leverage. Leverage can be defined as the use of borrowed capital, or money, for an investment, with the expectation that the profits made will be greater than the interest required. The following are a few of the examples of good debt and how they can help you.

Student loan. Student loans are not a debt worth keeping for 25 years; however, they can be an amazing kick starter to pursue your aspirations and expand your opportunities in life. Education is a major driver for people's ultimate success in life along with a positive financial outlook. Many people need to borrow money to pay for that education. Be careful not to overborrow for education or to keep the note for the entire term at a higher-than-average interest rate. Refinance to a lower rate. Pay the note off as soon as possible. The IRS doesn't give you many tax advantages for student loan debt. Once you reach a certain income threshold the interest paid for educational loans is no longer tax deductible, therefore it serves you no purpose to keep paying interest unless you cannot afford to pay it down (or fully off) at the moment.

Business loan. Businesses are started because people need to make money to provide for themselves and their families. In most cases, obtaining debt is required to start a small business. Small businesses support countless people across the globe. People can earn a decent living or even grow to great levels of wealth through owning a small business. This form of debt can transform people's lives for the better and for generations. Having the ability to borrow money to start a small business is core to free markets and the opportunities it affords people. Remember that almost one-third of small businesses fail to survive their first two years. If you take out a business loan, be sure you have the proper ambition, savvy and hard work to succeed.

Rental real estate. There are many ways to make money in real estate. Rental real estate can be a significant source of income generation and cash flow. Rental real estate loans most commonly are standard mortgages, like when purchasing a personal home. There are also commercial notes, construction loans and more that offer the opportunity to acquire borrowed funds in order to purchase a real estate investment. This is considered a positive source of debt that can significantly improve an investor's life if they follow sound financial and business principles. Rental real estate has a much higher rate of success than a small business, though still requires active participation coupled with sufficient levels of hard work and grit.

Home ownership. It is nearly impossible to purchase a home in cash, unless you are a multimillionaire. Most people need to take out a mortgage in order to purchase a home. Homeowners in the United

States are 14x wealthier than renters. The main reason? Their home is an *investment* that can rise in value and provide other economic opportunities as a result. *Being smart* about purchasing a home is important to note here. Stretching your finances to buy a home or buying a home over value are unwise and can negatively impact your overall financial health in significant ways. Many savvy investors live in a home for a few years, fix it up, then sell for a profit and do it again with another home.

HOW REAL ESTATE IS A HUGE NET WORTH BOOSTER

Simply owning real estate does not make you wealthy. You are buying an asset. That asset is worthless unless you take action. Sure, the market may go up and after some time you could sell for a profit. It can also go down though. What you do from the moment you acquire a real estate asset makes all the difference in the world and this is how net worth can soar.

When I purchased my first rental property, I rented it at a $650 monthly cash flow. It was awesome! But I wasn't all of a sudden rich. I had to account for expenses, like repairs and turnover. I wasn't satisfied with the one, so I created a partnership and we started buying properties together just four weeks later. As of now, my business partner and I own 27 doors together, and I own another 10 doors on my own. In total, I have ownership in 37 rental doors that each provide additional monthly income and greatly contribute to my exponential net worth increases over the same time frame. I will break some of this down for you in the charts below to show what is possible with some focus, discipline and hard work.

This first chart represents my monthly and annual average cash flow by year along with the growing number of doors owned and operated. This is not actual, it is projected based on gross rents less repairs, insurance, debt service & utilities.

Year	Total Doors	Monthly Cash Flow	Annual Cash Flow
2016	3	$ 1,263	$ 15,150
2017	7	$ 3,234	$ 38,808
2018	10	$ 4,677	$ 56,124
2019	24	$ 9,014	$ 108,618
2020	30	$ 11,900	$ 142,800
2021	37	$ 14,000	$ 168,000

This second chart represents my personal net worth over the same five-year period from when I started investing in rental real estate.

Year	Total Doors	Personal Net Worth
2016	3	$ 195,500
2017	7	$ 387,351
2018	10	$ 535,785
2019	24	$ 973,796
2020	30	$ 1,476,476
2021	37	$ 1,535,721

There were multiple factors that played into the growth and expansion of my personal net worth, though each of them involved a component of the three-fold focus areas I've shared with you in growing net worth. My income increased significantly over that period of time. I started my rental portfolio of assets that grew over time. Then finally, I paid down various debts. The formula isn't complicated and truly isn't all that challenging to go after. What *is* challenging, however, is people taking the first step and then continuing down the path with consistency. This has been a theme throughout this book—consistency, that is. Be consistent in your approach and behaviors, then good things will happen for you. Net worth is the end result of your approach and behaviors. It is a lagging measurement of your personal financial success or failure. Focus on the formula and executing according to what you know is required.

BUILDING NET WORTH ONE DOOR AT A TIME

People constantly ask me, "Do you buy long-term rentals?" The answer is always *yes*. Real estate is a long game to me and so is net worth. Net worth in real estate is built steadily over time, one door at a time. There are specific action steps I cover below that you can start taking today to begin increasing your net worth through real estate.

Save money, raise capital or partner up. In order to become a real estate investor, you must either save your own money, raise capital from investing partners or partner with somebody that has money. Your credit also has to be solid with a good history in order for lenders to take a risk on you. This is where everyone starts and one option isn't better than another, it's just different. Whatever route you take is up to you, your resources, your network and your skillset.

Purchase a rental property. Once you have the money, capital or partner it's time to invest. Purchase a rental property that will produce cash flow and become a solid investment for you. Look at factors such as location, the local economic pillars, the housing market, the rental market, potential cash flow and CAP rate. I trust you have already completed these first two steps.

Generate income from your rental property. Purchasing the property is the easy part, as you've learned by now from this book. Now, go and make money off your property! Manage it right. Don't neglect it. Do what you can to maximize your return on investment and improve your financial model for profit. Businesses don't grow without profit, unless whoever is funding it has deep pockets. In your scenario, you are likely the person funding your rental real estate business and your pockets are unlikely too deep. At least *mine* weren't and still aren't! Be financially responsible and your business will benefit—as will the size of your financial coffers.

Put your rental property income to use. With the new property or multiple properties in your rental portfolio and a profitable income statement, you're ready to take the next step in your business. There are three standard paths you can go down.

1. **Pay down mortgage principal.** Paying down debt is always an option and never a dumb move. It is a good financial decision *most* of the time. However, when you are building your portfolio, paying down debt restricts your ability to grow. Keeping debt can work in your favor if you are a savvy investor who can multiply your rental properties and subsequent income which can eventually help pay down the debt faster. Some investors pay an extra sum off their principal debt balance each month, then use the rest to grow and operate their business.

2. **Buy more rental properties.** Rental property income is a great way to build capital for more rental property purchases. It is highly recommended to accelerate growth. Growing your rental portfolio will increase your ability to bring in more revenue, cash flow and ultimately profit. Using your rental property business income to grow your business is a solid play and what most large companies do each quarter when they report their financial statements. Reinvesting in your business is how your business will grow. It doesn't just happen.

3. **Create forced equity.** When you buy a property, the money you put down on the purchase, subtracted from the property value itself, becomes your instant equity. This number can grow over time through appreciation and other market factors, or it could decrease in value as a result of different factors. Forced equity is when you make improvements to the property itself and drive the increase in rental property value despite market conditions or other factors. Assuming all things remain equal, upgrading a bathroom, refinishing a kitchen and repainting the property are going to increase property value. The term is called 'forced equity' because *you* are the *force* behind the equity change.

Leverage your rental property or properties for more growth. Your rental property portfolio is open for business. You are generating monthly cash flow and each month paying down the principal debt service. You also want to grow but aren't sure how. An incredible growth-generator may already be in your back pocket. Your rental property or your rental property portfolio can be used as leverage to obtain more capital. There are three primary methods for this:

1. **Get a Home Equity Line of Credit (HELOC).** If you have a certain loan-to-value ratio and good credit, you can likely get a line of credit on properties within your portfolio. Your rental property or properties become(s) collateral for the loan. You can get access to cash within a relatively short period of time. A line of credit can be used for anything, really. So why not use it to acquire more rental properties? If you didn't get the strong hint, I'm suggesting you look into it. Of course, you can pay down the line of credit when you don't need it and then use it again in the future. It's like a revolving lender without having to apply each time assuming you pay down the balance.

2. **Cash-out refinance.** Another common practice is to refinance your property and take out any available equity as part of the transaction. A word of caution here not to just refinance blindly to get cash. Carefully assess your current note terms vs what you can qualify for on the refinance. If your current rate is 4.0% and your refinance quote is 4.5%, consider twice before pulling the trigger. Typically, a refinance is done to move to a lower interest rate and more favorable overall terms. Not always, but mostly. Don't go into worse debt unless your cash return and potential investment are winners.

3. **Upgrading through a 1031 Exchange.** Another great way to grow is to sell your current property through a tax-deferred 1031 Exchange and purchase a bigger or multi-family property using the proceeds within six months of the sale. Look closely at

the IRS law here to ensure you follow the correct process. Many investors hire a tax accountant to help with the transaction because the penalties can be fierce. However, don't be scared. A lot of people take advantage of this wonderful tax loophole. For example, you could sell a single-family property and upgrade to a duplex or quadplex with the proceeds, tax free.

Repeat this cycle again. The above recommendations for growing your net worth through real estate are proven to work. When something is proven to work, why not try it yourself? There is no reason to start from scratch and carve your own path through the jungle. Just walk down the path that scores of others have made for you which shows you the way to success. When the cycle works, repeat the cycle until it no longer works. The same applies here. There is a level of skill and hard work required, plus some market factors and a little dumb luck that ultimately determine how successful you become. Proven best practices implanted by other successful investors are a smart way to proceed in any business.

START TRACKING YOUR NET WORTH TODAY

Simply reading about net worth is not going to benefit you much. Net worth is not just for the rich and famous as a token of pride to share how much they are worth. It is for *every* single person that cares enough to track their personal financial scorecard. I'm a golfer. I absolutely love the sport. I have four kids ages eleven and under, so I don't play nearly as much as I'd like to. However, I keep score every time I play. Not keeping score of your personal financial score (net worth) is like not keeping score on a round at the course for a golfer. How will you ever know if you are improving? The short answer is: *you won't*. Firmly rooted in my personal beliefs is the mantra of *constant growth and improvement*. The way to know whether I am growing and improving is through consistent measurement. At the corporate workplace, measurement is completed on what are called Key Performance Indicators, or KPIs. Each KPI is an indicator of performance, good or bad. Net worth is the personal KPI that every person should be tracking if they have any desire to become financially free. Throughout my life and career, I have come across many who have a personal goal of becoming financially free or independent. This is a great goal, *wonderful*, in fact. However, less than 10% of those people are actually tracking their personal net worth. How much money do you have to earn, save or be worth before you consider yourself financially free or independent? If you have a number,

How To WIN In Rental Real Estate AFTER The Deal

fantastic. How will you know whether you are making progress toward reaching that number? Tracking your net worth is the answer. If you aren't tracking your net worth you will likely never become financially free or independent.

The formula is **'total assets – total liabilities = net worth'**. It is easier to track your net worth with a tool, or a worksheet. Given this, I am providing you with a very simple, easy to complete worksheet for tracking your net worth. Remember, we are all about *taking action*. This worksheet will show you the power of your behavior and financial decision-making over time. If your liabilities equal your assets, your net worth is zero. Obviously, the paying down of your liabilities and the increase in your assets is the right method.

The 'Personal Net Worth Worksheet':

Personal Net Worth Worksheet					
	1/1/XXXX	4/1/XXXX	7/1/XXXX	10/1/XXXX	YTD% Increase
ASSETS					
Retirement Accounts					
Equity Grants					
Stocks					
Bonds					
Annuities					
Total Equity Investments	$ -	$ -	$ -	$ -	0%
Cash/Savings					
Business Accounts					
Insurance					
Collectibles					
Personal Property					
Real Estate - Personal					
Real Estate - Investment					
Notes Receivable					
Other Assets - ie cars, boats					
TOTAL ASSETS	$ -	$ -	$ -	$ -	0%
LIABILITIES					
Car Loans					
Credit Card Debt					
Mortgage Debt					
School Loans					
Real Estate Invesment Debt					
HELOC					
TOTAL LIABILITIES	$ -	$ -	$ -	$ -	0%
NET WORTH	$ -	$ -	$ -	$ -	0%
Annual Cash Flow (Earned)					
Annual Cash Flow (Unearned)					

240

Now, how you go about this is what makes the biggest impact. Let's compare two scenarios together.

Scenario A

Andy has a net worth of $50,000. He has $20,000 in cash to use that is in a savings account. He has a $20,000 student loan. Andy decides that his best option is to pay off his student loan throughout the year. He pays off $5,000 every quarter. At the end of the year, his student loan is now $0.00 and his cash is now $2,000. Andy accomplished his goal. However, his overall net worth only increased by $2,000.

Andy accomplished his target, he paid off his student loan in just one year. That's great! However, the student loan was only collecting 4% interest with a monthly payment of $500. Andy was also deducting $1,000 per year in student loan interest to reduce his tax liability. That can no longer be used. Overall, his net worth improved by just $2,000 because he used all of his cash to pay down an existing, low-interest-yielding debt.

Scenario B

Andy takes his $20,000 in cash from his savings account to purchase a rental property. He contributes $18,000 toward the acquisition of the property. The monthly payment for this property is $500 and he finds a tenant in the first month who pays $1,100 in rent for a gross cash flow of $600/month. He also purchased the property 10% below market value for an instant equity boost. Throughout the year he paid down the mortgage by $2,000 and was now able to deduct $4,000 in interest paid toward his tax obligation. He continued to pay down his student loan and also deducted the additional interest expense toward his tax bill. He also was able to save cash by not paying down that massive amount of cash toward his student loan liability beyond the monthly payments due. Assuming a 90% occupancy rate, 10% repair rate and 10% other expense rate on the rental property, Andy brought in an additional $5,040 in cash. At the end of the year, Andy's net worth increased by $30,000.

The increase in Andy's net worth between the two scenarios is a direct result of how he chose to *use* his cash on hand. In scenario B, instead of using the money to pay down debt, like was done in scenario A, Andy chose to invest his cash into an income-producing asset. Now there is nothing wrong with paying down debt. In fact, that's a very good choice. Dave Ramsey would be very proud of that decision. Also, there is no guarantee that the income-producing asset will actually produce income or that the asset will be purchased at 10% below market value. This is all based on one's ability to buy right and manage right. By following the principles and teachings in this book, the likelihood of success increases significantly. Based on my experience and that of many thousands over, this investment strategy is a very good one. There are equity benefits, income benefits, tax benefits and of course, net worth benefits.

The reality of net worth is that there are winners and there are losers. There are fast, intelligent and proven ways to increase your net worth and there are other ways to slowly increase your net worth. Here is the path that many have chosen, including myself:

- Increase your earning power.
- Build a strong credit profile.
- Accumulate savings.
- Use your cash and good credit score to obtain a loan in order to acquire an income-producing asset below market value.
- Reinvest your cash flow into more income-producing assets.
- Repeat the above.

Along the way you pay down the outstanding debt. As you complete this cycle, and you do it intelligently, there is a high likelihood of your net worth soaring to new heights in just a few years. Remember though, this is not a get-rich-quick scheme. This requires hard work, dedication and a commitment to discipline in order to find true success. Anybody can get lucky and anybody can go broke. Follow the path laid out before you and your chances of success skyrocket.

Net worth is an individual's grade report for their financial coursework. Listen. Study. Do your homework. Prepare diligently for your exams. Put forth your best effort based on what you've learned in the classroom and you are more likely to succeed.

LET'S WRAP A BOW ON THIS CHAPTER

Congratulations, you've finished Chapter Fourteen and learned something new to improve your rental real estate business! The focus of this chapter is to educate you on the personal financial metric 'net worth' and how real estate can take your personal net worth to greater heights. This requires discipline and a true understanding of debt, then how to successfully leverage debt to build a business, real estate preferred, to grow your net worth.

What is net worth and why does it matter. Net worth is the single metric that signifies your overall financial health. It is a barometer to your financial success or failure.

How to build your net worth and improve your financial health. Net worth can be built via three important steps; increase your income, build up your assets and pay down your debts. Increasing your income allows for you to build up more assets and pay down your debts faster. The assets that help your net worth grow are income-producing. There is good debt and bad. Get rid of the bad debt and leverage yourself with good debt to build your business.

Building net worth one door at a time. Grow your net worth one door at a time by following proven strategies for acquisition, business operations and expansion. Do what others before you have done successfully time and again. Find out what works for you and go for it.

How real estate is a huge net worth booster. Real estate has the potential to increase your net worth in significant ways. Real estate boosts your net worth through cash flow, tax reduction, depreciation and appreciation. When done correctly, real estate produces income while simultaneously increasing in value over time.

Start tracking your net worth today. Measure what you want to improve. Start using a net worth tracker *today*. This metric is your personal Key Performance Indicator of your financial wellness. Update your net worth at minimum annually, though I recommend quarterly.

FIFTEEN

SUCCESS IS THERE FOR YOU—IF YOU EARN IT

A s we come to the conclusion of this book, I want to commend you for getting this far! Many people that pick up a book and start reading it, never make it half-way through! That may be a different statistic for the "Harry Potter" or "Hunger Games" book series. Though it is more common for books where the intention is to teach others about a trade, how to improve their life or how to build a business. I wrote this book to help other investors like myself have a better chance at success. As a result, I found it appropriate to close the book around the topic of success.

So, what *is* success? In short, success is accomplishing something you set out to accomplish. That could really be anything. Also, the level of success is relative. Every person achieves a certain level of success in their lives. Comparably to others, it may be more, less or equal. As long as you are alive, you will either live to accomplish your *own* aspirations and dreams or be used as a resource to accomplish those of another. Rental real estate can help propel your aspirations and dreams, making them a reality instead of just a pipe dream.

How you define success ultimately drives what you end up achieving in your rental real estate business and in life. With your rental property business, success is relative: to your goals, appetite for risk and the amount of work you are willing to put in. Some investors reading this book simply want an extra $1,000 per month in disposable income or have a goal of 10 total doors for extra cushion during retirement. Others want to build a million-dollar gross revenue business or have a goal of 500 doors and a full-time real estate empire. Success can be defined differently for each of these endeavors and that's wonderful, assuming you know what you are shooting for. My personal ambition has been high since I was a child, though I doubted my abilities to achieve anything truly great. As I've done hard things over the years and achieved targets that I didn't realize I could achieve, my confidence has risen to new heights! The same goes with my personal ambitions for my family, my business and ultimately my life. If you follow the principles and best practices shared in this book, your confidence and ambitions should increase as well.

THIS IS NOT EASY—THOUGH NOTHING WORTHWHILE IS

The title of this book is "How To **WIN** In Rental Real Estate **AFTER** The Deal". It's not titled, "How To *Get* The Deal" or "*Finding* The Best Deal." The focus is on what is required as an owner of rental real estate *after* you formally close, or purchase the property in order to find success. The phrase that entered my head was "this is not easy— though nothing worthwhile is." We've all heard this stated in one way or another. Hard work, commitment, grit and perseverance are required in order to find true success and fulfillment in any endeavor. Grant Cardone nailed it again when he said, "Success is not something that happens *to* you; it's something that happens *because* of you and *because* of the actions you take." You are the creator and author of your own life's success. Understanding this is important because there is no ceiling to your success. Take the actions necessary to reach new heights in your life. Because *you are worth it*.

Being average at something requires an average amount of effort. Being great at something requires a much higher level of commitment and effort. Being the *very best* at something, well, that takes a *lifetime*. When we think of names associated with a particular trade, say Tiger Woods for example. We don't say, "Tiger Woods: the best golfer, basketball player, inventor and polo player of all time!" Tiger Woods is famous for the sport he mastered, *golf*. He was fully committed at a very young age and continues today that same level of commitment to be the greatest of all time, or the G.O.A.T. Are you reading this book to become the greatest landlord or rental real estate business owner of all time? Unlikely, I know. However, you may be reading it because you want to be more than average or even great. Personally, I am pursuing greatness. One day I will achieve it. I am writing this book as a stepping stone to that higher tier that requires extra, focused effort. I'll share with you more of my personal story as we round things out.

This Happened to Me – My pursuit of something greater

My story is one of ambition, hard work, lots of mistakes, commitment, self-doubt, grit, a wife who became my catalyst, higher education, sacrifice, dreams, kids that became my motivation, positivity, belief in God and never giving up.

I became the neighborhood paperboy for the "Seattle Times" when I was a mere eleven years old. I didn't come from wealth, had no allowance and still wanted material things that my parents just couldn't buy for me with six kids. I took over half the route from my thirteen-year-old brother at the time. Within six months the entire route was mine. My income doubled, but so did my workload! I would deliver those papers *every* day after school and each morning on the weekends, including Christmas, New Years and other holidays. I was committed and did what was required. I became a pretty good paperboy. I did save up enough to buy that 13" TV/VCR combo for my bedroom I wanted so badly, but I had bigger dreams in life.

I learned hard work as a boy from my old man, who is one of *nine* kids. The paper route was a bonus in that regard. My dad taught me to work hard, not take anything for granted and to do a quality job. I'll never forget Saturdays growing up, because they were the worst! Dad was home all day and that meant chores (and lots of them)! I was always tasked with picking weeds in the backyard. Growing up in the Pacific Northwest, it is beautiful because it rains more than most places. Rain, however, turns into weeds. They literally grow everywhere *non-stop*. Our backyard was decent-sized and my dad loved his garden, so the kids had to keep it from being invaded by unwanted weeds. I would spend multiple hours picking weeds, filling bucket after bucket, and hating every second. The positive aspect of it all? I could see my progress in real-time. As weeds were removed, the beauty of what remained became clearer. It was not something I loved at the time, but certainly something I look back on with gratitude and appreciation for all the lessons I learned at such a young age. Now, ironically, I am quite the green thumb myself and I think my dad is proud of that.

My mom taught me how to persevere and rise above your circumstances. She is the youngest of seven and overcame some really tough life challenges. Mom did her best to compensate for the cards she was dealt by making her own kids feel loved and appreciated. Always wanting something *greater* started when I was young and continues to the present moment. I don't settle. Not because I'm ungrateful or because somebody told me. I don't settle because I know there is *more* that I can do. I know there are *more* people I can reach. I know there are *more* ways to make a difference. Deep inside, I know the pursuit of something greater is personal and purposeful. I know there is more for me to do as I pursue not just greatness, but the greatest impact *for good*.

LEARN FROM YOUR MISTAKES—EVEN BETTER THE MISTAKES OF OTHERS

Mistakes, missteps and imperfections are everywhere to be had. Mistakes are OK. They are actually expected. Everyone makes them and nobody is immune. Jesus Christ is the one exception, but newsflash, you aren't Jesus! Robert Kiyosaki said, "Don't waste a good mistake...learn from it." Learning from your mistakes is the key to your success in life and in your rental real estate business. Mistakes in and of themselves are an opportunity to improve, to learn and to do better the next time around. As children, we consistently made mistakes as we learned how to crawl, talk, walk, run and just how to do life. This is expected and part of the growth process. As adults, we learn new things. We start new jobs. We begin new relationships. We start new businesses. We have children. Each of these new adventures comes with learning and growth, typically through mistakes and consistent improvement over time. Your rental real estate business is no different. Get it in your head right now: you *will* make mistakes, likely many of them. This is okay and expected. The key is to learn from the mistakes you make, limit the number of mistakes and to avoid the catastrophic mistakes that could tank your business.

This Happened to Me – The 'young happy couple' illusion

Tenants are the lifeblood of a rental real estate business. I've found out the hard way that unlike a friendship or a significant other, compatibility is not a requirement with your tenants! I've learned that it isn't how much you like somebody or jive with them that matters when they are your tenant. In the first two years of being a landlord, I looked positively on young, friendly and likeable couples. You know, like my wife and I! We gravitated toward them because they were like us and we thought we were pretty cool and would want a landlord to give us a shot too. This ended up burning us multiple times. It would start out positive. It would be good for about four to six months, before heading south.

One young couple we chose as tenants was from a remote town in Oklahoma. They were friendly, had great stories to tell and had great income. Their references were solid and their social media accounts didn't scare me. The girl of the couple had a brother who was going to live with them. They were each listed on the lease agreement. In the first few months, they were incredible at communicating, always paid rent on time and had all the appearances working in their favor. I even did multiple stop-by inspections in the first six months and the place was kept clean and smelling nice!

After about month ten, the behavior changed. Rent wasn't being paid on time. The communication decreased. I had a neighbor call me to make a complaint about noise. After the year mark, rent was late again one month and I inquired about the reason why. No response. In fact, nothing from the couple who were the primary communicators in the property. I had a scheduled visit there the next week and heard nothing until I stopped by the property. To my surprise, the brother was sitting outside by himself with a beer in hand, smoking a cigarette. We started talking and after I inquired about why rent was late, he mentioned he was 'trying' to get a hold of me but didn't know how. My phone number was on the lease agreement and we'd communicated before (but that's beside the point). After more digging, he stated that he was going to be paying rent himself. His sister and her boyfriend had apparently up and skipped town one day a few weeks back. He didn't even know where they had gone.

They had signed an 18-month lease and were six months shy of completing their agreement. The brother insisted that he would be staying at the property and paying rent himself. I was skeptical because it went from three people sharing rent to just one, who worked at a call center in town. He did pay rent for about two more months, but it was always late and never a full payment. I knew it wasn't going to end well. I told him he needed to vacate the place by the end of the next month and I'd forgive him the rest of the lease. He seemed relieved! So was I. He moved out; we moved on. As I am conducting an open house to fill the property with new tenants, I discovered why the couple left town so abruptly. The police department was searching for the girl of the couple for a serious felony offense! I never did find out what she did, but I also never heard from them again. Mistake made. I have learned from it and gotten better.

Choosing tenants is still my single biggest challenge of being a landlord and in full disclosure the most important business decision you will make as a landlord. Regardless of the successes or failures you've had in tenant selection, just know you will have more (of both). It is impossible to completely avoid bad tenants or bad behavior. The reason? Tenants are human beings and human beings are prone to make mistakes. Your goal is to learn from the mistakes and do your best in choosing better tenants. Follow what you know to be sound best practices and you will successfully limit the bad tenants while avoiding the catastrophic tenants that can ruin your business.

There are two components of mistakes that are worth covering, yours and those of others. Eleanor Roosevelt is quoted for saying, "Learn from the mistakes of others. You can't live long enough to make them all yourself!" I agree wholeheartedly with this statement and want to talk more about it with you. I have never been drunk. I have never consumed marijuana of any kind. I have also never consumed crack, cocaine, heroin, meth or acid. I have avoided all of these substances because I chose to learn from those that either lived before me or around me. I also had access to television, books, magazines, movies and even the internet later in my childhood years. I had access to information and enough real-life examples to make early decisions around whether or not to participate in consuming these substances. I never had to try any of them to understand the true consequences of consumption. Whenever my parents took us to downtown Seattle, I would witness the sad life choices of others who did choose to go down the drugs & alcohol route. It wasn't pretty. In fact, it was downright scary! Why try something that is proven to destroy your body and wreck your life? I never understood the need of others to indulge themselves in reckless choices and behaviors when there are countless other examples around them of what the end result is. To each their own I suppose. However, for me, I choose to be better. I choose the path that is more likely to result in achievement, health, happiness and success. Which path will you choose?

When it comes to rental real estate, the same principles apply. Learn from the mistakes you make. Don't repeat the same mistakes over and over. Learn from them and become better the next time around. This is how we grow into better versions of ourselves, better landlords and better business owners. I implore you to learn from the mistakes I have shared throughout this book from my own experiences as a landlord. In rental real estate, sometimes we get lucky and other times—not so much. This primarily relies on what our tenants choose to do or not do. Some mistakes are covered up because we have a great tenant or get lucky. Other mistakes become colossal failures because of a bad tenant or unfortunate luck. My point of telling you this is that as a rental real estate business owner, you must focus on *limiting* your mistakes and avoiding the catastrophes. Get the right insurance coverage. Screen people properly. Conduct thorough assessments before choosing a tenant. Don't buy before you understand what you are buying. Enforce your rules with tenants. Don't trust others without verifying. Be careful who you choose to go into business with. Don't be wasteful. Run the numbers, then run them again. Be honest and decent. Rely on trustworthy professionals. Obey the law. Be a good person. Following this advice would be wise and help you limit mistakes while avoiding catastrophes. However, it is ultimately up to you. Learn from the mistakes of others if you want to find personal success.

CONSISTENCY AND FOCUSED EFFORT MAKE ALL THE DIFFERENCE

James Clear wrote the book titled "Atomic Habits", a best-seller. His book is written with a focus on creating and maintaining positive habits that benefit your life. He explains that "Habit formation is the process by which a behavior becomes progressively more automatic through repetition. The more you repeat an activity, the mere structure of your brain changes to become efficient at that activity." In short, consistency and focused-effort make all the difference! They are required in order to create and maintain effective habits in your life and in your rental real estate business.

Grant Cardone, in his extremely popular and best-selling book "The 10X Rule" teaches the following, "Don't be confused by what looks like luck to you. Lucky people don't make successful people; people who completely commit themselves to success seem to get lucky in life." Sure, some people get 'lucky' in the sense that maybe they bought an investment that doubled, tripled or more in market value because they bought at the right time. The irony there is that they made the investment. They took that step and were rewarded for it. Grant goes on to say, "Success tends to bless those who are most committed to giving it the most attention." I implore you to give attention to your business. Commit to the success of your rental real estate business and revel in your eventual life success.

I don't believe in overnight successes. Having money is important in life and in business. I have no issue with the pursuit of money. However, I *do* take issue with people who expect something in return for nothing or for very little effort. That isn't winning. That's called being lazy and entitled. Consistent, focused effort over a period of time yields results. My parents taught me how to work hard and earn my keep, which meant no allowance because my chores were how I paid rent and contributed to the family household! If I wanted something outside of Christmas or my birthday, I had to pay for it. So, I did just that! I was taught the value of hard work at a very young age that has served me well up to this day.

This Happened to Me – Consistency in rental real estate

I shared a lot of my story earlier in this book as to how I got to where I am today. What I didn't share was the *key* to it all. I truly believe that consistent and focused effort are my keys to success. Each and every day I worked at building my rental real estate business. Each new place, each new tenant, each turnover, each repair, each and *every thing* that was required along the way that taught me. I never gave up on any of it. I had more than a few tough days and boiling-over frustration at times over careless and inconsiderate people that happened to be tenants of mine. Though through it all, I remained focused and consistent in my efforts.

I began writing this book last year. The year 2020 brought along with it some major challenges and unprecedented mayhem. We had a few disastrous repairs that showed their ugly faces, including a $24,000 foundation repair. We had multiple deals fall through, which hadn't happened before. We had some crazy tenants and some crazy reality TV show-like situations to manage our way through. Despite the craziness, I managed to reach my goal of hitting 30 doors. Austin and I purchased all six doors in October. Nine months passed without a single new door in. I didn't stop working along the way to strengthen my business, find new properties and reach the goal of 30 doors. It wasn't an overnight success. My success is owed to consistent and focused effort.

2021 has started off rather quickly as I became a multi-state investor right out the gate. With the new acquisition of seven doors in 2021, my rental real estate portfolio is now 37 doors deep. I aspire to reach 45 doors in 2021. I will get there through consistency and focused effort.

I share my stories with my own rental real estate business because I believe the best lessons learned are from stories, both successful and unsuccessful. I hope that you learn a thing or two from my journey. You too can build a successful real estate business. What's holding you back? Certainly, it isn't the want-to or you wouldn't have purchased this book. It can't be that you don't have money because you can get started in this business with very little money as long as you are willing to put forth the effort. If there is anything holding you back, it's your mindset or your willingness to do the hard work. If that's the case, either you jump over those hurdles or you choose another path. Owning and operating a rental real estate business is not for the faint of heart. It's for those with grit, with focus, with commitment and with the willingness to give a consistent effort over time. Why not you? Why not now?

ADD TO YOUR LEGACY THROUGH YOUR RENTAL REAL ESTATE BUSINESS

When I embarked on my rental real estate journey, my motivation wasn't just wealth. Wealth is certainly a component. My true motivation is rooted within the walls of my home. My wife and kids mean *everything* to me. I strive each and every day to provide them with the life they deserve. I want to be an example of prudence, hard work and achievement to my kids. I want them to know that their daddy worked tirelessly to provide them with a greater opportunity to pursue their dreams.

I am in the process of building my legacy. This legacy is not for me; it is for the people that follow. While I'm still here, I want to share in success with my family and enjoy life to the fullest. When I'm gone, I want to be sure I leave behind something of significance. My rental real estate business is rocket fuel for making this a reality. I make it a point that this is a 'family business' and I involve each of my children in the work. Each time I show a property I have at least one of my children with me, sometimes all of them! Each time I close on a new property, I have one of more of my children with me. Often, we get to spend several hours or even an entire day together, without the normal distractions of life. There are long car rides and long days. Many times, they moan and groan, though I know behind the scowls they are watching and learning. The extra time I am privileged to spend with them is priceless. I am creating memories that I hope they look back on as fondly as I already do. I consider it a duty of mine to show them the way instead of just telling them what to do. I want them to be involved, to feel involved and to be a part of the journey. My rental real estate business has been a blessing in educating my children about the principles of hard work, diligence, perseverance, trials and finding success.

My wife and I made a goal together that we would leave each of our children the keys to one single-family rental property from our portfolio when they get married. Up until 2020 we had just two properties that we owned without a business partner. In 2020 we acquired our third. I am happy to share that we will have hit our goal of four, and actually more, in 2021! Our kids don't know this yet. This is another reason why involving them in the business is so important to me. This is part of my personal legacy. What will yours be? Have you thought about it? Have you thought about what you could truly accomplish by building a successful rental real estate business? I certainly have; and it is my motivation, better yet my drive to continue onward with optimism and faith.

BUCKLE UP AND ENJOY THE RIDE

To close out this book, I want to both commend you and leave you with some final words of wisdom. Congratulations for doing what it takes to win. Success doesn't just happen by relaxing, complaining or wishing upon a star. It happens because you dreamed about success and then took action in making your dreams a reality. I commend you for being a dreamer and a doer. Life rewards these types of individuals.

I've done my best to outline how to win in rental real estate after you've officially become an investor. These "15 Keys to Mastery and Ultimate Success in Your Rental Real Estate Business" are guidelines, recommendations and best practices for you. They are not a guarantee of success. However, if followed, your likelihood of success is significantly greater. In fact, by following these *keys* in detail your chances of success are very high. Remember, there is no need to carve out your own path in the jungle. Follow the path that many before you have taken to success. Avoid the pitfalls and catastrophic mistakes I warn about in these pages. Work hard. Be diligent. Be consistent. Treat others with kindness and respect. Follow the proven methods and go get it!

Finally, buckle up and enjoy the ride! I received some wise counsel once that happiness doesn't come at the end of the journey, once you've achieved great success and riches. Happiness *is* the journey. Learn to enjoy the ride, appreciate the hard work and the struggles along your path to success. It takes the proper perspective. Realign yours until you can appreciate the crazy. If you don't, when you do reach the pinnacle, it won't magically create happiness inside of you. That's because happiness is a choice each person makes for themselves and their life. For me personally, I compare it to my incredible children. Each phase of their childhood is special. Though each phase brings its unique challenges, waiting for the next phase is not the answer. You'll miss the glorious and amazing moments along the way. I choose to enjoy each phase of my children's lives because each is temporary and fleeting. I no longer have another chance to relish the newborn phase as my youngest is almost three and we are not having any more children. Four is enough for us! I do miss it though. I wish I could hold my tiny babies again and snuggle them tightly until they fall asleep in my arms. It goes by so fast, so enjoy the ride each step of the way.

You can do this. I believe in you. Believe in yourself. Take action today. Create your story of success. That story continues right now!

LET'S WRAP A BOW ON THIS CHAPTER

Congratulations, you've finished Chapter Fifteen and learned something new to improve your rental real estate business! The focus of this chapter is that despite the challenges, you can succeed with consistency and following proven best practices. Enjoy the journey and choose happiness!

This is not easy—though nothing worthwhile is. Your pursuit of honorable things will not be easy, nor should it be. We don't learn from easy things. We learn from challenges, from trials, from mistakes, from falling down and persevering through it all.

Learn from your mistakes—even better the mistakes of others. Mistakes are great learning opportunities, not guarantees of improvement. Take an honest assessment and learn from your mistakes. Even better, learn from the mistakes of others and increase your chances of less painful success.

Consistency and focused effort make all the difference. Overnight successes are a mirage of the true, hard work and focused effort that happens behind the scenes. Nothing happens overnight. Consistency and focused effort are the keys to true, lasting success.

Buckle up and enjoy the ride. I want to commend you for reading the entire book! I've outlined a path to success. The choice is yours whether you'll take action and learn from this book. Enjoy the journey—even the challenges. Everything that happens is a learning opportunity. *Choose happiness* my friends!

ABOUT THE AUTHOR

Casey Denby is a loving husband and father to four wonderful children. He resides in the state of Colorado with his family. He speaks fluent Spanish after fulfilling a service mission in Ecuador for two years, which experience shaped his life. Casey is the Vice President of Learning & Education at RE/MAX World Headquarters. He has worked in progressive leadership roles during his corporate career at Dish Network, Comcast Corporation, The Western Union Company and RE/MAX HQ. Casey began investing in rental real estate in early 2016. He has since built a respectable multi-state portfolio of 37 total doors that he primarily self-manages along with his business partner. He is passionate about real estate and strives to provide a safe, quality place to live for each tenant that resides in his properties. Casey wrote this book to give back to other rental real estate investors by sharing his experiences and learnings that could help them along their own journey in this great adventure.

Follow our REI journey on Instagram

@the_rental_property_dudes

REFERENCES

1. Average renter in years

https://www.businessinsider.com/millennials-renting-for-very-long-time-2015-8

2. Renters vs homeowners
https://ipropertymanagement.com/research/renters-vs-homeowners-statistics

3. Pet statistics

https://www.aspca.org/animal-homelessness/shelter-intake-and-surrender/pet-statistics

4. Renters with pets

https://www.humanesociety.org/resources/increasing-housing-options-renters-pets

5. Legal entities

https://www.accruit.com/blog/selecting-entity-real-estate-purchase-%E2%80%93-part-1

6. Service dogs vs emotional support animals

https://www.floridatoday.com/story/life/2019/01/14/service-dogs-vs-therapy-dogs-vs-emotional-support-animals/878753002/

www.ingramcontent.com/pod-product-compliance
Lightning Source LLC
Chambersburg PA
CBHW030612220526
45463CB00004B/1267